D1448277

Steve Stugg

Wellcome Unit for the
          History of Medicine
Manchester University
March 1990.

Scientists in Whitehall

Scientists in Whitehall

PHILIP GUMMETT

MANCHESTER UNIVERSITY PRESS

© Philip Gummett 1980

Published by
Manchester University Press
Oxford Road, Manchester M13 9PL

British Library cataloguing in publication data

Gummett, Philip
   Scientists in Whitehall.
   1. Science and state – Great Britain
   I. Title
   509'.41   Q127.G7

   ISBN 0–7190–0791–7

Typeset by
Northern Phototypesetting Co., Bolton
Printed in Great Britain by
Redwood Burn Limited, Trowbridge & Esher

Contents

List of tables

List of figures

Acknowledgements

The work presented in this book began in 1971 in the form of an MSc and later a PhD dissertation in the Department of Liberal Studies in Science at the University of Manchester. Special thanks are therefore due to F. R. Jevons and to Roger Williams, who set me off on this course of study and whose guidance, encouragement and example, then and later, have been invaluable. A further part of the work was begun while working as a research fellow under Michael Gibbons, to whom also special thanks are due.

The structure of the book has been influenced by a most helpful correspondence with Professor F. F. Ridley, and the information and analysis contained in it would have been much poorer without the generous assistance of many 'scientists in Whitehall' whom I have interviewed, or with whom I have corresponded over the past eight and a half years. They are too numerous to list in full, but my debt to the following must be gratefully acknowledged: Sir Douglas Black, Dr G. H. O. Burgess, Mr M. Daniel, Mr J. B. Dick, Dr P. Drath, Lord Flowers, Sir Harold Himsworth, Mr F. H. Jacob, Sir Peter Kent, Mr A. C. Ladd, Sir Harry Melville, Mr J. W. Nichols, Mr E. M. Nicholson, Professor W. S. Peart, Sir Charles Pereira, Dr R. Press, Mr. W. J. Reiners, Dr L. E. J. Roberts, Mr A. Silverleaf, Sir Frederick Stewart, Lord Todd, Dr T. L. V. Ulbricht, Dr C. A. A. Wass and Lord Zuckerman.

For reading and commenting on all or part of the typescript, my thanks go to Geoffrey Price and, again, to Michael Gibbons and Roger Williams. None of the people named above is, of course, in any way responsible for what I have done with his information or advice.

I wish to thank the Controller of Her Majesty's Stationery Office for permission to reproduce Crown copyright material; the editor of *Nature* for permission to adapt the *Nature* guide, 'How Britain runs its science'; Mr Keith Pavitt for permission to draw in chapter five on material previously published in *Research Policy*, and for other permissions; Professor S. Eilon for permission to draw in chapter five on material previously published in *Omega*; Mr David Croom of Croom Helm Ltd for permission to draw in chapters two and five on material previously published under his copyright; the Science Research Council and the Social Science Research Council for permission to use the diagrams presented in figure 6.1; and Professor E. Shils for permission to draw in chapter seven on material previously published in *Minerva*.

Typing of various drafts has been skilfully and swiftly done by Yvonne Aspinall, Judy Jara, Eleanor Willis and, especially, Edna Foster. The staff at Manchester University Press have dealt admirably with the business of turning a typescript into a book.

Finally, some acknowledgements nearer to home. My thanks go to Bernard and Nicola Gummett, without whose timely help during a minor domestic crisis this book would probably not yet be complete; to Karen, for patience during more years of research into science policy than she would care to remember; and to Hannah for not proving too distracting.

P.J.G.

Manchester, November 1979

List of abbreviations

ABRC	Advisory Board for the Research Councils
ACARD	Advisory Council for Applied Research and Development
ACSP	Advisory Council on Scientific Policy
ACT	Advisory Council on Technology
ADAS	Agricultural Development and Advisory Service
AEA	Atomic Energy Authority
ARC	Agricultural Research Council
ASTMS	Association of Scientific, Technical and Managerial Staffs
AUT	Association of University Teachers
BRE	Building Research Establishment
BRS	Building Research Station
CCR	Committee of Civil Research
CERN	European Centre for Nuclear Research
CPRS	Central Policy Review Staff
CSP	Council for Scientific Policy
DAFS	Department of Agriculture and Fisheries for Scotland
DES	Department of Education and Science
DGR	Director General of Research (in DOE, *infra*.)
DHSS	Department of Health and Social Security
DOE	Department of the Environment
DOI	Department of Industry
DRPC	Defence Research Policy Committee
DRR	Directorate of Research Requirements (in DOE, *supra*.)
DSIR	Department of Scientific and Industrial Research
DTI	Department of Trade and Industry
GeV	Giga electron volt

HRS	Hydraulics Research Station
IPCS	Institution of Professional Civil Servants
IRC	Industrial Reorganisation Corporation
IRDA	Industrial Research and Development Authority
JCO	Joint Consultative Organisation (of ARC, DAFS and MAFF)
MAFF	Ministry of Agriculture, Fisheries and Food
MOT	Ministry of Transport
MPBW	Ministry of Public Buildings and Works
MRC	Medical Research Council
NERC	Natural Environment Research Council
NIRNS	National Institute for Research in Nuclear Science
NRDC	National Research Development Corporation
PESC	Public Expenditure Survey Committee
QSE	Qualified Scientists and Engineers
R&D	Research and development
SAC	Scientific Advisory Committee (to War Cabinet)
SISTERS	Special Institutions for Scientific and Technological Education and Research
SPATS	Senior Professional Administrative Training Scheme
SRC	Science Research Council
SSRC	Social Science Research Council
TRRL	Transport and Road Research Laboratory
UGC	University Grants Committee

Introduction

Throughout this century, but particularly since the second world war, governments everywhere have sought to harness science and technology to their national interests. Special institutions have been established to foster science and technology and to relate them to the work of government. Yet despite the novel political pressures created by science, and despite the argument by some scientists that the nature of scientific research requires it to be treated in a uniquely open-handed way by governments, in Britain the institutional structures and administrative procedures employed by successive governments for the promotion and use of science and technology have largely remained true to traditional principles of British public administration.

In particular, the principle of the responsibility of a minister for the work of his ministry has led time and again to resistance to the idea that governmental programmes in science and technology should be co-ordinated in any but the minimal sense of avoiding undue duplication. The idea of a deliberate 'science policy' has been explicitly rejected. A natural corollary of this attitude, in scientific affairs as elsewhere, has been a reluctance to plan from the centre. This reluctance has been intensified by strong support for that freedom of research which characterises at least the academic world. Secondly, and recent discussion of more 'open government' notwithstanding, the concept of accountability which prevails in all areas of British government, including scientific affairs, is one of ex post facto accountability to Parliament for the proper spending of funds provided for in the departmental Votes. Decision-making continues to be a highly secret business and the prevailing attitude in Whitehall remains one of revealing very little of the influences upon any particular decision, and of involving outsiders in decision-making only where this is considered politic. Thirdly, traditional attitudes towards the relations between generalists and specialists within the civil service have only recently shown signs of any significant response to pressure from scientists for greater recognition of their role in government. Finally, the selection of scientists from outside the civil service to serve as advisers seems to have depended as much on the mysterious processes governing admission to the list of 'the great and the good' as has the selection of any other kind of outsider to serve as an adviser, except party political ones.

These are the main themes which underlie the substantive subjects of this book, but before outlining the structure of the book, a few words about its intellectual location (at least in the eyes of its author) may be helpful.

On one dimension, this study can be seen as falling within the field of the social studies of science and technology, the elements of which include sociology and social history of science, the social and economic conditions of technological change and the philosophy and psychology of science.[1] Further elements of that field include technology assessment[2], and the political sociology of science[3], the latter overlapping with this study in so far as both share a concern with the origins and functions of science advisers.

More specifically still, this study can be located at the intersection between a further constituent of the social studies of science and technology – namely, the field of science policy studies – and the study of government, especially the area of policy studies. Although in the United States the inhabitants of this particular intellectual conjunction tend to have approached from the side of government studies, in Britain the opposite is more usual. (True to form, Manchester has led the world by creating a joint chair of government and science policy, with one foot institutionally in each field.)

Within the field of science policy studies (alternatively called science and government studies, or science and public policy studies), scholars and practitioners have been concerned with the political functions of scientists and technologists, the effects of science and technology on various aspects of public policy, and governmental policies for the promotion and regulation of science and technology themselves.[4] This diversity of subjects belies the apparent simplicity of the term 'science policy', and indeed, following from a study published by the Organisation for Economic Co-operation and Development in 1963, it has been generally agreed that:

The term 'science policy' is ambiguous. It too often connotes only a policy limited to the needs of science *per se* and excludes the effects of science and technology on the full spectrum of national policies in such disparate fields as agriculture and industry, defence, education and domestic and foreign political affairs.[5]

Following from the recognition of this ambiguity it has become conventional to define science policy as meaning:

The collective measures taken by a government in order, *on the one hand*, to encourage the development of scientific and technical research and, *on the other*, to exploit the results of this research for general policy objectives.[6]

Thus one speaks of 'science policy' as meaning the complementary activities of policy *for* science (the provision of an environment fostering research activities), and policy *through* science (the exploitation of science and technology in various sectors of government). Where I do not specify which sense of the term is intended, then it should be understood, unless the context clearly suggests otherwise, that both senses are intended. It should also be noted that very often the word 'science' will be used to mean 'science and technology', and I hope that here too the context will make the meaning plain.

From the perspective of government studies, this book is perhaps loosely connected with the tradition of writing about the specific political problems of advanced industrial (and therefore highly technological) states.[7] More immediately, however, it is related to what in Britain is the still relatively undeveloped field of policy studies. This approach implies that the emphasis in the book is on describing what policy is, and how it is formulated and implemented, 'policy' itself being understood to be 'a purposive course of action followed by an actor or set of actors in dealing with a problem or matter of concern'.[8] Thus policy-making is distinguished from decision-making, which is concerned with making choices among competing actions. Its study involves the examination of policy-makers and their environment, of how policies are formed, adopted and implemented, and of what their eventual effects are.

It follows that other aspects of the study of government, such as electoral behaviour, the distribution of power within societies, or the role of political parties, are not at all central to policy studies, although they may be relevant to particular policy issues. This implied focus away from some of the more traditional concerns of the study of government is particularly relevant to the study of science policy because, although science policy has sometimes become the subject of major political debate,[9] more generally, as Brickman has observed, it has remained

> removed from the contrasting sets of ideological principles on which political systems are founded and over which electoral battles are often fought. By and large, the growing responsibilities of government in [research and development] have seldom polarized professional political opinion along the usual partisan lines; and from one industrialized nation to another, to quote one well-placed observer, 'all science policies are very similar, whatever the political regime'.[10]

This book explores certain aspects of science policy-making in Britain, in both senses of the term. It begins by setting the stage, as it were, with a brief introduction to British government. This may safely be passed over by readers who are already familiar with the subject, but may be helpful to others. The second chapter is also concerned with stage-setting, and consists of a review of the main features in science–government relations in Britain from the nineteenth century to 1979. The object of this chapter is to establish in broad outline what those features have been, leaving more detailed treatment of most of them to later chapters; to change the metaphor, it provides a small-scale map of a large area, the better to see the relation of one feature to another before going into greater detail on particular features later.

Chapters three and four, somewhat arbitrarily divided, are concerned not with the institutional stage of science–government relations but with the actors on that stage. Chapter three examines the history of the scientific civil service in Britain, concentrating particularly on the so-called specialist–generalist division within the civil service as a whole, and drawing some comparisons in this regard with French practice. Chapter four is concerned with the individuals who are drawn into Whitehall from outside as scientific advisers, either on advisory committees or as individual advisers to ministers, and is also concerned in a more general way with the problems involved in acting as an expert adviser in government.

Chapters five, six and seven move on from the actors to the play – to what is done within science–government relations, and how (although, not surprisingly, the distinctions between stage, actors and play are not clear-cut; further information about machinery of government, for instance, can most conveniently be introduced in this part of the book). Chapter five falls on the 'policy through science' side of science policy, and is concerned with how government departments in general (concentrating on three in particular) have sought to get done that research which has been considered essential to their overall policy objectives. Some comparison is made with United States practice. Chapter six deals with 'policy for science' and examines the research council system, through which the bulk of British basic scientific research is funded. Finally, chapter seven addresses certain underlying themes of the book as a whole. The first of these is the rejection in British government of the idea of a co-ordinated, national science policy. The second is the way in which the environment that surrounds science policy-making has been affected by the changing level and nature of the public and political interest in science and technology, by the limited degree to which scientists have been encouraged to involve themselves in government, and by the limited extent to which scientists are organised for political influence.

This book does *not* deal with the problems of formulating and implementing policies in the area of 'Big Technology' – principally aerospace, computers and nuclear power – although no sharp distinction can be made between science policy and technology policy. These are enormous subjects in their own rights, and there is a limit to what can be done in one volume. For similar reasons, coupled with the added difficulty of obtaining information, the defence sector is likewise largely ignored. Also missing is any discussion of the burgeoning field of governmental regulation of science and technology.[12] Even with these omissions, much is left that is worth examination.

Although one of the arguments to be made in this book is that the style of science policy-making in Britain has not, in essence, changed in at least the last sixty years, times have changed in another respect. In 1969 Hilary and Steven Rose wrote:

> Prior to 1964, when a crusading political party promised that the new socialism would be 'forged in the white heat of the scientific revolution', an election in which a principal political issue was how to harness science and technology to the nation's needs was almost unthinkable. Now it is hard to imagine an election in which it would not be.[13]

Yet twice in 1974, and again at the general election in 1979, political debate about science and technology in Britain (micro-electronics and the future of the National Enterprise Board apart) was almost non-existent. Perhaps it is time for that debate to begin again. After all, if less developed countries need to husband their limited resources in science and technology, developed countries arguably will need to do the same in the 1980s because their *other* resources are so limited. Both circumstances point to the need for careful analysis and a measure of planning. Academics, fortunately, are spared the responsibility of making decisions on matters of national policy. But perhaps, by describing what is presently going on, they can help to inform the policy-making process and try to ensure that the right questions are asked. In the field of science policy, that is one of the larger hopes behind this book.

Notes

[1] Good introductory essays on these subjects can be found in Ina Spiegel-Rösing and Derek de Solla Price (eds.), *Science, Technology and Society: A Cross-disciplinary Perspective* (Beverly Hills, California: Sage Publications, 1977).

[2] A good introduction to the field of technology assessment is given by Michael Gibbons, 'Technology Assessment: Information and Participation', in Ron Johnston and Philip Gummett (eds.), *Directing Technology: Policies for Promotion and Control* (London: Croom Helm, 1979).

[3] See Stuart S. Blume, *Toward a Political Sociology of Science* (New York: The Free Press, 1974).

[4] From a large field, see Jean-Jacques Salomon, 'Science Policy Studies and the Development of Science Policy', and other essays in Spiegel-Rösing and de Solla Price, *op. cit.*; Harvey Sapolsky, 'Science Policy', in F. Greenstein and N. Polsby (eds.), *Handbook of Political Science*, vol. 6 (Reading, Mass.: Addison-Wesley, 1975), pp. 79–110; B. C. Denny, 'Science and Public Policy: A Literature in Search of a Field', *Public Administration Review*, **25** (1965), pp. 239–48; R. Rettig, 'Science, Technology and Public Policy', *World Politics* (1969), pp. 273–93; L. K. Caldwell, *Science, Technology and Public Policy: A Selected and Annotated Bibliography* (Bloomington, Indiana: Indiana University, three volumes, 1968, 1969, 1972); Jean-Jacques Salomon, *Science and Politics* (Paris: Editions du Seuil, 1970; London: Macmillan, 1973, translated by Noel Lindsay); and T. Dixon Long and C. Wright (eds.), *Science Policies of the Industrialised Nations* (New York: Praeger, 1975).

[5] P. Piganiol, *Science and the policies of governments; the implication of science and technology for national and international affairs* (Paris: OECD, 1963); cited in Alexander King, *Science and Policy: The International Stimulus* (London: Oxford University Press, 1974), p. 37.

[6] Salomon, 'Science Policy Studies and the Development of Science Policy', *loc. cit.*, pp. 45–6.

[7] A good introduction to this literature is given in Roger Williams, *Politics and Technology* (London: Macmillan, 1971).

[8] The definition is from James E. Anderson, *Public Policy-Making* (London: Nelson, 1975), p. 3. This book also provides a good introduction to policy studies.

[9] As in Britain in 1959–64. See Norman J. Vig, *Science and Technology in British Politics* (Oxford: Pergamon, 1968).

[10] Ronald Brickman, 'Ideological and Partisan Factors in Science Policy: A Cross-national Assessment', paper presented at ninth World Congress of Sociology, Uppsala, Sweden, August 1978, p. 1. The quotation is from Salomon.

[11] A good initial appreciation of these subjects, and further references, can be obtained from Keith Pavitt, 'Governmental Support for Industrial Innovation: The Western European Experience', and Roger Williams, 'The Development of Nuclear Technology', both in Johnston and Gummett, *op. cit.*

[12] On regulation, see Dorothy Nelkin, 'Technology and Public Policy', in Spiegel-Rösing and de Solla Price (eds.), *op. cit.*; Roger Williams, with Robin Roy and Vivien Walsh, *Government and Technology*, Open University Control of Technology Units 3–4 (Milton Keynes: Open University Press, 1978); and the essays in Part Two of Johnston and Gummett, *op. cit.*

[13] Hilary and Steven Rose, *Science and Society* (Harmondsworth: Penguin Books, 1970; first published by Allen Lane, 1969), p. xii.

I
BRITISH GOVERNMENT

In order to discuss how Whitehall has dealt with the formulation and implementation of policy in respect of science and technology, it is necessary first to understand how British government works. This chapter provides a brief introduction to that subject, which may already be familiar to some readers. It is not in the least exhaustive, and is entirely derivative, being concerned simply to prepare the way for the more detailed examination later of science–government relations in Britain.

The department

The principal operating units in British government are called either departments or ministries, although some (such as the Treasury and the Home Office) lack those terms in their titles. For most purposes the two names can be used interchangeably. Departments, or ministries, are responsible for some defined aspect of governmental business, such as defence, education, transport, or the management of the economy. At their heads are politicians drawn from the party with the largest number of seats in the House of Commons, the politicians themselves coming from the Commons or the Lords. The political heads of the more important departments have the title of secretary of state; in lesser departments they have the title of minister, and in both cases there will be one or more further ministers of lower rank. The political head of a ministry is regarded as responsible to Parliament for the work of his or her ministry, and that responsibility is jealously guarded against any real or apparent attempts by other ministries to interfere in what a particular minister regards as his or her area of jurisdiction.

Ministers come and go with changes in the balance of parties within Parliament, but the civil servants, or officials, who staff the ministries usually stay indefinitely in their jobs, except at the most senior levels, where there is a significant, but variable, amount of movement between the parts of a ministry and between one ministry and another. The staff of a ministry may total anything up to about 200,000 (including so-called 'industrial civil servants' who are employed in such places as ordnance factories and naval dockyards). Thus in 1979 the Ministry of Defence had 225,100 staff, the Department of Education and Science had 2,700, the Ministry of Agriculture, Fisheries and Food had 14,200, and the Treasury 1,100. Corresponding to the political head of a ministry is the permanent secretary, or official head. Just as there may be more than one minister, so large ministries or ministries (like the Treasury) where most of the work is at the highest levels of policy-making, have more than one permanent secretary.

Ministries are internally divided into sub-units, variously termed divisions, directorates, branches or, confusingly, departments, each of which is responsible for a particular aspect of the work of the ministry. Thus in 1978 the sub-units of the Department of Education and Science included the Arts and Libraries Branch, several Higher and Further Education Branches, and the Science Branch; of the Department of Energy: the Atomic Energy Division, the Energy Technology Division, and the Energy Policy and Conservation Division; and of the Department of Industry: the Concorde Division, the Research and Development Requirements Division, and the Machine Tools and Mechanical Engineering Division.

Most of the decisions which are made by a ministry will emerge from within these sub-units and, even though they will go forth in the name of the minister, they will never have been referred to him for approval. This is possible because most of the subjects on which ministries have to make decisions are either routine matters, where clear rules or well established precedents may dictate the response, or else are subjects on which the minister has already indicated what general line is to be taken; only the most important, or most sensitive, issues are referred up to him. Officials are encouraged to take decisions at the lowest level in the hierarchy at which they can confidently do so; unless this is done, decisions are said to 'drift upwards', adding to the workload of already heavily burdened senior officials and ministers. The general position in this regard was well summed up by the official head of the Foreign and

Commonwealth Office in 1968:

> All officers should assume the maximum responsibility and take the largest number of decisions that they properly and rightly can. ... Where Ministers have laid down clear lines of policy, decisions within them should be possible at the working level.
>
> Obviously the more a problem lies outside, or casts doubt on, established lines of policy, the closer it will need to come to Ministers. Equally, the greater the chance that a problem will catch the eye of the public, Parliament or the press, the greater the need for Ministers to be consulted, or at least to be informed of action that has been taken. This is an important instinct to develop, and refine. Where the implications are wide, a senior official with wider responsibilities and contacts and greater experience may be better placed to see the problem in perspective than a junior. But the rule is: if you can rightly decide, do so.[1]

Although this approach to decision-making relieves ministers of much work, it also creates problems for them in ensuring that their views on all the major areas of departmental policy are well known throughout the department. This is a matter of organisation and communication, and different ministers adopt different methods (such as regular meetings with staff down to quite junior levels, or frequently examining a sample of all the correspondence issued from the ministry) to try to ensure that their officials are acting as they themselves would have done.[2] The role played by officials in governmental decision-making has led to some debate about the degree to which ministers, as opposed to officials, are able to influence policy. Some have argued that such is the volume and complexity of government business that ministers, who may well be inexperienced in the subjects of their departments, and who, however intelligent and diligent, nevertheless have limited intellectual and physical resources, rapidly become pawns in a Whitehall chess game in which the major pieces are the senior civil servants.[3] Against this, others (who probably constitute the majority among informed commentators) speak highly of the integrity of British officials, and of their willingness and ability to develop new policies to suit new ministers. These commentators often also observe that, where a minister knows what he wants, his officials will do it if it is humanly possible, and that when difficulties arise this is generally because ministers do not always have clear and well worked out policies in mind, or have failed to convey them properly to their officials.[4]

Inter-departmental co-ordination

Although the department is the principal operating unit in Whitehall, and although ministers, as has been said, jealously guard their autonomy, there are many issues which cannot be resolved within a single ministry. An issue might require the co-operation of two or more ministries, or might involve competition between departments (as over their shares of the national budget), or might be of such political sensitivity and importance that no single minister might feel justified in taking a decision on his or her own initiative. In addition, ministers are constrained in the amount of money which they can spend on any one item without Treasury approval, from which constraint derives the Treasury's commanding position among the departments. They are also constrained as to the kinds of overseas activity in which they can engage without the approval of the Foreign and Commonwealth Office, and as to the numbers and types of staff whom they can employ without the approval of the Civil Service Department.

Various mechanisms have been developed to deal with these kinds of issues. Ad hoc interdepartmental committees, composed of representatives from the relevant ministries, deal with many of the relatively non-contentious matters which arise from time to time. Close contact is maintained by officials at all levels in the spending departments with their Treasury counterparts, the role of the latter being to ensure that departmental spending is according to previously agreed plans, to monitor changes in plans, and to agree, where possible, to any changes which the spending department might wish to make. If officials at the working level cannot agree about such changes, the matter is referred upwards, perhaps to be eventually resolved by discussion between the Chancellor of the Exchequer and the minister concerned.[5]

This constant 'horizontal' cross-referral between Treasury (and Foreign and Commonwealth Office and Civil Service Department) and spending departments is one of the principal means of co-ordination in Whitehall. But it is chiefly a process for monitoring the implementation of existing policies and dealing with deviations from them. The plans themselves are constructed by a process of deliberation at various levels within each department, followed by wider discussion and approval, amendment or rejection within the Cabinet network. The phrase 'Cabinet network' is used because decisions which are often loosely referred to as having been taken by 'the Cabinet' have more often than not been taken in some other forum than the usual Thursday morning meeting of Cabinet ministers. The Cabinet network comprises the Cabinet itself, a number of cabinet committees, and the Cabinet Office.

Although the full Cabinet, under the chairmanship of the Prime Minister, is the principal decision-making body within the government, most of its business is conducted at cabinet committees. The names and duties of these committees have traditionally been regarded within Whitehall as secret, despite references to them in the press[6] and by former members of Cabinets.[7] It is, however, known that past cabinet committees have had such titles as Home Affairs, Food Policy, Civil Defence, Machinery of Government, Atomic Energy, Nuclear Defence and Foreign Affairs. Breaking with tradition, Mrs Thatcher announced in 1979 the establishment of four standing committees of the Cabinet: a defence and overseas policy committee, an economic strategy committee, a home and social affairs committee, and a legislation committee. The membership and terms of reference of these committees and their sub-committees remain secret.[8]

There are ministerial cabinet committees, composed of ministers (not all of whom need be members of the Cabinet) and appointed by the Prime Minister, and official cabinet committees, which mirror at official level the duties and composition of the ministerial committees. Generally, a ministerial committee meets only after its agenda has been discussed by the corresponding official committee. Decisions made by the ministerial committees, if unanimous, are usually regarded as carrying the weight of full Cabinet decisions, and are implemented without further discussion by the full Cabinet. Thus only issues on which agreement is not reached at cabinet committees or which are so important that the Prime Minister wishes them to be discussed by the entire Cabinet, go to the Thursday Cabinet meetings.

The Cabinet and its committees are served by the Cabinet secretariat, the head of which, the Cabinet secretary, ranks among the top handful of civil servants. The secretariat, in turn, is part of the Cabinet Office, a 600-strong staff which includes the Central Statistical Office and the Central Policy Review Staff (or Cabinet 'Think Tank') and which provides another channel of co-ordination throughout Whitehall as it collects material for the

Cabinet and its committees, and as it checks on the implementation of Cabinet decisions. Cabinet Office staff are also often members, and frequently chairmen, of official cabinet committees.

Because it, or more precisely its one-time head, will feature significantly in later chapters, a little more should be said about the Central Policy Review Staff (CPRS). It was set up in February 1971 with the following terms of reference:

> Under the supervision of the Prime Minister, it will work for Ministers collectively; and its task will be to enable them to take better policy decisions by asking them to work out the implications of their basic strategy in terms of policies in specific areas, to establish the relative priorities to be given to sectors of their programme as a whole, to identify those areas of policy in which new choices can be exercised and to ensure that the underlying implications of alternative courses of action are fully analysed and considered.[9]

Lord Rothschild, the Head of the CPRS from 1971 to 1974, has reproduced the following 'translation' of the above, written by an un-named member of his staff. The tasks of the CPRS are:

> Sabotaging the over-smooth functioning of the machinery of Government.
>
> Providing a Central Department which has no departmental axe to grind but does have overt policy status and which can attempt a synoptic view of policy.
>
> Provide a Central reinforcement for those Civil Servants in Whitehall who are trying to retain their creativity and not be totally submerged in the bureaucracy.
>
> Try to devise a more rational system of decision-making between competing programmes.
>
> Advise the Cabinet collectively, and the Prime Minister, on major issues of policy relating to the Government's Strategy.
>
> Focus the attention of Ministers on the right questions to ask about their own colleagues' business.
>
> Bring in ideas from the outside world.[10]

With about sixteen to nineteen relatively youthful staff, of which about half are career civil servants on secondment from their departments and about half come from universities, industry, financial institutions and international organisations, the CPRS acts within Whitehall as a somewhat provocative entity.[11] It produces periodic reviews of governmental strategy as a whole, conducts major studies on selected subjects,[12] participates in the more important formal reviews of departmental policy, prepares collective briefs for the Cabinet and, since mid-1976, has provided the central focus for scientific advice to the Cabinet.

The Cabinet Office as a whole is sometimes referred to as the Prime Minister's department, with the Cabinet secretary as its official head, and the growth of this office to its present size, coupled with the other powers of the Prime Minister (he or she appoints the members and controls the agenda of the Cabinet and its committees, and can call an election and risk the political future of his or her colleagues) has led some commentators to write of prime ministerial rather than cabinet government.[13] Against this, it has been argued that the Cabinet Office serves the whole Cabinet, and not the Prime Minister only, that Prime Ministers can be, and have been, overruled by their Cabinets, that they need to carry their party and their colleagues with them, and that the need to reflect within the Cabinet the balance of interests in the party makes it difficult to dismiss some ministers.[14]

Parliament

The Prime Minister is also the leader of the majority party in the Commons, and although this book is concerned with the executive machinery, not the legislature, this is an appropriate point to say a little about how Whitehall relates to Westminster.

Whereas in, for instance, the United States, the three main elements of the government – the legislature, the executive and the judiciary – are elected or appointed through channels which are largely independent of one another, and are each capable of raising formidable barriers to unwelcome acts by the others, in Britain this is not so, at least as regards relations between legislature and executive.[15] As Walter Bagehot put it in 1867:

> The efficient secret of the English Constitution may be described as the close union, the nearly complete fusion, of the executive and legislative powers. . . . The connecting link is *the Cabinet*. . . . [i.e.] a committee of the legislative body selected to be the executive body. . . . A Cabinet is a combining committee – a *hyphen* which joins, a *buckle* which fastens, the legislative part of the State to the executive part. . . . In its origin it belongs to the one, in its functions it belongs to the other.[16]

Despite the closeness of the link, however, there can be no doubt that once Parliament (or, more particularly, the House of

Commons) has enabled a Cabinet to be formed, the initiative then passes to the executive, and this has remained true despite the increase in parliamentary assertiveness which occurred between 1974 and 1979. Parliament, nominally the supreme authority in the land, in practice spends most of its time examining, criticising and passing legislation which has been proposed by the executive. This sometimes results in changes to those proposals, but on major issues, and the vote of no confidence which brought down James Callaghan's government in March 1979 notwithstanding, governments rarely have difficulty in obtaining the necessary majority in the House. This does not mean that the House of Commons has no role to play, for it has an important indirect influence upon the legislation which is placed before it in so far as ministers will not usually frame legislation which they know will be unacceptable to their parliamentary supporters. Furthermore, it occasionally exerts direct influence and insists upon changes in bills. In addition, it serves as a testing ground for would-be ministers. But in the main it remains the case that Parliament *responds* to executive initiatives. As Hanson and Walles put it; 'The House of Commons is essentially a body in which the back-bench Members ratify decisions taken elsewhere. It legitimises but does not legislate.'[17]

Some of the closest scrutiny of governmental activity comes not on the floor of the House but in the hearings of House of Commons (or House of Lords) select committees. These committees, composed of members selected in proportion to the strength of their parties in the Commons, seek to examine the administration rather than the politics of governmental activity in as cool and non-partisan a way as possible. The most powerful and most respected of these committees has been the Public Accounts Committee, which examined past government expenditure. Although, as Hanson and Walles again observe, the committee has usually examined the expenditure of money voted by Parliament at least two years previously and may, therefore, at times have looked like a 'watchdog barking outside an empty stable', nevertheless its existence has been an important check on bureaucratic mismanagement. Furthermore, 'while the horse may have been stolen, the Committee's revelations may lead to the return of the beast, or at least a substantial part of it'.[18] For instance, the charge by the committee in 1964 that Ferranti had made excessive profits on a government contract for the Bloodhound missile resulted in the return of a considerable sum of money to the Treasury.

Also worthy of mention are the Expenditure Committee (formerly the Estimates Committee), which has scrutinised current government spending plans, and the Select Committee on Science and Technology, which has examined such matters as the UK nuclear industry, oil pollution around the British coast, defence research and development, the computer industry, and the support of science in the universities.[19] Important changes in the structure of the select committee system took place in June 1979, with the abolition of the existing specialist committees and their proposed replacement by a set of departmentally-oriented committees. Precise details of the new arrangements were not available at the time of writing.

Select committees operate by requesting written memoranda from departments on the subject of the inquiry, by taking oral evidence from officials, and sometimes from ministers and from non-governmental witnesses, and by having briefing documents prepared for them by the clerk to the committee, and possibly also by outside experts. The Public Accounts Committee has also been powerfully aided by the reports of the Comptroller and Auditor General, whose staff audit the accounts of government departments. In general, though, the degree of preparation of committee members, and hence the penetration of the inquiry, leave much to be desired. Compared, for instance, with the research facilities available to Representatives and Senators in the United States Congress, where a Representative may have a staff of six and a Senator a dozen or so, where committees have their own substantial staffs, and where they have available the largest library in the United States, the Library of Congress, with over 200 staff, some of whom have received PhDs for particularly detailed research studies conducted for Congress, British MPs have no staff beyond a secretary, and a library whose staff is measured in tens, not hundreds. A select committee will have only one clerk to assist it, and may also appoint an outside expert as part-time specialist adviser. Furthermore, in accordance with the separation of executive and legislative powers in the United States, Congressional committees have substantial power vested in them, and members of Congress generally do not seek to enter the executive branch. In Britain, by contrast, MPs collectively have very much less power, and individually usually seek appointment to ministerial office; the latter ambition is not well served by over-zealous criticism of governmental activity, and this leads to a relative lack of attentiveness on the part of many MPs to select committee work. Nevertheless, the select committees remain a useful source of information about governmental activity, and do at least provide some detailed scrutiny of the executive.

Notes

[1] Sir Paul Gore-Booth, 'Decision-Taking in the Foreign and Commonwealth Office and the Submission of Papers', in Sir Richard Clarke, *New Trends in Government* (London: HMSO, 1971), pp. 123–4.

[2] See R. J. S. Baker, *Administrative Theory and Public Administration* (London: Hutchinson University Library, 1972) chapter 7.

[3] Left-wing Labour politicians seem particularly drawn to this argument. See, for instance, Barbara Castle, 'Mandarin Power', *The Sunday Times*, 10 June 1973; Anthony Howard (ed.), *The Crossman Diaries: Selections from the Diaries of a Cabinet Minister 1964–1970 Richard Crossman* (London: Magnum Books, 1979), pp. 92, 298, and *passim*; and Michael Meacher, 'The men who block the corridors of power', *The Guardian*, 14 June, 1979.

[4] See, for instance, Edmund Dell, *Political Responsibility and Industry* (London: George Allen and Unwin, 1973), pp. 183–4; and William Plowden, letter to *The Guardian*, 20 June 1979 (replying to Meacher article cited above). For further discussion of this issue and some proposals to increase the responsiveness of officials to ministers, see *The Civil Service: Eleventh Report from the Expenditure Committee together with minutes of evidence taken before the general subcommittee in sessions 1975–76 and 1976–77 and appendices* (London: HMSO, 1977).

[5] Hugh Heclo and Aaron Wildavsky, *The Private Government of Public Money* (London: Macmillan, 1974).

[6] An excellent article on cabinet committees is Bruce Page, 'The secret constitution', *New Statesman*, 96 (No. 2470), 21 July 1978, pp. 72–6.

[7] For instance, Patrick Gordon Walker, *The Cabinet* (London: Fontana, 1972; first published 1970); Richard Crossman, *op. cit.*, *passim*; Harold Wilson, *The Governance of Britain* (London: Weidenfeld and Nicolson and Michael Joseph, 1976; my references below are from Sphere Books, 1977, edition).

[8] Reported in *New Scientist*, 14 June 1979, p. 937.

[9] White Paper on *The Reorganisation of Central Government* (London:HMSO, Cmnd 4506, 1970), cited in 'The Role of the Central Policy Review Staff in Whitehall', memorandum submitted by the CPRS, in *Eleventh Report from the Expenditure Committee: Session 1976–77, loc.*

cit., vol. II, p. 603.

[10] Victor Rothschild, *Meditations of a Broomstick* (London: Collins, 1977), pp. 112–3.

[11] The flavour of the CPRS is well caught in James Fox, 'The brains behind the throne', *The Sunday Times Magazine*, 25 March 1973.

[12] A list of CPRS studies to 1974, and a general account of the Staff's work, are given in Christopher Pollitt, 'The Central Policy Review Staff 1970–1974', *Public Administration*, **52** (winter 1974), pp. 375–92. More details on the CPRS are contained in Heclo and Wildavsky, *op. cit.*, and Harold Wilson, *op. cit.*

[13] E.g. John MacKintosh, *The British Cabinet* (London: Methuen, 1962); Richard Crossman, Introduction to Walter Bagehot, *The English Constitution* (London: Fontana, 1963), pp. 51–3. Page, *op. cit.*, explicitly attributes the outcome of two cabinet committees to packing of the committees by the Prime Minister.

[14] See Gordon Walker, *op. cit.*, chapter 5; A. H. Hanson and M. Walles, *Governing Britain* (London: Fontana, 1970), pp. 110–16; and, most recently, Wilson, *op. cit.*, pp. 12–24, who offers a direct refutation of Crossman and MacKintosh.

[15] For an argument that the British judiciary is not as independent as is often claimed, see J. A. G. Griffiths, *Politics of the Judiciary* (London: Fontana, and Manchester University Press, 1977).

[16] Bagehot, *op. cit.*, pp. 65, 66, 68.

[17] Hanson and Walles, *op. cit.*, p. 68.

[18] *Ibid.*, p. 75.

[19] See Roger Williams, 'The Select Committee on Science and Technology: the First Round', *Public Administration*, **46**, (1968), pp. 299–313; and Roger Williams, 'Towards the scientific ombudsman', *New Scientist*, 6 July 1972, pp. 13–15.

II
THE GOVERNMENT OF SCIENCE IN BRITAIN: A REVIEW

The machinery of British government has developed slowly over the centuries. It has been a gradual evolution, with no analogue to the constitution-building exercises which have taken place in, say, France and the United States. The introduction into that machinery of mechanisms for the promotion, regulation and utilisation of science and technology has, in the main, occurred relatively recently, but still in sufficiently gradual a way as to require no fundamental shake-up of the overall pattern of governmental institutions or practices.

In this chapter we make a preliminary review of the history of the government of science in Britain. The review is not intended to be exhaustive, but simply to acquaint the reader with sufficient general background to enable him to fit together and follow the more substantive chapters which are to follow. Accordingly, this chapter is largely derivative, and usually brief, in its treatment of individual developments. Where, however, an issue or event seems of some interest and is not going to be discussed in detail later in the book, then it receives rather fuller treatment in this chapter.

The nineteenth century

The establishment of the Royal Observatory at Greenwich in 1675 is generally taken as the starting point of governmental support for science in Britain, but it was not until the nineteenth century that such support acquired any momentum, with the setting up of the Geological Survey in 1832 and what later came to be called the Laboratory of the Government Chemist in 1843, initially set up to perform analyses for the Inland Revenue Department on imported perishable goods. In 1850 the government decided to award an annual grant of £1,000 to the Royal Society, to encourage the pursuit of research. One year later the Great Exhibition of Industry of all Nations not only demonstrated to the world Britain's technical and engineering skill but also yielded a financial surplus which, together with money voted by Parliament, led in 1872 to the establishment of the Royal College of Science (now the Imperial College of Science and Technology) at South Kensington.[1]

A Department of Science and Art was set up in 1853, with Lyon Playfair as science secretary. Playfair returned from the Paris International Exhibition of 1867 to argue that, by international standards, British technology had made little progress in recent years. This led to the creation, in 1868, of a Select Committee on Scientific Instruction which, *inter alia*, recommended the foundation of new colleges on the lines of Owens College, Manchester. Following further pressure from the British Association for the Advancement of Science (founded in 1831) a Royal Commission on Scientific Instruction and the Advancement of Science was set up under the chairmanship of the Duke of Devonshire. Among other things, the commission recommended the establishment of State-run laboratories, increased research grants for private scientists, and a Ministry of Science and Education advised by a Council of Science. No clear-cut governmental response was, however, made to these proposals, and it is hard even to find any substantial discussion of them in the official records of the day: the proposals appear to have fallen into a policy vacuum.[2]

Poole and Andrews suggest that there were three elements on which nineteenth-century science policy was based.[3] First, grants were awarded for pure research, either to individuals or through the Royal Society, for the funding of expeditions or specific pieces of research, such as solar physics. International expeditions 'consumed a perhaps disproportionate amount of money and were in many ways analogous to the present-day international space race'. Second, although the Treasury was in general reluctant to invest in scientific research, there was an 'explicit faith in the integrity of the Royal Society. This alliance with the establishment, and the fear of being identified as politically partisan, prevented the Royal Society from more energetically supporting the [scientific] community's demands for more money.' Third, however, was the ready availability of money for expensive utilitarian research, such as the Geological Survey, the Ordnance Survey and the technical branches of the Local Government Board (e.g. in public health), the Home Office (e.g. explosives) and the Board of Trade (e.g. lighthouses). In each of these departments, write Poole and Andrews,

> the 'scientific expert' was becoming a common phenomenon. The work of such pioneers as Sir John Simon, the first medical officer of the Privy Council, who was responsible for scientific investigations into disease and public health, and Dr. Angus Smith, the government's first Alkali Inspector, marked the beginning of a new era in public service. The public health inspectors, factory inspectors, scientific advisors to the Board of Trade and expert advisors to the Royal Commissions formed a first impressive section of the new expert class.[4]

The nature of the relationship between government and science underwent a significant change in 1899, with the foundation of the National Physical Laboratory.[5] Following German example, the Laboratory was devoted to the task of bringing scientific knowledge to bear upon everyday industrial and commercial practice. It opened the way to substantial State support for scientific *research* (as opposed to the routine application of scientific techniques in, for instance, the Laboratory of the Government Chemist), and research which, moreover, would be conducted in State-owned laboratories. Further initiatives in the agricultural and medical fields followed a decade or so later. After Lloyd George's Liberal budget of 1909, a Development Fund was created to provide for the scientific development of forestry, agriculture and fisheries; this resulted by 1914 in the establishment of twelve major agricultural research institutes in England and Wales, together with improvements in agricultural education.[6] Finally, under the National Insurance Act of 1911, whereby all wage-earners compulsorily contributed to health and unemployment insurance, one penny per insured person was allocated to a fund for medical research, to be administered by a body called the Medical Research Committee.

The first world war

The first world war brought wider recognition of the importance of science and technology, and a tightening of the bonds between science and government. The claims which had been made since the late nineteenth century about the poor state of British manufacturing industry received disturbing support in the first few months of the war with the realisation of how dependent the country was on German drugs, dyestuffs, optical equipment and other materials needed for the war effort. As an immediate response to this problem the government established in 1915 an Advisory Council on Scientific and Industrial Research. The council was initially composed of eminent scientists, though industrialists were added in later years.

At first, it was proposed that the new council should report to the Board of Education, but as the authority of the Board was restricted to England and Wales, and as it was thought that the council should have a United Kingdom jurisdiction, the government turned, in the words of Chester and Willson, to that 'ancient but extremely flexible body', the Privy Council,[7] on which a little explanation is needed.[8]

The Privy Council is composed of present and past holders of high governmental or political office, such as Cabinet ministers and leaders of the main political parties, together with other persons of distinction who are not necessarily politicians. Originally the king's advisory council, its main business today is the transaction of certain formal acts of State. Its leading ministerial member is the Lord President of the Council, who is always a senior member of the government. The Lord President has no departmental duties and is available for whatever duties the Prime Minister cares to give him, such as chairing a large number of cabinet committees. As we shall see, from 1915 until about 1970, when he was succeeded in this respect by another non-departmental minister, the Lord Privy Seal,[9] one of the Lord President's duties was the general oversight of government policy towards science and technology.

What was done in 1915, then, was to make the Advisory Council on Scientific and Industrial Research responsible to a small committee of the Privy Council, under the chairmanship of the Lord President. This was a highly convenient arrangement, for it provided the Advisory Council with a constitutional basis for its existence and with a Cabinet minister to look after its interests, while at the same time leaving it free to think and act largely independently of ministerial control. For, as Chester and Willson observed of the use of Privy Council committees to supervise not only scientific and industrial research but also, in later years, medical, agricultural and nature conservancy research, the committees were 'elaborate but transparent screens' which never concealed the fact that the Lord President was their operative member. The committees rarely met, and the Lord President was never regarded as the working head of the research organisations in any way comparable to the position of a minister at the head of a department.[10]

In 1916 it was decided that the new arrangements for scientific and industrial research would be improved by the constitution of a separate department of State, and the Department of Scientific and Industrial Research (DSIR) was set up, advised by the Advisory Council on Scientific and Industrial Research and operating under the loose supervision of the Lord President and the Privy Council Committee on Scientific and Industrial Research.[11]

DSIR came to have three main functions. First, it operated its own laboratories, which, on its dissolution in 1965, numbered fifteen and included the National Physical Laboratory (for which it assumed responsibility from the Royal Society in 1918),[12] the Building Research Station, the Fire Research Station, the Forest Products Research Laboratory and the Road Research Laboratory. Second, it administered the industrial research association scheme. This scheme was the brainchild of the Advisory Council during the war, and provided for governmental support from the so-called 'Million Fund' for research laboratories set up co-operatively, and partly funded by firms within a sector of industry.[13] Finally, the department awarded research grants to postgraduate students and to university staff. Its policies and priorities were rooted from the start in economic and social needs, and its initial emphasis on research of value to the war effort gave way in the 1920s and 1930s to programmes on such problems as the more efficient use of fuel, the development of home-grown timber, industrial fatigue, and building research.[14]

The arrangements for the constitution and supervision of DSIR soon became of considerable importance, as they provided the model for what came to be known as the research council system in Britain and, indeed, throughout the Empire. The report of a committee of inquiry into the machinery of British government, written under the chairmanship of Lord Haldane in 1918, was the instrument whereby the DSIR model became replicated.[15]

The Haldane committee placed considerable emphasis upon the need in modern government for access to what it called 'intelligence and research'.[16] This phrase embraced all kinds of statistical data (such as social and economic statistics) together with scientific research available both in the form of the results of past work and in the form of facilities for solving new problems of interest to government. The reports distinguished between research that was needed for the specific purposes of a particular department, and research which was for the general use of all departments. The former, it said, should continue to be done under the supervision of the department in question; many departments which had no provision for such work might remedy that deficiency with great advantage. The latter, however, was best not supervised by an administrative department, precisely because it was of value to more than one department and needed somehow to be related to all potential beneficiaries in a flexible way.

The committee went on to say that as regards the method to be adopted for supervising research of general use, a form of organisation on the lines already laid down for DSIR would prove most suitable. One advantage of this arrangement was that it made possible an authority whose jurisdiction would cover the whole United Kingdom (whereas attachment to a ministry often entailed jurisdiction over England and Wales only). Another was that it placed responsibility to Parliament in the hands of a minister who 'is in normal times free from any serious pressure of administrative duties, and is immune from any suspicion of being biased by administrative considerations against the application of the results of research'.[17] The clear implication of this sentence was that departmental ministers might, because of departmental pressures, sometimes find it inconvenient to support certain kinds of research, or to publish or use the results. By placing responsibility for research of general use with the Lord President, the Haldane committee hoped to avoid even the possibility of this eventuality. The sentence is doubly noteworthy, however, because it is the root of what, in later years, has been called the 'Haldane principle of research council autonomy'. It is worth emphasising that neither Haldane himself nor his committee ever used such a phrase, and also that the intention of the sentence was to free from direct ministerial control only that research which was of value to more than one department.

A further recommendation of the committee was that the Medical Research Committee should be reconstituted analogously with DSIR, under the nominal control of the Lord President and a Privy Council committee.[18] This recommendation was implemented in 1920 with the creation of the Medical Research Council (MRC). Although modelled on DSIR, MRC also differed from it in not being a government department, in appointing its own chief executive, or Secretary (that of DSIR being appointed by the Lord President), and in having staff who were not civil servants. Whereas DSIR worked through its own laboratories, the industrial research associations and research grants, MRC set up no equivalent to the research associations, spent a relatively smaller amount of money on individual research grants, and concentrated its resources into a small number of central laboratories (such as the National Institute for Medical Research) and a large number of research units attached to universities and hospitals, all staffed by MRC personnel.[19]

This is a convenient place to move ahead of the chronology and add that, in 1931, an Agricultural Research Council (ARC) was set up, followed in 1949 by the Nature Conservancy, both responsible to the same Privy Council committee and to the Lord President. Together with DSIR and MRC, they constituted until 1965 what came to be called the four 'research councils'.

Haldane's 1918 report also suggested that as the amount of general research conducted for government grew it might become impossible for the Lord President to supervise it adequately in addition to his other duties. It was thought that there might one day be a need for a minister 'specifically appointed on the ground of his suitability to preside over a separate Department of Intelligence and Research, which would no longer act under a Committee of the Privy Council, and would take its place among the most important Departments of Government'.[20] Haldane took a variant of this proposal to Ramsay MacDonald, after the election of the first Labour government in 1924, his plan now being that a central advisory committee should be established to which the Cabinet could refer technical questions.[21] According to MacLeod and Andrews, the proposed committee was to have three objects:

> First, to ensure that critical problems were brought to the attention of the government and studied on a statistical basis; second, to assist the government of the day with an organisation, 'stable but not rigid,' for exploring the problems in which it was interested, without the need for improvising machinery of coordination; and third, to utilise to the

greatest advantage the existing research facilities of government departments.'

MacDonald was initially enthusiastic, but his enthusiasm waned and no action was taken until after the return of Baldwin's government in 1925, and the reappointment of Balfour as Lord President. Roughly coinciding with the election, something of a national outcry was aroused by revelations of poor British administration of research in East Africa. Balfour, who had a deep sense of the importance of scientific research, took this opportunity to resurrect Haldane's proposal, with the result that the Committee of Civil Research (CCR) was established in June 1925. The task of this committee was to give 'connected forethought from a central point of view to the development of economic, scientific and statistical research in relation to civil policy and administration, and [to] define new areas in which enquiry would be valuable'. It was to be an advisory body, and was to co-ordinate, on the civil side, economic, scientific and statistical work. It was to have no statutory members except the Prime Minister, and its procedures were to be flexible in the extreme.

The CCR proceeded, through a series of sub-committees, to examine a wide variety of home and imperial affairs.[22] The composition of the sub-committees varied, some being restricted to Cabinet ministers, others consisting largely or wholly of government scientists or outside experts. Some of the topics were selected on Balfour's initiative, but more usually the committee responded to departmental initiatives. In the climate of the late '20s and early '30s, the CCR could not, however, survive without support from powerful allies to countermand the general apathy towards science. Balfour's declining strength consequently weakened the committee considerably, and in 1930 it was transformed into a new Economic Advisory Committee on which science was soon forced into second place.

To sum up the inter-war period, we may say that those years saw a steady build-up in governmental support for research. In addition to the developments already recounted, the Ministries of Agriculture and Fisheries, Health, and Fuel and Power, the Post Office, the Colonial Office and the Service departments all strengthened their research facilities so that, whereas in 1920 government expenditure on civil research and development (R&D) totalled about £1·3 million, by 1939 it had reached about £4 million.[23] The research councils accounted for a major share of this expenditure, DSIR being, throughout this period, the largest single source of government support for civil R&D.

Looking back on this period, Lord Zuckerman, who, as we shall see, played a major role in government–science relations during and after the second world war, considered that it was then that the research councils firmly established the tradition of operating autonomously from government, in accordance with the so-called 'Haldane Principle'.[24] He suggests that a consequence of this was that 'a kind of intellectual barrier developed between "Royal Society," "Research Council," and "University Science" on the one hand, and the scientific laboratories of government departments and industry on the other, the former assuming a far higher prestige'. Few complained about this; most departments 'were still run by men most of whom had graduated in the classics or the humanities'. In any case, by modern standards government expenditure on science was tiny during the inter-war period.

Yet, as Vig has observed, this expenditure was nevertheless 'undoubtedly high' by contemporary international standards.[25] In his view, other Western governments had made no greater progress in co-ordinating research programmes, and there was no evidence that the British machinery of government 'was especially deficient in view of the limited goals pursued'. Thus, with the major reservation that she lacked scientists and other specialists in senior positions in public administration, Britain can at least be said to have caught up with other Western nations in the institutionalisation of science by the start of the second world war.

The second world war and after

That war, as Vig describes it, was 'the great turning point in government–science relations in Britain as elsewhere'.[26] He adds that one immediate result of the war was that scientists, economists and other specialists were integrated into government administration and planning in a way they had not been previously. This point can be supported by reference to the mass of publications describing the development of operations research[27] and the work performed by scientists in, for instance, the development of radar, not merely as a technical device which would work in the laboratory, but as an operational tool which would work in combat conditions.[28] It can also be supported by reference to the debate about the role of scientific advisers, as epitomised in the pre-war and wartime conflicts between Sir Henry Tizard, then chairman of the Air Ministry's Committee for the Scientific Survey of Air Defence, and Professor F. A. Lindemann (later Lord Cherwell), Churchill's friend and scientific adviser, over the priority to be given to radar research and other matters.[29] (See chapter four.)

That the introduction of scientists to high office within government even in time of war was not, however, without considerable difficulties is well illustrated by the history of the Scientific Advisory Committee to the War Cabinet, the background to which goes back before the second world war.

During the 1930s there developed an increased awareness within at least some sections of the scientific community of the idea of the social responsibility of scientists. This awareness was in turn part of the wider climate of intellectual soul-searching generated by the conjunction of the depression and the rise of communism and fascism.[30] One of the standard-bearers among the scientists was J. D. Bernal, who argued in his book *The Social Function of Science*[31] that science should be planned so as to serve social needs. The book was highly controversial[32] and came under attack from the Society for Freedom in Science, which was started in 1940 by J. R. Baker, M. Polanyi and others. Against them, Zuckerman suggested that the attackers misunderstood Bernal's position. He considered *The Social Function* to be a 'fascinating challenge',[33] and in a favourable review written in 1939 he argued that Bernal's attitude towards the social role of science was 'a very strong reflection of a change which has come over most scientists during the past few years'.[34] As convener of the curiously named Tots and Quots dining club,[35] at which 'radical' and 'reformist' scientists[36] met and discussed the social relations of science, Zuckerman was in a good position to make such a judgment.

After the unprecedented political activity of at least some of their number during the '30s, it would have been surprising if scientists had not tried to gain access to the highest counsels of war. One proposal to that end came from Sir Henry Tizard, who, in addition to his Air Ministry post mentioned above, was also Rector of Imperial College, and had been secretary of DSIR. Tizard's proposal, made in July 1938, was for a Central Scientific Committee under the Minister for the Co-ordination of Defence, and included provision for the committee to initiate research under certain conditions.[37] It came to nothing, as did a proposal from the Royal Society almost a year later that, in effect, a small group of leading fellows of the society might place themselves at the disposal of the Committee of Imperial Defence.[38] In September 1939 the society proposed instead that its two secretaries might serve as liaison officers between the Cabinet and the scientific world.[39] It was not until twelve months later, following further representations, that the Scientific Advisory Committee to the War Cabinet (SAC) was brought into existence.[40]

The committee's first chairman was Lord Hankey, and its members were the president and two secretaries of the Royal Society, and the secretaries of the three research councils. Its terms of reference were:

(a) to advise the Lord President on any scientific matter referred to it;
(b) to advise government departments, when so requested, on the selection of individuals for particular lines of scientific enquiry, or for membership of committees on which scientists are required; and
(c) to bring to the notice of the Lord President promising new scientific or technical developments which may be important to the war effort.'[41]

There has been no detailed study of the SAC, but a number of observations have been made about it, chiefly by Clark.[42] He noted that the committee studied 'a wide range of ad hoc problems varying from the need to secure the country's food supplies to reports that the enemy was building a Channel Tunnel. It was in a good position to collect evidence, and it controlled a number of specialist Panels and Sub-Committees.' He felt, though, that its organisation was inadequate, and that Churchill tolerated it only on the understanding that 'we are to have additional support from outside rather than an incursion into our interior'. Clark caught this reluctant aquiescence well in Tizard's remark that 'the Prime Minister did not like at all the suggestion of the setting up of the Committee under a Cabinet Minister, but he thought it politically wise to do so'. And he added Tizard's opinion that the SAC was 'really very ineffective' since, while it did some 'useful but not outstanding work', it was not 'particularly concerned with the needs of the fighting Services'. As Clark observed, Tizard's opinion is valuable because, although not a member of the SAC, he was at the time Foreign Secretary of the Royal Society and was naturally in close contact with the committee's members – so much so that his position was to become 'the paradoxical one of unofficial adviser to the advisers'.

Clark also concluded that the committee was at times 'either ignored or short-circuited by the one-man recommendations of Professor Lindemann'. In this respect, it is noteworthy that R. A. Butler, who succeeded Hankey as chairman of the SAC, recalls discussing the committee with Lindemann while on a journey in March 1943. Lindemann, he said, thought 'it was a pity that this committee had ever been appointed, that it had been called into existence only to appease the *amour propre* of the scientific establishment, and that he himself did not think it worth a moment of his worry'.[43] Butler adds, however, that the committee seemed 'to be worth more than a moment of our journey'. He has since remarked that, in his view, the SAC did useful work in acting as a focus for scientists, and that Lindemann's polemical remarks were not only unjustified but ungenerous.[44] But this remains a subject for investigation.

ACSP and DRPC

In January 1947 the SAC was replaced by the Advisory Council on Scientific Policy, which had the function of advising the Lord President in the exercise of his responsibility for the formulation and execution of government (civil) scientific policy.[45] It was paralleled on the defence side by the Defence Research Policy Committee (DRPC), advising the Minister of Defence. The debate within Whitehall which accompanied this change will be discussed in chapter seven, and for now it suffices to note that the Advisory Council was composed of scientists and industrialists from outside the government service, the heads of the research councils, a representative from the Treasury, and a few others, meeting under the chairmanship of Sir Henry Tizard. Sir Henry was also appointed chairman of the Defence Research Policy Committee and became, in effect, the government's chief scientific adviser. To aid co-ordination, there was some overlap in the staff of the two committees. Professor Zuckerman soon became deputy chairman of the Advisory Council.

Tizard, who had been reluctant to accept these posts,[46] began to plan his retirement in late 1949, and proposed that Professor (later Sir) John Cockcroft, Director of the Atomic Energy Research Establishment at Harwell, should replace him on both DRPC and ACSP. The Labour government accepted this proposal, but the return to power of Cherwell (with the election of a Conservative government in 1951) led to changes.[47] In 1952 Cockcroft did succeed Tizard as chairman of the DRPC, while remaining Director of Harwell, but this arrangement lasted only until August 1954, when he was replaced on the DRPC by Sir Frederick Brundrett, who had served as deputy to both Tizard and Cockcroft. Brundrett in turn was replaced by Zuckerman in 1960. On the civil side, Tizard's successor on the ACSP was A. R. (later Lord) Todd, Professor of Organic Chemistry at the University of Cambridge, who remained chairman from 1952 until 1964, when the Advisory Council ceased to exist.

Not much is known about the work of the DRPC. In 1947 Tizard told the Estimates Committee that while the DRPC looked weak on paper, the direct access which its chairman had to the Minister of Defence, by-passing the Chiefs of Staff, made it strong in practice.[48] At the same time he added that, on the civil side, the new ACSP would act as a 'clearing house' and a co-ordinating centre; it was in a 'very strong strategic position because it has the responsibility of initiating work. It does not wait to meet until somebody asks its advice.'[49]

Despite Tizard's optimism, the new machinery faced several difficulties from the beginning. First, in the post-war euphoria over science (which, having won the war, was now – some said – going to 'win the peace'), it was possible that too much might be expected too fast from science. Tizard warned of this danger, and was echoed by the Estimates Committee.[50] Second, Tizard was never content with the 'domestic arrangements' for the two advisory bodies – that is, protocol, transport, and so on. Clark relates how, despite Tizard's stipulation that he be provided with adequate transport, he was met to be taken to the Ministry by a car of 'little dignity and considerable age. It is claimed that Tizard took one look at it and exclaimed: "Call a cab".'[51] But perhaps most important was the extremely limited extent to which the new bodies were responsible for advising on the defence and civil applications of atomic energy.

Between 1947 and 1954 responsibility for the atomic energy programme was divided between the Prime Minister (Attlee, then Churchill) and the Ministry of Supply. Decision-making focused sharply on a series of ministerial cabinet committees, assisted by a confusing and changing array of official and advisory committees. The ACSP itself in 1948 set up an advisory committee on atomic energy but this was never one of the key committees within Whitehall on the subject.[52]

As for the DRPC, it had no responsibility at that time for the development of atomic energy. In the confusion which plagued the atomic energy machinery, Tizard was kept out of touch with atomic matters.[53] While the ACSP's limited role in atomic energy affairs was a possible constraint upon its effectiveness, in the case of the DRPC the matter was much more serious. As Hayward has argued, since the DRPC was not party to the most crucial aspect of Britain's defence research, it lacked the necessary scope and influence to have much real effect on the course of that research.[54] Although the situation was apparently rectified by 1956,[55] this early gap in the matrix of responsibilities which were supposedly co-ordinated by, and between, the ACSP and the DRPC was serious.

More is known about the ACSP than the DRPC, if only because it published a report each year of its life (1947–64), as well as additional reports by its chief committee – the Committee on Scientific Manpower, under the chairmanship of Professor Zuckerman.[56] The reports attracted a good deal of interest in the press (Nature devoted at least part of a leading article to each report; The Times covered each report with a leading article or at least a summary; The Guardian reported all but two of the reports),[57] and were also generally favourably received and much quoted in Parliament.[58] Contemporary commentators were on the whole favourably disposed towards the council. Thus, when Tizard retired, Nature commented that Professor Todd was taking over 'a going concern with a record of achievement and with a high prestige in Whitehall'.[59]

Yet later commentators were less enthusiastic. Dr Alexander King, who had been the council's first secretary (later becoming Director General for Scientific Affairs at OECD), thought that it declined in status after Tizard resigned, reasoning that Todd's part-time appointment inevitably restricted his scope for contact with ministers, and that his responsibility for civil science only also weakened his position.[60] The doyen of science journalists, J. G. Crowther, however, considered that after 1952 a new forthrightness and emphasis appeared in the council's reports, although he also thought that the council became 'more a commentator on, rather than a leader of, scientific policy, in spite of many penetrating . . . pronouncements'.[61]

Vig has offered a lengthier analysis, based on his opinion that, with the exception of the work of the Committee on Scientific Manpower, 'generally the Council had little influence'. While the council had achieved some success under Tizard, 'whose unique experience and dual role as chief military scientist carried considerable authority', its position was later weakened. This was partly because separate chairmen were appointed to the ACSP and the DRPC, and partly because the element of overlap in their staffs was removed. The effect of these changes, said Vig, citing 'a former official intimately involved', was to destroy the system of co-ordination built up by Tizard, and to contribute to 'a marked deterioration in relations among the various civil and military research agencies, greatly undermining the position of ACSP as well'. Vig also considered that the council's 'vague terms of reference restricted it to occasional advice on general problems (aside from certain specific matters of lesser import)', and that its lack of authority on budgetary matters and on overall planning, together with the fact that atomic energy was outside its scope, contributed to its lack of influence. And while, in Vig's opinion, the appointment (see below) of Lord Hailsham as Minister for Science led to 'broader scope' becoming apparent 'in the ACSP's considerations of the national balance of research, and sharper conclusions in its advice on certain allocational difficulties', nevertheless the council continued to be restricted by 'its purely advisory status, its limited working brief, and its lack of staff assistance'.[62]

Similar arguments have come from others. Hilary and Steven Rose also considered that co-ordination between defence and civil science policy did not outlast the dual chairmanship of Tizard, and that the council's advisory status prevented it becoming a major force in policy-making. They suggested, however, that the trouble was that the ACSP conflicted not so much with its political masters as with the civil service:

The Secretariat of the new Council seems early to have run into opposition from those mandarins within the Civil Service – particularly within the Treasury – who resented the passage of power into the hands of an essentially non-Civil Service body; it was, for the eighteen years of its life, to be hampered by an inadequate machinery for either obtaining information on which to base its advice, or having its advice heeded once given.[63]

This argument cannot, however, be sustained from the official record, at least at the outset of the council's life. On the contrary, the tone of senior Treasury and Cabinet Office staff was one of cordial welcome for the council; E. M. Nicholson, the head of the Office of the Lord President at the time, and no friend of the Treasury, has said that the Treasury made no difficulties over the council's staff – again, at the outset.[64] Whether subsequent changes took place cannot yet be assessed from the official record, although as will be seen below, a high-ranking government committee, with Lord Todd among its members, was to argue in 1963 that the council's secretariat was inadequate to the tasks it then faced.

These generally negative commentaries on the value of the Advisory Council (to which one may add that of Professor Lord Blackett[65]) usually made an exception for the council's work in persuading successive governments to increase dramatically the provision of places in higher education (principally in the universities) for the study of science and technology. Lord Zuckerman has claimed that this was one of the council's more successful areas of activity,[66] and Gannicott and Blaug have described the manpower committee and its post-ACSP successor as being a (successful) 'science lobby in action'.[67] The record of achievement is certainly clear. The committee pioneered the collection of statistics about the supply of scientists and engineers in Britain, and also pioneered work on forecasting the demand for them.[68] Their arguments were acknowledged by the government to underlie the sharp expansion in higher education places for science and engineering which began in 1956, and which raised the supply of new graduates and holders of degree-level diplomas in science and technology from 7,688 in 1955 to 14,150 in 1964.[69]

But to claim that this was the only area in which the council's advice was influential seems unduly restrictive. The appointment of a number of departmental chief scientific advisers in 1947–48, an expansion in 1954 in the role of the National Research

Development Corporation (a government-funded body set up in 1949 to aid the development of inventions), the curtailment of plans for Britain to become involved in manned space flight and the establishment of the Natural Environment Research Council (see below) are only some of the issues on which ACSP advice can be fairly firmly held (in the absence of access to the official records) to have been strongly influential.[70] Furthermore, of the issues discussed in the ACSP reports, it can be shown that the council got what it wanted on about half of them.[71] Of course, to say that the outcome of an issue corresponded with the ACSP's advice does not prove that the advice was the influential factor in the government's mind. But this finding does raise a doubt over the conventional hasty dismissal of the ACSP and suggests that further analysis when enough of the official records are open to examination may modify the conventional wisdom on this subject.

Other pre-1964 developments

We now retrace our steps to the years immediately following the establishment of the ACSP and the DRPC and briefly summarise the other main developments in the field of science–government relations up to 1964, when a major transformation took place.

The establishment in 1949 of the Nature Conservancy has already been mentioned. A second early post-war development was the establishment of the National Research Development Corporation (NRDC), the function of which, as also mentioned above, was to give financial assistance for the development of inventions.[72]

Thirdly, from 1954 the Lord President's scientific duties expanded to include responsibility for atomic energy. Research in this field had begun during the war under the auspices of DSIR, and therefore under the political control of the Lord President, but after the war it was decided that such a defence-oriented subject should be entrusted to the Ministry of Supply. It was later decided to make the development of atomic energy the responsibility of a non-departmental authority, and in January 1954 the statutory powers of the Minister of Supply in this respect were transferred to the Lord President. On 1 August 1954, following pressure on the Cabinet by Lord Cherwell,[73] the UK Atomic Energy Authority (AEA) came into existence, under the supervision of the Lord President. It was responsible for research into, and the production of, fissile material; for the study of the industrial applications of atomic energy; and for supplying weapons under contract to the Ministry of Supply. After the resignation in March 1957 of the Lord President, Lord Salisbury, his functions with respect to atomic energy were transferred to the Prime Minister, where they remained until November 1959, when they passed to the newly created Office of the Minister for Science.[74]

The creation of that office appears to have owed more to political pressure than to administrative need. Chester and Willson offer as reasons for this development 'the increasing popular awareness of the importance of scientific advancement for the national well-being; the widening of the actual group of government organisations dealing with scientific research, and the financial and high policy aspects of that widening; and the attractiveness of a dramatic sounding new office with the General Election at hand'.[75] A further factor was pressure from within the government to turn the Ministry of Supply into a Ministry of Technology.[76] The result, however, was little more than a return to the position during Lord Salisbury's lord presidency, there not even being a change in the operative minister, since the then Lord President, Viscount Hailsham, was immediately appointed Minister for Science. Dissatisfaction with this apparent lack of purposeful action was freely expressed in Parliament.[77]

To conclude this discussion of events up to 1964, the development of R&D from the war to 1964 may be described quantitatively. Total government expenditure on both civil and military R&D was somewhat less than £10 million in 1939 (having risen from about £0·6 million in 1913).[78] Expenditure by private industry on R&D at that time was somewhat over half that figure.[79] By 1947–48 government expenditure had grown enormously. Civil R&D was costing about £9 million, with a further £7 million spent on research in the universities (via the UGC), and defence expenditure had reached about £60 million.[80] The defence component continued to dominate government R&D expenditure for many years to come. Government also continued to provide the major share of the total national R&D outlay, although the industrial contribution grew from a little under a quarter in 1955–56 to just over a third in 1961–62. But although government always provided most of the money for R&D, industry, at least from 1955 and probably from 1945, did most of the work.[81]

Atomic energy and aviation apart (see table 2.1), the major dispensers of public expenditure on civil R&D in the twenty years after the war were the research councils, especially DSIR. The only civil departments with significant R&D budgets were the agriculture departments. Clearly, however, expenditure on aviation R&D was comparable in scale to that on the research councils and the universities, and, buried in the defence statistics, the support given to atomic energy research was probably greater still.

The number of economically active qualified scientists and engineers (QSEs) grew by about 50 per cent between 1956 and 1965 to a total of 301,000.[82] The great majority of QSEs, at least from 1956, worked in industry, with the education sector taking second place and government third. But whereas most engineers were employed in industry, the largest sectoral employer of scientists was education. Of the QSEs in industry, a very high proportion worked in a very small number of industries, so that in 1956, for example, one-third of the QSEs in industry were in the aircraft, chemical or electrical industries.[83] About one-third of QSEs in industry as a whole were engaged on R&D, the proportion being higher (about 55 per cent) for scientists and lower (about 25 per cent) for engineers. Of the QSEs engaged in R&D, about 40 per cent in 1956 were on defence work in either industry or government establishments, this figure falling to about 25 per cent by 1959.[84] As recently as 1965 about 10 per cent of the QSEs in manufacturing industry were engaged upon defence work.[85]

Overall, therefore, R&D in the UK from 1945 to 1964 was mainly financed by government but performed by industry. The number of QSEs grew fairly steadily, these people being engaged to a large degree upon defence work, with industrial activity being particularly concentrated in the aircraft, chemical and electrical industries. Within the civil government sector, the main agencies were those concerned with civil atomic energy and aviation, followed by the research councils and the universities.

Table 2.1
Estimated government expenditure on civil R&D, 1945–46 to 1963–64
(£ million)

Source of expenditure	A 1945–6	B 1950–1	C 1955–6	D 1960–1	E 1963–4
1. DSIR[a]	2·3	4·9	7·5[b]	16·0	25·4
2. MRC	0·3	1·7	2·3	4·5	7·0
3. ARC	0·3	0·8	1·2	5·6	7·2
4. Nature Conservancy	*	0·08	0·2	0·5	0·7
5. Total–research councils	2·9	7·5	11·2	26·6	40·3
6. Universities and learned societies[c]	1·5	8·3	11·0[d]	19·4	31·2
7. Development Fund	0·03	0·3	0·4	0·5	0·7
8. Agricultural departments [a, e]	0·6	2·0	4·5[f]	3·7	5·1
9. Other civil departments [g]	0·9	3·0	6·0	6·4	4·6
10. Navy department	0·05	0·2	0·3	0·5	0·7
11. Air department	0·6[h]	0·4	0·6[i]	1·2	1·0
12. Ministry of Aviation[j]	n.a.	8·0	n.a.	16·8	31·2
13. NIRNS[k]	*	*	*	5·2	7·8
14. AEA[l]	*	*	n.a.	n.a.	45·0
Total 5–11	6·58	22·0	34·0	58·3	83·6
Total 5–12	n.a.	30·0	n.a.	75·1	114·8
Total 5–13	*	*	*	80·3	122·6
Total 5–14	*	*	*	n.a.	167·6

n.a. Figure not available.
*   Not applicable.

Notes

a   Includes expenditure on buildings by Ministry of Public Buildings and Works, and other allied services.
b   Taken from ACSP, ninth report, appendix III, table B.
c   The UGC does not record research expenditure separately. The items in columns A, B, D and E are estimates based upon a special inquiry made in 1961–62.
d   This figure has been computed from the item on learned societies given in ACSP, ninth report, appendix III, table A, and the item on university research in S. Blume, 'Research Support in British Universities', *Minerva*, 7 (1969), p. 651, table 1.

Changes in the 1960s

Important changes in the machinery for the government of
science in Britain took place in the 1960s. By the early years of the
decade the high cost of research in such fields as space, high-
energy physics and radio-astronomy was forcing serious thought to
be given to the problem of priorities, particularly within the
research council system.

Questions also began to be asked about the wisdom of the non-
directive approach of successive governments to the research
councils, and about the relation of the research councils to the rest
of what was by then a fairly elaborate governmental R&D system.
These kinds of questions had been an issue in the 1959 election, and
the subsequent appointment of a Minister for Science, aided as he
himself put it by only a busful of civil servants, satisfied few.
Worsening economic conditions, a growing debate about the role

---

e Includes National Agricultural Advisory Service and programmes in
Scotland under the direction of the ARC.
f Computed from items on Agriculture and Fisheries in ACSP, ninth
report, appendix III, table A.
g The figures in columns A, B and D include research expenditure by the
Post Office prior to its becoming independent of Exchequer finance.
h Includes total amount spent on meteorology, both operational and
research, since separate figures are not available for 1945–46.
i Based on Air Ministry's contribution to Medical and Meteorological
Research as itemised in ACSP, ninth report, appendix III, table A.
j The figures for 1945–46 and 1955–56 are not distinguishable within the
total research expenditure of the Ministries of Aviation and of Supply.
The figure for 1950–51 was calculated on an undisclosed basis. The
DSIR and Ministry of Aviation figures for 1960–61 and 1963–64 include
an element towards space research which is not distinguishable.
k The National Institute for Research in Nuclear Science (NIRNS) was
established in 1958 to provide highly expensive research facilities in
nuclear physics for use by all British universities. It was financed
through the Atomic Energy Vote.
l Civil expenditure by the AEA is not separately distinguishable before
1961–62.

Sources. Columns A, B, D, E from Council for Scientific Policy, Report on
Science Policy, (Cmnd 3007, 1966), appendix II. Column C from
ACSP, ninth report, (Cmnd 11, 1956), appendix III, table A, with
two exceptions as detailed in notes b and d.

which science and technology should play in the modernisation of the economy, and on top of that the so-called 'brain drain' whereby British scientists were believed to be emigrating in large numbers, set the scene for a major political and administrative debate.

The internal politics and the electoral image of the Labour Party provided the final impetus to set this debate going. The party was concerned to improve its image, having lost three consecutive general elections. It was also internally torn on the issue, not unrelated, of whether to drop clause IV of its constitution, the clause which embodied Labour's commitment to nationalisation. The solution to both problems was seen by Harold Wilson as being to 'redefine our socialism in terms of the scientific age. Instead of nationalising old, ailing sectors of the economy, we should apply public ownership at the growing points of industry – in the manufacture, for example, of products created by Government-sponsored research and development.'[86] This left-wing argument clearly implied a more *dirigiste* approach to government-sponsored R&D. At the same time, as Vig argues, identification with science also suited the right-wing revisionists in the party: 'how better to improve Labour's backward, working-class image and appeal to new professionals?'[87]

The result of both streams of thought was the commitment by Harold Wilson in 1960 to harness socialism to science and science to socialism, a commitment which was mobilised when he became leader of the party in January 1963,[88] and which led to a clear differentiation between the policies of the major parties in the run-up to the 1964 election. Whereas Labour, by now, was talking of setting up a Ministry of Technology and of making dynamic and purposeful use of science and technology, Conservative policy for science and technology, despite the dissent of some MPs (Aubrey Jones and Robert Carr in particular) was still cast in the *laissez-faire* mould of Quintin Hogg (formerly, and later, Lord Hailsham), the Minister for Science. Science, according to the Conservative campaign guide, was not in general a proper field for detailed government control and planning. Individual creativity, flexibility and freedom from centralised administration were the watchwords.[89]

The government was, however, under clear pressure on the political front to take some action to improve the way in which science and technology articulated with economic and other goals.

Internally, too, there was pressure for change. The ACSP was becoming increasingly concerned about the problem of priorities. It had no authority itself to advise upon the distribution of resources to the research councils and other scientific bodies. Because the research councils each negotiated their budgets individually and directly with the Treasury (and did not go through the Minister for Science), the only forum within government in which the competing claims of scientific bodies could be heard was the Treasury, and officials there were becoming decreasingly content with that arrangement.[90]

Accordingly, in March 1962, the government set up a committee of inquiry into the organisation of civil science. The chairman was Sir Burke Trend, a senior Treasury official who was soon to become secretary to the Cabinet. Among the six other members were Lord Todd and three other people (the chairman of the UGC, a university scientist and a Treasury official) who were, or had recently been, members of the ACSP.

The Trend committee was appointed to consider three issues.[91] The first was the desirability of changes in the functions of the agencies for which the Minister for Science was responsible, and in particular whether any new agencies were needed. The second was the arrangements 'for determining, with appropriate scientific advice, the relative importance in the national interest of the claims on the Exchequer for the promotion of civil scientific research in the various fields concerned'. The third was whether any changes were needed in the existing procedures by which the agencies were financed and held accountable for their expenditure.

The committee found that the various agencies concerned with the promotion of civil science did not, 'in the aggregate, constitute a coherent and articulated pattern of organisation'; and that 'the arrangements for co-ordinating the Government's scientific effort on a rational basis are insufficiently clear and precise'.[92] One major recommendation of the committee was that DSIR should be divided into a Science Research Council (SRC) and an Industrial Research and Development Authority (IRDA).[93] This recommendation, with its concomitant criticisms of the unwieldy structure of DSIR, can be taken as a reflection upon the inability of the ACSP to make similar criticisms of the research councils. The Trend committee touched upon that point obliquely when it said that the 'mixed membership' of the council was a handicap, since it was 'inconsistent with the conception of an advisory council that it should include official members' who necessarily represented 'the several policies' of their own organisations.[94] Two other organisational defects which the committee found in the ACSP were that, as the financing of the various agencies fell outside its purview, it had little means of influencing priorities, and that the small size of the secretariat handicapped the collection of information and the detailed study of major problems of policy.

The committee considered that the Minister for Science needed wider powers to enable him to play 'a more positive and effective part than hitherto' in promoting R&D.[95] It therefore recommended that he should assume responsibility 'for assessing the financial requirements of the agencies, for settling with the Treasury the funds to be made available for the promotion of civil scientific research and development and for allocating these funds as grants-in-aid among the agencies'. The existing system by which the Treasury decided between the claims of the research councils might have sufficed, said the committee, as long as the total outlay of the councils and other agencies was small. But with research council expenditure alone running at about £35 million per annum, and when a single new item might cost £1 million or more, it was necessary both that there should be more central co-ordination and that the co-ordinating minister should be fortified in his judgment by 'a full assessment of the scientific case for each project involved in relation to the needs not of one, but of all the agencies for which he is responsible'.

The minister was, therefore, to be advised by a reconstituted ACSP.[96] Its terms of reference would be similar to those already operating, except that it would be authorised to advise the minister on the allocation of resources to the agencies under his control. This would be done at the level of general recommendations about the forward programmes of the agencies, rather than through detailed examination of the budgets of the individual agencies. In order to carry out these functions the new ACSP would require a considerably strengthened secretariat. The council itself would consist of independent scientists and industrialists, at least one economist and some persons with wide experience of public affairs, and its meetings would be attended by assessors from the research councils and appropriate departments.

One other recommendation which must be mentioned is that

the committee endorsed an ACSP proposal for the establishment of a Natural Resources Research Council, based on the Nature Conservancy but taking over also some of the functions of DSIR.[97]

With the exception of a proposal to transfer NRDC from the Board of Trade to the Minister for Science, the Trend proposals were accepted by the government in July 1964, and at the same time the ministerial division of responsibility between education (higher and lower) and science was resolved with the announcement that a Department of Education and Science (DES) was to be set up, merging the Ministry for Science with the Ministry of Education. Implementation of the Trend blueprint, which was the product of discussions within the closed confines of Whitehall, was, however, considerably upset by the intrusion of party politics upon this arena. For, in accordance with its electoral pledges, the newly returned Labour government placed the industrial side of DSIR not under an IRDA but under a new Ministry of Technology. Perhaps fearing the worst, Lord Todd resigned the chairmanship of the ACSP on 1 October 1964,[98] fully two weeks before the general election. Yet, while party politics determined the broad structure of the new government science organisation, the detailed structure was in many ways faithful to the Trend plan. A Natural Environment (not Resources) Research Council (NERC) and the SRC were set up, financial responsibility for the research councils devolved to the DES, and the Secretary of State for Education and Science was to be advised on his responsibilities for science policy, including the allocation of resources to the research councils, by a new Council for Scientific Policy (CSP), composed wholly of independent scientists and industrialists. Thus the machinery for determining priorities between the research councils was established, but this was considerably less than the machinery which Trend had proposed for determining priorities across a much wider spectrum of civil R&D.

The Ministry of Technology

The Labour manifesto of 1964 stated that the promised Ministry of Technology would 'guide and stimulate a major national effort to bring advanced technology and new processes into industry'.[99] Initially the ministry was very small: it comprised mainly the

Atomic Energy Authority, the National Research Development Corporation, and the so-called industrial research establishments of DSIR; it also had responsibility for the industrial research associations and for the machine tool, computer, electronics and telecommunications industries. It had its own Advisory Council on Technology, chaired by the minister and with Professor Blackett as deputy chairman. The ministry was based on the beliefs that Britain's economic problems were largely due to a failure to apply technology sufficiently rapidly in industry, and that a civil technology ministry could help redress the distortions introduced into British technology by defence requirements.[100]

The ministry had a shaky start. It was small, and it was new on the Whitehall scene; it had difficulty getting staff from other departments;[101] its ministers (Frank Cousins, formerly secretary of the Transport and General Workers' Union, and Lord (C. P.) Snow, the novelist and former scientist) were not experienced in the ways of either Whitehall or Westminister. Mr Cousins had no seat in the Commons until January 1965. The ministry was reinforced in 1966 by its assumption of responsibility for the shipbuilding and engineering industries, but also lost Frank Cousins in July 1966, when he resigned over the government's incomes policy. He was succeeded by Anthony Wedgwood Benn.

It had already been agreed within Whitehall that the ministry needed strengthening, and a merger had been planned between the Ministry of Technology and the Ministry of Aviation. As the permanent secretary from 1966 (Sir Richard Clarke) put it, it had been 'rather absurd to talk about a "Ministry of Technology" with no say in the government's biggest stake in advanced technology, which was aircraft and electronics; and experience had already proved that to be responsible for so-called "sponsorship" of the electronics industry . . . was meaningless in practice when another department was responsible for very large R&D and procurement orders in the electronics industry'.[102]

Aviation was duly incorporated into Technology in February 1967. The staff immediately grew from 6,000 to 36,000 and was organised into three groups: Aviation, with responsibility for the development of civil aircraft (including Concorde), for space technology, and for procurement of defence aircraft and electronics (costing about £550 million a year); Research, comprising sixteen research establishments, two factories, the AEA (making altogether the biggest R&D force under one financial control in Western Europe), as well as NRDC and the officials responsible for supporting forty-six industrial research associations; and Engineering, which chiefly involved the government's responsibilities for the engineering, vehicle and shipbuilding industries. As Sir Richard Clarke observed,

> the centre of gravity of the new Ministry was industrial. Aircraft and atomic energy, much the biggest recipients of government industrial money ... were brought within the mainstream of industrial and economic policy ... the idea that 'science' should be kept at arm's length from the governmental machine in order to preserve the 'integrity' of research had been abandoned: the task was seen as one of bringing industry and the government-owned research establishments together in order to get the best possible cross-fertilization and orientation to market needs.[103]

A further expansion took place in October 1969, taking the staff to 39,000. This expansion, unlike its predecessor, was due not to the needs of the Ministry but to the Prime Minister's new policy of concentrating greater areas of responsibility into relatively fewer giant departments, so as to try to establish clearer lines of authority and co-ordination. 'MinTech' now took over responsibility for textiles, chemicals and other manufacturing industries, regional policy, the whole of the work of the Ministry of Power, and the Industrial Reorganisation Corporation, of which more below.

From a primarily research-oriented department, based on the industrial responsibilities of DSIR together with the AEA, Mintech had become in all but name a Ministry of Industry, responsible for all the manufacturing, mining and energy industries, public and private, except for printing and publishing, food and drink, building materials and pharmaceuticals. It had at its disposal a variety of policy instruments which included advice and services (in particular, of a scientific or technological nature), legal regulations (such as setting performance or quality standards which could only be met through the use of up-to-date technology), and finance (in the form of procurement, grants, loans, development contracts and pre-production orders – these last being orders placed by the government for production, before a commercial market had been established, of a few samples of, say, a machine tool, which could then be tried out at no risk by potential purchasers). Finally, from 1969, it had responsibility for the work of the Industrial

Reorganisation Corporation (IRC).

It was the IRC that most clearly fitted Young's observation that the 'fundamental importance of the growth of MinTech was the institutionalisation of the principle of discrimination, and the overturning of the traditional attitude of neutrality, of "holding the ring" '.[104] Selective, discriminatory intervention at the level of the firm (as opposed to industry sectors) was the watchword of the corporation.

Set up in 1966 under the Department of Economic Affairs (another new Wilson government ministry), the IRC was a para-governmental body run by a part-time board of industrialists and bankers, with a full-time executive staff and funds of £150 million. Its rationale is sometimes said to have been some calculations by Blackett, who estimated that, if firms could spend only a certain proportion of their turnover on R&D, then, comparing that figure with the estimated sum of money needed to mount the minimum viable industrial R&D programme, it turned out that relatively few British firms could be expected to do any R&D, and hence most would become technologically backward.[105] The solution was to encourage mergers. This the IRC did by catalysing mergers between companies that were interested in amalgamating, by applying persuasion in some mergers where one party was unwilling, and, rarely but notoriously, by entering the market place and buying shares so as to force through particular mergers, a tactic which the Conservative opposition dubbed 'back-door nationalisation'. Among the better-known cases of IRC activity were its assistance in the formation of International Computers Ltd, the merger between General Electric Company and Associated Electrical Industries, and the purchase of Cambridge Instrument shares so as to prevent a take-over by the Rank Organisation and encourage one by George Kent. Despite initial industrial suspicion, the IRC eventually gained the confidence of industry and was somewhat missed when, in fulfilment of an electoral promise, it was wound up by the Conservatives after their victory in the 1970 election.[106]

Other developments, 1964–70

Some other developments under the 1964–70 Labour

governments must now be briefly mentioned before, finally, going on to more recent events. Contrary to the recommendations of the Trend report, the research councils, now within the ambit of the Department of Education and Science, were institutionally separated from the organs of government-sponsored industrially-oriented research. Within the DES, as has been noted already, a new Council for Scientific Policy (CSP) was formed, to advise the Secretary of State on his responsibilities for the formulation and execution of scientific policy. The council, initially under the chairmanship of Sir Harrie Massey (a space scientist) and later under Sir Frederick Dainton (a chemist), was composed in accordance with the Trend proposals and had no official members, though the executive heads of the research councils attended its meetings as assessors. Unlike its predecessor, the ACSP, the CSP was required to advise the Secretary of State on the distribution of the Science Budget (or Science Vote) among the research councils. Inevitably this gave it a measure of influence over the policies of the research councils which the ACSP had never had.[107] At the same time, however, the CSP was restricted in the scope of its advice to matters falling within the purview of the Secretary of State for Education and Science.

The CSP's task of advising on the distribution of the Science Vote was not helped by the fact that it took office at a time when it had already become clear that the financial resources which the research councils had been enjoying in the immediate past could not indefinitely grow at such high rates as 12 or 13 per cent per annum. This point was reinforced by the onset of a series of economic crises, culminating in the devaluation of the pound in late 1967. (This was in the days before 'floating' exchange rates had come into widespread use; to devalue the pound was then regarded as a major political and economic step.) Unusually for a scientific body, the CSP acknowledged that science could not expect to continue to grow at a rate much greater than the national income, and it devoted considerable effort to the task of trying to devise criteria for selecting the most worthwhile research projects.[108]

It was far, however, from being wholly defeatist about the state of science. The council vigorously promoted the cause of basic scientific research, and enthusiastically declared in 1967 that 'Basic research provides most of the original discoveries and hypotheses from which all other progress flows'.[109] In an attempt to elucidate the mechanisms whereby the relationship between progress and research developed, and in an attempt also to elucidate other problems of science policy, the council set in train a series of studies of science policy,[110] the results of some of which led to an appreciation that the linkages between research and economic progress are in fact far from clear-cut. As the council's working party on the economic benefits of basic research reported in 1970, 'Curiosity-oriented research is only rarely the mainspring of substantial innovation'.[111]

The CSP advised on the research council system, and the Advisory Council on Technology advised on work within the Ministry of Technology. Co-ordination between the DES and the Ministry of Technology came (apart from a degree of overlap between the memberships of the advisory councils) through the usual Treasury and Cabinet Office channels, aided by the appointment in 1964 of Sir Solly Zuckerman, formerly deputy chairman of the ACSP, chairman of the DRPC, and chief scientific adviser to the Minister of Defence, as chief scientific adviser to the Cabinet. Zuckerman's remarkable career will be discussed later. For now, it should be noted that his was the first ever formal appointment of a permanent, full-time scientific adviser to the Cabinet. Tizard informally filled this role between 1947 and 1952, and Cherwell advised Churchill and perhaps the Cabinet in his time, but neither was formally appointed as scientific adviser to the Cabinet. Zuckerman's appointment, with the rank of permanent secretary – the top rung of the civil service ladder – clearly signified the importance attached to science in Whitehall in the mid-1960s.

Zuckerman was succeeded in 1971 by Sir Alan Cottrell, a distinguished metallurgist, who was also appointed at permanent secretary level. Cottrell was succeeded in 1974 by Dr Robert Press, who unlike his predecessors was a career scientific civil servant. Press had been deputy to both Zuckerman and Cottrell, and was appointed at the same rank as he had held while acting in that capacity, namely deputy secretary. After he retired the post of chief scientific adviser was moved into the Central Policy Review Staff, and Professor John Ashworth was appointed at deputy secretary level. The move to the CPRS, implying that the scientific adviser would now have to seek access to the Prime Minister through the head of the CPRS, thus continued the sideways movement of the cabinet science adviser which had begun after Sir Alan Cottrell's resignation. Interestingly, it was paralleled by a similar reduction in the status of scientific advice in the United States. A presidential science adviser had been appointed by Eisenhower in 1957; in 1973 the current incumbent of the science advisory post resigned and was not replaced by President Nixon, who said that he would seek whatever scientific advice he needed from the Director of the National Science Foundation. The reasons given for these moves were similar in both countries, namely that scientific advice was so freely available in all the departments and agencies of government that, it was said, the need for a strong advisory voice at the centre had decreased (although the formal reasons do not take account of the deteriorating relationship between President Nixon and the various scientists who advised the White House).

Returning briefly to the late 1960s, a final point must be added about the Labour machinery for the government of science. Following criticisms that the institutional split between science and technology could lead to a serious gap in communications, a Cabinet-level Central Advisory Council for Science and Technology was appointed in 1967 under the chairmanship of, again, Sir Solly Zuckerman. The membership came largely from the CSP and ACT. According to H. and S. Rose, the council's first item for study was the more effective distribution of skilled manpower within government and other public laboratories, and the better articulation of civil and defence research.[112] The only published work of the council was its report of 1968 on technological innovation, in which it recommended that government and industry should promote measures designed to link R&D, production and marketing into a single operation, to plan programmes of innovation related to market opportunities, to encourage effective technological management, to shorten lead times between R&D and its utilisation, and to make a balanced use of scientific and technological resources over all stages of the innovation process.[113] It is not known whether any specific governmental action followed from this report.

1970 and after

The general election of 1970 led to a number of changes in the machinery described above. The Ministry of Technology was transformed into the Department of Trade and Industry by the addition of most of the responsibilities of the Board of Trade and the loss of some aviation responsibilities which went temporarily to the Ministry of Aviation Supply before it in turn was incorporated into the newly formed procurement executive of the Ministry of Defence. The procurement executive is responsible for defence R&D at its own research establishments and through contracts placed with industry and universities, and is also responsible for the procurement of defence equipment (in particular, sea, land and air weapon systems).[114]

The Department of Trade and Industry survived only until 1974 when, first, in the midst of the energy crisis a Department of Energy was split off in January, with responsibility for the AEA and the fuel and power industries. Then, after the February election, and the return of a minority Labour government, the remainder of DTI was broken up into a Department of Industry (responsible for much governmental support of aviation and space research, research of value to industry, a number of research establishments and NRDC), a Department of Trade and a Department of Prices and Consumer Protection.

In 1970, Edward Heath, the new Prime Minister, had set in motion a series of reviews of the functions of all the government departments. One of the outcomes of that act (though not, by any means, of that act alone, as we shall see later) was a report in 1971 by Lord Rothschild, head of the recently formed Central Policy Review Staff, on the organisation and management of government R&D.[115] Lord Rothschild made many recommendations which were widely applauded, such as that all departments with a significant interest in science and technology should appoint chief scientists at a senior enough level to have access to ministers and to be able (and sufficiently equipped with staff) to advise them on scientific matters in general, and specifically on the formulation of departmental research and development policy. Responsibility for executing those R&D policies, Rothschild argued, should be attached to a separate official, the Controller R&D. These proposals were designed to clarify lines of responsibility and accountability in Whitehall. So also was the much-publicised 'customer–contractor principle' whereby applied research, 'that is, R&D with a practical application as its objective, must be done on a customer–contractor basis. The customer says what he wants; the contractor does it (if he can); and the customer pays.'[116]

This would have been uncontroversial had Rothschild not sought to apply it to the research councils, by asserting that 25 per cent in money terms of the work of the councils was on applied research and should, therefore, be commissioned by ministers. The 25 per cent was concentrated in the MRC, ARC and NERC, and Rothschild proposed to transfer this money to the relevant ministries, the money so transferred to continue to be spent in the research councils but on work commissioned by the ministries. This proposal was widely perceived as an attack upon the autonomy of the research councils and, as will be seen in chapter six, a major and unprecedented outcry burst forth from the scientific community. In the end Rothschild's proposals were more or less implemented,[117] with consequences for the research councils which we shall consider later. One consequence which must be mentioned here is that the Council for Scientific Policy was replaced by the Advisory Board for the Research Councils, which had almost identical terms of reference to its predecessor. The main difference between the two was that the ABRC had a composition more or less the same as that of the former ACSP (that is, a mixture of independent scientists, industrialists, heads of research councils and government scientists), and was so composed without regard to the solemn words of the Trend report about the proper composition of advisory bodies, previously noted. It was initially chaired by Sir Frederick Dainton, who was succeeded in 1973 by Sir Frederick Stewart, a professor of geology and, until then, chairman of the Natural Environment Research Council. Sir Alec Merrison, a physicist, succeeded to this post in 1979.

The final changes in machinery which need to be outlined here concern the Cabinet machinery for co-ordination of and advice on the research and development activities of government. In a memorandum [118] submitted by the Lord Privy Seal to the Select Committee on Science and Technology in May 1976 it was stated that the Science and Technology Group within the Cabinet Office performed a number of functions. First, it provided a focal point for advising, or ensuring that advice reached ministers, on the science and technology aspects of government policies. Subjects on which concerted advice had been arranged through the Cabinet Office machinery included UK policy towards international (and particularly European) collaboration in science and technology, the development of a code of practice for the genetic manipulation of micro-organisms, and the implications of domestic nuclear policies and programmes for international agreements, and vice versa. Second, the Science and Technology Group initiated studies on certain transdepartmental issues involving R&D, such as future world trends, environmental standards and marine technology. Third, the group monitored and advised on how the arrangements for the management of government applied R&D were working, and fourth, it assembled information for publication about departmental R&D programmes.

Although these arrangements, which dated from the early 1970s, had worked well, the government now thought that some changes could usefully be made with a view to keeping pace with the evolution of departmental arrangements for science and technology. It therefore announced that it proposed, first to amalgamate the secretarial functions of the Cabinet Office Science and Technology Group with the Economic and Industrial Secretariat in a multi-disciplinary group. The advisory role of the Science Group would be moved to the Central Policy Review Staff, and a Chief Scientist would be appointed there. Third, in order to ensure an overall view of R&D and other scientific matters at top official level, a Committee of Chief Scientists and Permanent Secretaries from the departments concerned would be established under the Secretary of the Cabinet. In addition to its co-ordination function, the committee would be responsible for seeing that scientific questions were brought before ministers collectively as appropriate, and that scientific priorities reflected those of the government as a whole. Hitherto it had been envisaged that a chief scientific adviser would play this role, but experience since 1972, particularly in respect of the increasing importance attached to scientific advice in departments, had led the government to believe it to be impracticable to focus such a role upon an individual who would himself have no responsibility for the programmes concerned. Finally, in order to 'improve interface' between government and outside organisations on applied R&D matters, it was proposed to set up an Advisory Council for Applied Research and Development (ACARD). This council was to advise ministers on applied R&D in the UK in both the public and the private sectors, on the articulation of this R&D with scientific research supported through the DES, on the future development and application of technology, and on the role of the UK in international collaboration in the field of applied R&D. The members of ACARD were not, in fact, finally appointed until December 1976. Under the chairmanship of the Lord Privy Seal and the deputy chairmanship of Sir James Menter, Principal of Queen Mary College, London, and formerly director of R&D at Tube Investments, they included six industrial managers, two representatives of public enterprises, a trade unionist, two academics and the chairman of the Advisory Board for the Research Councils.[119] At the time of writing, ACARD had produced only two reports, one on microprocessors, in which the council urged the government to encourage British industry to develop microprocessor applications, and another on industrial innovation.[120]

The picture today

The evolution of science–government relations in Britain has not followed a particularly clear-cut course; still less has it followed any prescribed plan. Like Topsy, it 'just growed', although always within the framework of existing machinery and practices. To conclude this review of the government of science it may be helpful to summarise the current state of the relevant governmental machinery and to set it into a broader statistical context.

Figure 2.1 outlines the main organisational features of the governmental arrangements for science and technology as at August 1979. The financial details are taken from the Supply Estimates for 1979–80, which show that in April 1979 the government planned to spend a total of £2,141 million on research and development in 1979–80, distributed principally as shown in the figure.

The most up-to-date figures for total national expenditure on R&D are for 1975. These are given in table 2.2, together with the corresponding figures for 1964 and 1969. The table shows that the overall distribution of R&D spending by performer and by source of funds has not changed markedly since 1964. Government performs about one-quarter of all R&D and industry about two-

Table 2.2
R&D spending in the United Kingdom, 1964–75 (£ million; percentages –
rounded – in brackets)

Spending at historical prices	1964	1969	1975
Performer			
Government	212 (28)	263 (25)	566 (26)
Universities and further education establishments	47 (6)	80 (8)	179 (8)
Industry	489 (64)	680 (65)	1,340 (62)
Others	20 (3)	22 (2)	66 (3)
Total	768 (101)	1,045 (100)	2,151 (99)
Funder			
Government	412 (54)	529 (51)	1,117 (52)
Industry	316 (41)	449 (43)	877 (41)
Other	40 (5)	67 (6)	157 (7)
Total	768 (100)	1,045 (100)	2,151 (100)

Source. Central Statistical Office, *Economic Trends (July 1979)*, (London: HMSO, 1979), table A.

thirds, while government provides about 10 per cent more than industry of the total national resources for R&D.

Concealed within the table, however, is evidence of a decline in spending on R&D. Thus the percentage of gross national product devoted to R&D fell from 2·32 in 1964 to 2·09 in 1975. Expressing the figures in 1975 prices shows that total spending fell by £49 million between 1964 and 1975, while the value of the R&D performed in industry fell by about 11 per cent between 1969 and 1975. Recent OECD figures[121] show that Britain is the only major OECD country to have experienced a clear decline in privately funded industrial R&D between 1967 and 1975, and as table 2.3 shows in columns 5 and 6, the decline can be seen in the level of industry-financed R&D as a percentage of the domestic product of manufacturing industry, as well as in absolute terms. As the table also shows, however, government support for R&D in Britain remained strong

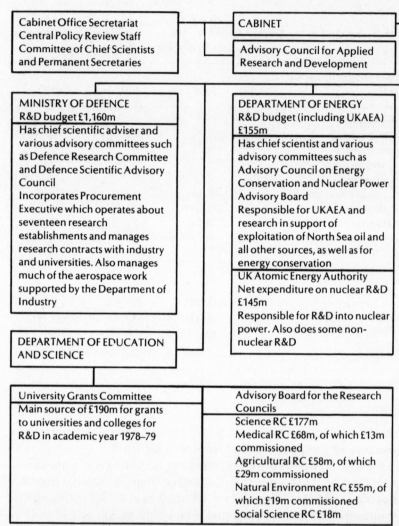

Fig. 1 **The main government organisation for science and technology in Britain, 1979.** *Source.* The structure of the figure and some of the notes are from the *Nature* guide 'How Britain runs its science' (London: Macmillan Journals, 1978). Budgetary details are from *Supply Estimates, 1979–80, Memorandum by the Chief Secretary to the Treasury* (London: HMSO, Cmnd 7524, 1979), table 7, and *Supply Estimates, 1979–80, Class X, Education and Libraries, Science and Arts* (London: HMSO, HC 266, 1979). Further details of departmental arrangements can be found in *Review of the Framework for Government Research and Development (Cmnd 5046)* (London: HMSO, Cmnd 7499, 1979).

| PARLIAMENT | Unofficial Parliamentary and Scientific Committee |

DEPARTMENT OF INDUSTRY
R&D budget £132m

Has chief scientist and engineer and various advisory committees and research requirements boards on, for instance, chemicals and minerals, computers, systems and electronics, and engineering materials
Operates six research establishments including National Physical Laboratory. Responsible for research of value to industry and for civil aerospace

National Research Development Corporation
Finances development of good research ideas

MINISTRY OF AGRICULTURE, FISHERIES AND FOOD
R&D budget £50m

Has chief scientist and Joint (with ARC) Consultative Organisation with boards on, e.g., animals, arable crops and forage, and horticulture
Incorporates Agricultural Development and Advisory Service which operates four research centres. MAFF also operates a Food Science Laboratory and several Fisheries Laboratories, and commissions work from ARC

DEPARTMENTS OF THE ENVIRONMENT AND TRANSPORT
R&D budget £59m

Has director general of research and advisory committees and research requirements committees in the areas of planning and transport, construction and housing, and environmental pollution.
Operate Building Research Establishment, Hydraulics Research Station and Transport and Road Research Laboratory. Commissions work with research councils and places contracts with British Rail, universities, etc. Responsible for R&D for a whole range of functions which affect the environment

Nature Conservancy Council
Runs nature reserves and advises DOE and other departments on nature conservation. Supports some research

DEPARTMENT OF HEALTH AND SOCIAL SECURITY
R&D budget £33m

Has chief scientist whose research committee advises on the whole programme of R&D for the department
Most of its R&D is commissioned with MRC or universities

by international standards in 1973, though it would almost certainly look weaker if comparative 1979 figures were available and was in any case heavily concentrated on big technology.

Table 2.3
Some comparisons of R&D activities in ten OECD countries

	1	2		3	4	5	6
				1967	1975	1967	1975
Belgium	0·3	17·5	(30·8)	1·0	1·1	n.a.	2·1[a]
France	0·7	43·8	(58·1)	5·9	6·0	n.a.	2·0
F.R. Germany	0·9	26·0	(33·4)	11·4	12·6	2·2	2·7
Netherlands	0·8	8·7	(14·0)	2·4	2·1	3·5[b]	3·6
Italy	n.a.	29·5	(39·8)	2·4	2·8	n.a.	n.a.
United Kingdom	1·0	56·0	(68·4)	10·4	7·4	3·3	2·7
EEC total	n.a.	n.a.	(n.a.)	33·5	40·0	n.a.	n.a.
Sweden	0·7	32·1	(39·9)	1·2	1·7	2·7	3·2
Switzerland	n.a.	30·9	(37·6)	2·3	1·7	n.a.	n.a.
Japan	0·6	16·1	(22·3)	11·7	17·8	2·4	3·0[a]
USA	1·3	70·4	(70·9)	49·6	42·6	3·5	4·2
Total	n.a.	n.a.	(n.a.)	100	100	n.a.	n.a.

a 1973.
b 1969.

Column 1. _Government R&D expenditures as a percentage of GDP, 1973._ Source: OECD document DST1/SPR/76.29 (Paris, September 1976).

Column 2. _Percentage of Government R&D expenditures on big technology, 1975._ First number comprises defence, space and energy (mainly nuclear) R&D. Second number in brackets also includes R&D specifically for industrial development, most of which is in fact spent on civil aviation and advanced electronics. Source: OECD document DSTI/SPR/77.8 (Paris, March 1977).

Columns 3 and 4. _Percentage of ten countries' industry-financed R&D, 1967 and 1975._ Source: OECD.

Columns 5 and 6. _Industry-financed R&D activities as a percentage of domestic product of manufacturing industry._ Source: Information supplied by the Science and Technology Indicators Unit, OECD, Paris.

Source of complete table. Keith Pavitt, 'Governmental Support for Industrial Innovation: the Western European Experience', in Ron Johnston and Philip Gummett (eds.), _Directing Technology: Policies for Promotion and Control_ (London: Croom Helm, 1979), p. 22.

Against this general background, then, we move on to consider some substantive issues in science–government relations in Britain.

Notes

[1] For the history of science and government until the 1930s, I have drawn freely on J. B. Poole and Kay Andrews (eds.), *The Government of Science in Britain* (London: Weidenfeld and Nicolson, 1972), pp. 5–16. See also D. S. L. Cardwell, *The Organisation of Science in England: a Retrospect* (London: Heinemann, 1957); M. Argles, *South Kensington to Robbins: An Account of English Technical and Scientific Education since 1851* (London: Longmans, 1964); E. Ashby, *Technology and the Academics* (London: Macmillan, 1958); and W. H. G. Armytage, *The Rise of the Technocrats* (London: Routledge and Kegan Paul, 1965).

[2] The absence of governmental reaction to the Devonshire Commission's proposals is documented in P. Randman, 'Government Science in Britain 1875–1921' (Manchester University, unpublished MSc dissertation, 1977), pp. 23–7.

[3] Poole and Andrews, *op. cit.*, pp. 8–9.

[4] *Ibid.*, p. 9.

[5] On NPL, see R. Moseley, 'The Origins and Early Years of the National Physical Laboratory : A Chapter in the Pre-history of British Science Policy', *Minerva*, **16**(1978), pp. 222–50; E. Hutchinson, 'Scientists and Civil Servants: The Struggle over the National Physical Laboratory in 1918', *Minerva*, **7** (1969), pp. 373–98; and Sir Gordon Sutherland, 'The National Physical Laboratory', in Sir John Cockcroft (ed.), *The Organisation of Research Establishments* (London: Cambridge University Press, 1965).

[6] The early development of agricultural research is discussed in D. Snelling, 'The Establishment and Growth of an Agricultural Research System in Great Britain up to 1937' (Manchester University, unpublished MSc dissertation, 1976).

[7] D. N. Chester and F. M. G. Willson, *The Organisation of British Central Government 1914–1964* (London: George Allen and Unwin, for the Royal Institute of Public Administration, 1968), p. 256.

[8] The following paragraph is largely based on Chester and Willson, *op. cit.*, p. 254.

[9] It is not quite clear when the responsibility shifted to the Lord Privy Seal, but this seems to have occurred in the early 1970s. With the resignation of Lord Jellicoe from that post during the 1970–74 Conservative government, the responsibility returned to the Lord President. Early in 1976 the Select Committee on Science and Technology was under the impression that the Lord President still held this responsibility, but in seeking to call him to give evidence to one of their inquiries they found themselves involved in a confusing correspondence with the Prime

Minister, Harold Wilson, the upshot of which was a statement that the responsibility had returned, apparently unannounced, to the Lord Privy Seal. It seems possible that the incoming Wilson government in 1974 had overlooked the matter. (See *New Scientist*, **69**, 26 February 1976, p. 426.) To bring this confused story up to date, after a six month delay Margaret Thather's government indicated in November 1979 that, apparently, neither the Lord President nor the Lord Privy Seal would in future play a co-ordinating role, but that the Prime Minister would herself play one in 'appropriate cases'. Whether this means that she will play an active role or, as seems more likely, that she will only occasionally become involved in scientific matters in which, as Prime Minister, she might in any case have felt obliged to take an interest, remains to be seen. (See *New Scientist*, 8 November 1979, p. 418.)

[10] Chester and Willson, *op. cit.*, pp. 267–72.

[11] On DSIR see Sir Harry Melville, *The Department of Scientific and Industrial Research* (London: George Allen and Unwin, New Whitehall Series, 1962); R. M. MacLeod and Kay Andrews, 'The Origins of DSIR: Reflections on Ideas and Men, 1915–1916', *Public Administration*, **48** (1970), pp. 23–48; Ian Varcoe, 'Scientists, government and organized research: the early history of the DSIR, 1914–16', *Minerva*, **8** (1970), pp. 192–217; and Ian Varcoe, *Organizing for Science in Britain: a case-study* (London: Oxford University Press, 1974).

[12] Hutchinson, *op. cit.*

[13] Melville, *op. cit.*, pp. 75–8.

[14] *Ibid.*, pp. 31–6.

[15] Ministry of Reconstructon, *Report of the Machinery of Government Committee, under the chairmanship of Viscount Haldane of Cloan, OM* (London: HMSO, Cd 9230, 1918).

[16] *Ibid.*, chapter 4 of Part II.

[17] *Ibid.*, para. 67.

[18] *Ibid.*, p. 60.

[19] For details of the MRC, see Medical Research Council, *Half a Century of Medical Research*, written by A. Landsborough Thomson (London: HMSO, 1973), two volumes; and Fanny Mitchell, 'The Medical Research Council', in D. C. Hague, W. J. M. MacKenzie and A. Barker (eds.), *Public Policy and Private Interests: the Institutions of Compromise* (London: Macmillan, 1975), pp. 204–43.

[20] Ministry of Reconstruction, *op. cit.*, p. 35.

[21] The account given here of the Committee of Civil Research, including all unreferenced quotations, is taken from R. M. MacLeod and E. Kay Andrews, 'The Committee of Civil Research: Scientific Advice for Economic Development 1925–30', *Minerva*, **7** (1969), pp. 680–705. See also Chester and Willson, *op. cit.*, pp. 322–3, and Anthea Bennett, 'Advising the Cabinet – The Committee of Civil Research and Economic Advisory Council', *Public Administration*, **56** (1978), pp. 51–71.

[22] These included the states of the iron, steel, coal, dyestuffs and fishing industries, the shortage of radium, and the more efficient co-ordination of government research. The last-named study led to the establishment of the ARC.

[23] See *Government Organisation in the Civilian Field* (London: HMSO, 1951), appendix II.

[24] Lord Zuckerman, 'Government needs and expectations', *Times Literary Supplement*, 5 November 1971, p. 1385.

[25] N. J. Vig, *Science and Technology in British Politics* (London: Pergamon, 1968), p. 13.

[26] *Ibid.*, pp. 13–14.

[27] See, for instance, C. H. Waddington, *OR in World War 2: Operational Research against the U-boat* (London: Elek, 1973); R. W. Clark, *The Rise of the Boffins* (London: Phoenix House, 1962); Lord Zuckerman, *From Apes to Warlords: The autobiography (1904–1946) of Solly Zuckerman* (London: Hamish Hamilton, 1978).

[28] See, for instance, R. W. Clark, *op. cit.*, and R. W. Clark, *Tizard* (London: Methuen, 1965).

[29] C. P. Snow, *Science and Government* (London: Oxford University Press, 1961); R. W. Clark, *Tizard* (London: Methuen, 1965); Earl of Birkenhead, *The Prof in Two Worlds: the Official Life of Professor F. A. Lindemann, Viscount Cherwell* (London: Collins, 1961).

[30] See, for instance, N. Wood, *Communism and British Intellectuals* (London: Victor Gollancz, 1959).

[31] J. D. Bernal, *The Social Function of Science* (London: Routledge and Kegan Paul, 1939).

[32] For reviews of the debate over the planning of science, see G. L. Price, *The Politics of Planning and the Problems of Science Policy* (Leeds: SISCON, 1976), Gary Werskey, *The Visible College* (London: Allen Lane, 1978), William McGucken, 'On Freedom and Planning in Science: The Society for Freedom in Science, 1940–46', *Minerva*, **16** (No. 1, 1978), pp. 42–72, and John R. Baker, 'Michael Polanyi's Contributions to the Cause of Freedom in Science', *Minerva*, **16** (No. 3, 1978), pp. 382–96.

[33] Sir Solly Zuckerman, *Scientists and War* (London: Hamish Hamilton, 1966), p. 140.

[34] S. Zuckerman, 'Science and Society', *New Statesman and Nation*, **17** (1939), pp. 297–8.

[35] The name came from the Latin tag 'quot homines, tot sententiae'. Among the twenty members were C. P. Snow, Ritchie Calder, Bernal, C. H. Waddington, J. Huxley, J. G. Crowther and P. M. S. Blackett. For the fullest available account of the club, see Lord Zuckerman, *From Apes to Warlords, loc. cit.*, especially appendix 1; see also J. G. Crowther, *Fifty Years with Science* (London: Barrie and Jenkins, 1970), pp. 210–22; and H. and S. Rose, *Science and Society* (London: Allen Lane, 1969; my references to Pelican edition, 1970), pp. 55–6.

[36] The distinction between reformists and radicals is P. G. Werskey's, in 'British Scientist and "Outsider" Politics, 1931–1945', *Science Studies,* **1** (1971), pp. 67–83. See also his '*Nature* and Politics between the Wars', *Nature,* **224** (1969), pp. 462–72.

[37] Memorandum from Sir Henry Tizard, 'Proposals for a Central Scientific Committee under the Minister for Co-ordination of Defence', 13 July 1939, Public Record Office, CAB 27/711. For a thorough study of the origins of the SAC, see William McGucken, 'The Royal Society and the Genesis of the Scientific Advisory Committee to Britain's War Cabinet, 1939–1940', *Notes and Records of the Royal Society of London,* **33** (No. 1, 1978), pp. 87–115.

[38] Letter from Sir William Bragg, President of the Royal Society, to Lord Chatfield, Minister for Co-ordination of Defence, 13 July 1939, Public Record Office, CAB 27/712.

[39] Memorandum to the Cabinet by the Minister for Co-ordination of Defence, 'Proposals by the President of the Royal Society for the use of scientific knowledge', 25 September 1939, Public Record Office, CAB 66/2.

[40] Clark, *op. cit.* (1965), p. 274.

[41] Public Record Office, CAB 90/1, 8 October 1940.

[42] Clark, *op. cit.* (1965), pp. 274–5.

[43] Lord Butler, *The Art of the Possible: the Memoirs of Lord Butler* (London: Hamish Hamilton, 1971), p. 110.

[44] Lord Butler, private communication to author, 17 July 1973.

[45] *First Annual Report of the Advisory Council on Scientific Policy (1947–1948)* (London: HMSO, Cmd 7465, 1948), para. 1.

[46] Clark, *op. cit.* (1965), p. 383.

[47] This episode is recounted in Sir Mark Oliphant and Lord Penney, 'John Douglas Cockcroft', *Biographical Memoirs of Fellows of the Royal Society,* **14** (1968), p. 181. The date of Tizard's intention to retire is confirmed by Clark, *op. cit.* (1965), p. 401.

[48] *Third Report of the Estimates Committee, 1946–47, Expenditure on Research and Development* (London: HMSO, 1947), question 1716. For further information on the DRPC, see *Statement Relating to Defence* (London: HMSO, Cmd 7042, 1947), paras. 27–9; Chapman Pincher, 'Organization of Defence Research in Britain', *Nature,* **177** (1956), pp. 251–2; and Office of the Minister for Science, *The Management and Control of Research and Development* (the Gibb–Zuckerman report) (London: HMSO, 1961), *passim.*

[49] Estimates Committee, *op. cit.* (1947), question 1781.

[50] *Ibid.,* question 1835 and para. 75.

[51] Clark, *op. cit.* (1965), p. 387. Tizard was not the only scientist to be so treated. Professor Gowing recounts how Sir James Chadwick, Britain's leading nuclear physicist, once returned to Britain from extremely important government negotiations on atomic energy to be met at Southampton by a relatively junior official with a car which ran out of fuel

on the journey to London. Margaret Gowing, *Independence and Deterrence, Britain and Atomic Energy, 1945–1952* (London: Macmillan, 1974), vol. 1, p. 47.

[52] Gowing, *op. cit.*, chapter 2, especially pp. 31–2 and 58–9.

[53] *Ibid.*, pp. 33–7.

[54] K. Hayward, 'The British Nuclear Weapons Programme, 1945–1957' (Manchester University, unpublished MA thesis, 1971), p. 139.

[55] Pincher, *op. cit.*, p. 251.

[56] The council's annual reports began with the one already cited (note 45), and ended with *Annual Report of the Advisory Council on Scientific Policy 1963–1964* (London: HMSO, Cmnd 2538, 1964). The reports of the Committee on Scientific Manpower began with *Report on the Recruitment of Scientists and Engineers by the Engineering Industry* (London: HMSO, 1955) and ended with *Scientific and Technological Manpower in Great Britain 1962* (London: HMSO, Cmnd 2146, 1963).

[57] Fuller details are given in Philip Gummett, 'British Science Policy and the Advisory Council on Scientific Policy' (Manchester University, unpublished PhD thesis, 1973), p. 187.

[58] *Ibid.*, pp. 42–4 and 59.

[59] *Nature*, **169** (1952), p. 395.

[60] A. King, 'The Dilemma of Science Policy', *The Round Table*, No. 247 (1972), p. 346.

[61] J. G. Crowther, *Science in Modern Society* (London: Cresset Press, 1967), pp. 50–3.

[62] Vig, *op. cit.*, pp. 23–4 and 65–6.

[63] Rose and Rose, *op. cit.*, p. 74.

[64] See Philip Gummett and Geoffrey Price, 'An Approach to the Central Planning of British Science: the Formation of the Advisory Council on Scientific Policy', *Minerva*, **15** (No. 2, 1977), pp. 141–2.

[65] P. M. S. Blackett, 'Wanted: a Wand over Whitehall – Professionalising the Civil Service', *New Statesman*, **68** (1964), p. 346. See also his Tizard Memorial Lecture, 'Tizard and the Science of War', reported in *Nature*, **186** (1960), pp. 647–53.

[66] Sir Solly Zuckerman, 'Scientists in the Arena', in Anthony de Reuck *et al.* (eds.), *Decision-Making in National Science Policy* (London: J. and A. Churchill, for CIBA Foundation, 1968), pp. 8–13.

[67] K. G. Gannicott and M. Blaug, 'Manpower forecasting since Robbins: a science lobby in action', *Higher Education Review*, **2** (1969–70), pp. 5674.

[68] See G. L. Payne, *Britain's Scientific and Technological Manpower* (London: Oxford University Press, 1960) for further discussion.

[69] 1955 figure from *Annual Report of the Advisory Council on Scientific Policy 1956–1957* (London: HMSO, Cmnd 278, 1957), appendix III. 1964 figure from Council for Scientific Policy, *Report on Science Policy* (London: HMSO, Cmnd 3007, 1966), appendix IV; calculated by subtracting the figures given there for members of professional institutes.

For the government's acknowledgement of the role of the ACSP in the 1956 expansion, see House of Commons, *Debates*, **560** (1956), cols. 1750–3.

[70] See Gummett, *op. cit.*, especially p. 145, for further argument.

[71] *Ibid.*, p. 147, table II.

[72] See G. E. Haigh, 'The National Research Development Corporation: An Historical Study' (Manchester University, unpublished MSc thesis, 1970).

[73] See Birkenhead, *op. cit.*, Chapter 11; Gowing, *op. cit.*, pp. 421–36; and House of Lords, *Debates*, **172** (1951), cols. 670–9 and 684–708.

[74] Chester and Willson, *op. cit.*, pp. 272–3 and 371.

[75] *Ibid.*, p. 371.

[76] Vig, *op. cit.*, p. 31.

[77] For example: A. Bevan, House of Commons, *Debates*, **612** (1959), cols. 869–71; Debate on the Office of the Minister for Science, House of Commons, *Debates*, **615** (1959), cols. 41–104; and Lord Morrison, House of Lords, *Debates*, **220** (1959), cols. 206–8.

[78] 1939 figure from Vig, *op. cit.*, p. 13; 1913 figure from Zuckerman, *TLS* lecture, *op. cit.*, p. 1385.

[79] Vig, *op. cit.*, p. 10.

[80] Estimates Committee, *op. cit.* (1947), paras. 3–4.

[81] See Cmnd 278, *op. cit.*, appendix I; and Department of Education and Science, *Statistics of Science and Technology 1970* (London: HMSO, 1970), tables 1 and 2.

[82] For 1956 figures, see Cmnd 2146, *op. cit.*, table 5. For 1965 figures, see Department of Trade and Industry, *Persons with Qualifications in Engineering, Technology and Science 1959 to 1968* (London: HMSO, 1968), pp. 5–7.

[83] Ministry of Labour/Advisory Council on Scientific Policy, *Scientific and Engineering Manpower in Great Britain* (London: HMSO, 1956), para. 17. For criticism of this concentration, see M. J. Peck, 'Science and Technology', chapter 10 in R. E. Caves (ed.), *Britain's Economic Prospects* (Washington, D.C.: Brookings Institute, 1968).

[84] Committee on Scientific Manpower, *Scientific and Engineering Manpower in Great Britain, 1959* (London: HMSO, Cmnd 902, 1959), para. 52.

[85] Committee on Manpower Resources for Science and Technology, *Report on the 1965 Triennial Manpower Survey of Engineers, Technologists, Scientists and Technical Supporting Staff* (London: HMSO, Cmnd 3103, 1966), para. 27.

[86] Cited by Vig, *op. cit.*, p. 82.

[87] *Ibid.*

[88] *Ibid.*, chapter 5.

[89] *Ibid.*, chapter 4, and especially p. 80.

[90] *Annual Report of the Advisory Council on Scientific Policy 1960–1961* (London: HMSO, Cmnd 1592, 1962), paras. 32–8.

[91] Committee of Enquiry into the Organisation of Civil Science (London: HMSO, Cmnd 2171, 1963), para. 1.

[92] Ibid., para. 43.

[93] Ibid., pp. 32–4 and 38–42.

[94] Ibid., para. 51.

[95] Ibid., para. 105.

[96] Ibid., para. 113.

[97] Ibid., para. 84.

[98] The Times, 2 October 1964.

[99] Vig, op. cit., p. 102.

[100] See, for instance, Anthony Wedgwood Benn, The Government's Policy for Technology, special lecture given at Imperial College of Science and Technology, 17 October 1967 (London: Ministry of Technology, 1967).

[101] Sir Richard Clarke, 'Mintech in Retrospect', Omega, 1 (Nos. 1 and 2, 1973), pp. 25–38 and 137–63, at p. 28.

[102] Ibid., p. 31.

[103] Ibid., pp. 33–4.

[104] Stephen Young with A. V. Lowe, Intervention in the mixed economy: the evolution of British industrial policy 1964–72 (London: Croom Helm, 1974), p. 28.

[105] See P. M. S. Blackett, memorandum in Second Report from the Select Committee on Science and Technology, Session 1968–69, Defence Research (London: HMSO, HC 213, 1969), pp. 87–8, and also Alan G. Mencher, Lessons for American Policy Making from the British Labor Government's 1964–70 Experience in Applying Technology to Economic Objectives, Part I: The Scientific Opportunity Syndrome: Its Consequence and Cure (Washington, D.C.: National Science Foundation, 1975), appendix 2, p. 8.

[106] On the IRC see M. E. Beesley and G. M. White, 'The Industrial Reorganization Corporation: A Study in Choice of Public Management', Public Administration, 51 (1973), pp. 61–89; Stephen Young, 'Reshaping Industry: The IRC In Retrospect', New Society, 18 November 1970, pp. 906–8; and Young and Lowe, op. cit., Part II.

[107] Philip Gummett and Roger Williams, 'Assessing the Council for Scientific Policy', Nature, 240 (1972), pp. 329–32.

[108] See Council for Scientific Policy, Report on Science Policy (London: HMSO, Cmnd 3007, 1966), passim; and Third Report of the Council for Scientific Policy (London: HMSO, Cmnd 5117, 1972, para. 15–16 and appendix C.

[109] Council for Scientific Policy, Second Report on Science Policy (London: HMSO, Cmnd 3420, 1967), para. 45.

[110] Ibid., Part V; and Cmnd 5117, op. cit., appendices C and D.

[111] Cmnd 5117, op. cit., appendix D, para. 22. See also J. Langrish, M. Gibbons, W. G. Evans and F. R. Jevons, Wealth from Knowledge (London:

Macmillan, 1972).

[112] Rose and Rose, op. cit., p. 125.

[113] Central Advisory Council for Science and Technology, *Technological Innovation in Britain* (London: HMSO, 1968), pp. 16–17.

[114] See *Government Organistion for Defence Procurement and Civil Aerospace* (London: HMSO, Cmnd 4641, 1971).

[115] Lord Rothschild, 'The Organisation and Management of Government R. & D.', in *A Framework for Government Research and Development* (London: HMSO, Cmnd 4814, 1971).

[116] *Ibid.*, para. 6.

[117] *Framework for Government Research and Development* (London: HMSO, Cmnd 5046, 1972).

[118] Memorandum by the Lord Privy Seal, in Select Committee on Science and Technology (Science Subcommittee), *Industry and Scientific Research, Memoranda, Session 1975–76* (London: HMSO, HC 136, 1976), pp. 122–7. This memorandum also contains a useful review of the role of departmental chief scientists and of co-ordinating mechanisms for science and technology additional to those operated by the Cabinet Office. The views expressed in the memorandum were expanded in oral evidence by the Lord Privy Seal, accompanied by the head of the CPRS and Dr Robert Press on 6 July 1976. See *ibid.*, *Minutes of Evidence* (London: HMSO, HC 23–xx, 1976).

[119] *New Scientist*, **72** (1976), p. 572.

[120] Advisory Council for Applied Research and Development, *The Applications of Semiconductor Technology* and *Industrial Innovation* (both London: HMSO, 1978).

[121] OECD, *Trends in Industrial R&D* (Paris: OECD, 1979); cited in *New Scientist*, 9 August 1979, p. 428.

III
THE SCIENTIFIC CIVIL SERVICE

The idea that scientists, engineers and other technical experts have moved over the years ever closer to the centres of national power has been widely discussed in academic and popular circles. It arises in its strongest forms in theories of 'technocracy', or rule by experts, and in theories of post-industrialism which claim that advanced industrial societies are in the midst of a vast transition to a new social order that will be as different from industrial society as industrial society was from feudal society, and which will have theoretical knowledge as its axial principle, and professional people – particularly scientists – as its key citizens.[1]

The origins of these ideas can be traced to the early nineteenth century and the political thought of the French writer Saint-Simon.[2] His was one of the earliest visions of the significance of the industrial revolution and of the social changes that would be needed to realise the benefits of that revolution. Aristocrats, courtiers and other idlers would be replaced in the seats of power by scientists, industrialists and artists — that is, by those whose powers of discovery, of productive work or of expression were of value to the community. As industrialisation spread, so the power to create wealth would also spread, and the need for soldiers to undertake acquisitive wars (or to defend their country against would-be conquerors) would decline. Furthermore, science could be used not only to make discoveries about the natural world but also to lay bare the principles on which human society could and should be rationally and harmoniously organised. As Kumar puts it:

In all this Saint-Simon was proclaiming the end of political rule, the exercise of political power, as such. Industrial society had no need of coercion. The men who direct, the scientists and industrialists, do so not because they possess superior political or diplomatic skills, but because they have knowledge. They do not give orders, they only declare what conforms to the nature of things. The scientists state what is known on any particular question; the industrialists apply and execute it. Thus it is no longer a case of men controlling men. It is things themselves, through the mediation of those who understand them, that indicate the manner in which they should be handled.[3]

As the Saint-Simonian motto had it, 'from the government of men to the administration of things'.

Whereas Saint-Simon saw industrialisation as holding out the promise of progress through the application of science to social affairs, Weber, a century later, took a more pessimistic view of the effect of science on society with his concept of rationalisation. This concept is complex and difficult to summarise, and for convenience I once again draw upon Kumar's work.[4]

Weber considered that 'The fate of our times is characterized by rationalization and intellectualization and, above all, by "the disenchantment of the world"'. Rationalisation here meant the negative process by which the world was rid of magic and mysticism, but Weber also used the term to mean the positive embodiment of the method and substance of science in the institutions, practices and beliefs of a society. It implied, says Kumar, a studied and increasing mastery over the environment, both natural and social, and this tendency could be observed in, among other things, the elaboration of a rational system of laws and formal procedures for handling them, and in the rise of a rational system of administration with modern bureaucracy.

It was with the bureaucracy that the 'irrationality' of rationalisation became apparent. For while, in theory, rationalisation could imply a degree of liberation from inefficiency and waste, thereby improving the quality of life, in practice the growth of rationalised bureaucracies was costing Western man his political freedom. As Weber put it:

> No country and no age has ever experienced, in the same sense as the modern Occident, the absolute and complete dependence of its whole existence, of the political, technical, and economic conditions of its life, on a specially trained *organization* of officials. The most important functions of the everyday life of the society have come to be in the hands of technically, commercially, and above all legally trained government officials.

The trained official, in Weber's words, had become 'the pillar of both the modern State and of the economic life of the West', and bureaucracy, with its submission to the rationality of scientific expertise, had become the highest expression of the rationalising tendency in industrial society.

In all this, as Kumar rightly argues,[5] the theories of Saint-Simon and Weber were the forerunners of all the major elements of the theory of post-industrial society. Their emphasis on the key roles of scientific rationality and of experts in modern bureaucracies forms the theoretical backdrop against which, in this and the next chapter, we examine the status, roles, backgrounds and work of scientific experts in the government of Britain. It will be concluded, among other things, that for all that the Saint-Simonian and Weberian theories have been borne out, in general terms, in the West, in Britain at least these tendencies have been relatively slow to advance. Scientists have become more numerous and more significant in British government over the years, but they remain 'on tap, not on top'. British government depends on scientists, but is not ruled by them. As Weber also pointed out, indispensability should not be confused with power; if it were otherwise, in slave economies the slaves would have been the rulers.[6]

The origins of the civil service

The origins of the modern British civil service are generally taken to have been the Northcote–Trevelyan reforms of 1854 which introduced the idea of meritocratic selection for the elite of the service, the so-called 'first Division'. Entering by passing a common, service-wide examination, members of this elite group were to learn their duties 'on the job'. It was held that because the skills thus cultivated would be specific to a given department, officials could not easily be transferred between departments.[7]

Reforms in 1920 led to the reorganisation of the general group of civil servants into four classes. At the bottom were the clerical assistants, engaged on mechanical work. Next came the clerical class, who applied general rules to particular cases. Above them was the executive class, whose members dealt with difficult cases and with the overall management of the office. At the top was the administrative class, the first division, concerned with the formation of policy, the co-ordination and improvement of the machinery of government, and the general administration and control of departments. The administrative–executive–clerical trichotomy was to survive largely unchanged for half a century, and the degree to which it changed even then is arguable. It was with the 1920 reforms that there emerged the view that members of the administrative class, far from acquiring skills which were specific to a particular department, were in fact in possession of general administrative skills. This made them sufficiently versatile to be easily switched from one department to another, a versatility which in turn was said to be fostered by such transfers. The idea of the versatile, generalist administrator will be returned to later.

By the time of the 1920 reforms the upper levels of the civil service had ceased to be concerned merely with the administration or execution of policies which their ministers had laid down: they had themselves become intimately involved in policy-making. This shift was due to the fact that by this time ministers could no longer expect to be familiar with all the details of departmental business. The increasing complexity and volume of governmental business (due partly to the greater technical complexity of industrial society, and partly to the government, especially under Lloyd George, becoming more positively involved in all aspects of national life) forced ministers to delegate more and more responsibility to their officials, and lowered the level in the hierarchy at which decisions were taken.[8]

The rise of the specialist

If the volume and complexity of business was forcing administrative officials to become decision-makers as well as advisers on policy, it was also leading to a growth in the number of specialist civil servants. Whereas, it has been estimated, the government employed 137 scientists in 1890 and 154 in 1900, by 1910 the figure was 201 and by 1919 327 (112 in military and 215 in civil departments).[9] Growth continued to be rapid. In 1947 the professional, scientific and technical classes (a wider grouping than scientists alone) numbered 37,400, rising to 59,510 in 1978. This is to be compared with a total civil service of 684,000 in 1947 and 737,984 in 1978. Concentrating more specifically on scientists and engineers, in 1968 there were 15,000 'qualified scientists and engineers' (out of a national employed stock of 341,900) in the direct employ of government departments, with another 4,700 employed by the Atomic Energy Authority and a similar number by the armed forces. In 1978 the size of the Science Group was 16,667.[10]

The work of these specialists covers an enormous range of scientific and technological research in dozens of civil and defence research establishments (some of which have several thousand staff), inspection with regard to health and safety, inspection with regard to cost and quality control (as, for instance, over defence procurement contracts), the management of technical work within departments (such as highway engineering), and the provision of advice to other officials and to ministers on research policy and on the technical aspects of all kinds of policy.

In the 1920s and 1930s, as the numbers grew, the lot of the specialist civil servant became more and more confused. Recruitment was arranged departmentally rather than centrally, and the internal structure of the specialist classes became ever more elaborate, so that by 1930 there were over 500 distinct grades within the professional, scientific and technical classes, even though those classes represented less than 10 per cent of the service.[11] The conditions of the specialists were poor. They regarded themselves as underpaid compared with their administrative counterparts,[12] as unnecessarily bound by official secrecy, and as insufficiently listened to by those in authority. Bernal's judgment in 1939 was that 'The scientist in Government pay gets the worst of both worlds. He does not have academic privileges and he misses the possibilities of advancement and in many cases even the security of tenure of the Civil Servant.'[13]

The questions of working conditions (including official secrecy), pay, and the relative status of specialists and administrators, became the abiding concerns of a succession of committees of inquiry and royal commissions from the 1930s.

The difficulties associated with shrouding research in a veil of secrecy were succinctly stated by the Carpenter Committee on the Staffs of Government Scientific Establishments in 1931. Noting that the strictness with which the condition of secrecy was imposed varied considerably between departments, being most onerous in the armed services, the committee concluded:

> The necessity for this secrecy . . . is a matter of policy to be decided by the departmental authorities; nevertheless we cannot omit to note that it imposes a real disability on the scientific staff. A research worker can only achieve recognition in the scientific world . . . if additions to knowledge discovered in the course of his researches can be published

for the consideration of all concerned.[14]

This is a problem which, over time, has appeared to shrink in importance. It did not, for instance, feature in the report of 1969 by the Select Committee on Science and Technology on defence research.[15] A report of 1974 by a committee under the chairmanship of Sir Hermann Bondi, then chief scientific adviser to the Ministry of Defence, which examined the problems involved in the interchange of scientists between the civil service, on the one hand, and the research councils, the universities and industry, on the other, devoted one short paragraph to the question of confidentiality and concluded that interchanges of staff 'could usually be so arranged that no concern or embarrassment of this kind would arise'.[16] Finally, a study of fifty professional civil servants by Blume and Chennells found 'no evidence of conflict over restrictions on opportunity to publish'.[17] Whether the decreased emphasis upon secrecy is due to a decline in the proportion of secret work as the volume of government research has grown, or to a higher degree of insulation between government and academic scientists now than in the 1930s (of which the study by Blume and Chennells offered some indications), is an interesting matter for speculation, the truth probably being a mixture of both.

The effect of the pay and conditions then prevailing in the scientific classes was summarised in 1943 by the observation of the Committee on Scientific Staff under the chairmanship of Sir Alan Barlow, second permanent secretary to the Treasury, that the government 'had failed in peace-time to attract into and retain in its service a proper proportion of the best scientists produced by the Universities'.[18] Following the committee's report, considerable rationalisation of the scientific service took place, including a restructuring of the manifold classes into three categories, scientific officer, experimental officer, and scientific assistant, roughly parallel to the administrative, executive and clerical classes. Recruitment became a central rather than a departmental matter; machinery was set up to ensure a uniform standard for promotion; and a measure of inter-class promotion (e.g. experimental officer to scientific officer) was introduced.

At least as important as any of these steps was the alignment of the salaries of the scientific officer class with those of the administrative class. There, roughly speaking, they have remained,[19] although they have lagged behind the salaries of the corresponding generalist classes from time to time. A bitter public campaign about salaries was mounted in 1974 when, following an unprecedented half-day strike, an *ad hoc* 'scientists' central action group' placed advertisements in the national press in which anyone thinking of a career in the scientific civil service was advised to 'forget it!' on the ground that 'Discrimination in the latest pay offer leaves some scientists as much as 16 per cent behind ordinary civil servants'; but this was an unusual and short-lived campaign.[20]

Longer lasting, and even more bitter, was a dispute which peaked for about a month in June and July 1979. The dispute was initially about the bases of pay negotiations in 1979 – a transitional year before new arrangements came into force. The government had agreed in 1978 that, for the transitional year, scientists' pay rises would be linked to those received by administrators, but when it came to negotiating the 1979 rises the Civil Service Department argued that this had not been a firm agreement and offered the scientists considerably less than the administrators. The scientists' negotiators, the Institution of Professional Civil Servants (IPCS), refused the increase, and, although the government later offered the scientists the same rise as the administrators, it attached conditions which the IPCS could not accept. Furthermore, it later published an account of its offer in a way which, according to the IPCS, breached the normal confidentiality of negotiations and was misleading. By this time the issue had become bound up with what initially had been a separate set of negotiations about the pay of other groups of specialists represented by IPCS. The upshot was a series of strikes by all types of IPCS members, which included disruption at nuclear submarine bases, armament factories, government communications centres and the Royal Mint.[21] The scientists eventually accepted the same percentage increase as the administrators. The long-term effects of the dispute on the scientific civil service cannot be gauged at the time of writing.

Specialists and generalists

The 1945 changes, and the encouragement which was given to scientific civil servants to join more freely in the activities of their professional communities (such as attending conferences) went a considerable way towards breaking down the pre-war notion that, as it was put in the mid-'50s in evidence to the Priestley Commission, 'Government research establishments were considered rather indecent places to work in'.[22] But the third abiding concern, that of the relative status of specialist and administrative officials, continued to rankle, and in two respects. The first was the limited access which specialists had to ministers, and the second was their allegedly limited prospects of promotion to senior administrative posts.

In a pre-war formulation of the first of these themes, Menzler, a former chairman of the IPCS, noted that the permanent secretary in a ministry, supported by his administrative officers, characteristically presented to his minister lucidly drafted memoranda upon the pros and cons of the alternative policies from which he might choose, and implemented his decision once taken. Where, asked Menzler, did the technical expert come in? To what extent was he encouraged to assist the minister in taking decisions in a society which is increasingly technically oriented? To what extent was he allowed to see the minister and personally present his reasons for holding particular views about technical matters? Menzler's answer deserves quotation at length:

> ... prima facie evidence of an unsatisfactory state of affairs from the point of view of the intervention of the expert is afforded by the traditional structure of Whitehall administration itself. ... It cannot be denied that if some matter of public importance arises upon which the Minister desires advice, he will ordinarily go to the secretariat, for the simple reason that that is the machine. The secretariat will collect the facts and, if technical considerations are involved, may conceivably, but not necessarily, seek the views of the technical experts in the department, if any. The experts will draw up those memoranda so characteristic of Civil Service procedure, which will be forwarded to the appropriate member of the Administrative Class, possibly an Assistant Secretary but sometimes no more than a Principal, who will do his best to understand what it is all about; and in the light of such appreciation of the technical factors as he is able to attain (and sometimes the technical experts are not very helpful in this respect) and of non-technical factors of a political or administrative type, he will frequently draft another suitably peptonised report or minute or memorandum for the consideration of a Principal Assistant Secretary or perhaps even of the Permanent Secretary himself. After these successive processes of filtration the Minister gets something before him upon which to reach a decision.[23]

This is clearly a partisan statement, but it does convey the deep feeling which specialist civil servants have long held in relation to the administrative class, of being blocked from direct access to the centres of power by generalists. A somewhat similar sentiment was implied in Sir Henry Tizard's story of how he once received a file about a new invention. The file had previously gone through the hands of many able administrators. The invention was that 'of a mysterious liquid one drop of which added to a gallon of water would make a first-class aviation fuel. ... The able administrators had enlarged on the diminishing stocks of petrol, on the rate of consumption, the sinking of tankers, and so on. ... I returned the file to its source with what I think may have been the shortest minute ever written to a Minister.'[24]

This aspect of what later came to be called the specialist–generalist problem[25] had been discussed at least as early as 1923 by Sir Francis Floud, permanent secretary to the Ministry of Agriculture, who considered that

> if specialists are to be mainly employed as advisers ... they [should] have a right to demand that their advice should be sought. I have known cases in which administrative officers have come to decisions on technical questions without ever consulting the technical advisers of the Department.[26]

Nevertheless — and here Floud's remarks went to the heart of both aspects of the specialist–generalist problem — the technical adviser should not himself be the 'administrator'. The latter required the essential quality of 'adaptability', which was

> more likely to be found in men who have had a good general education and have been initiated at an early age into the daily routine of civil administration than in men who have become specialists in one particular branch of knowledge.

Such a man acquired a 'great capacity for seeing both sides of a question'; the specialist could be 'described as seeking for absolute truth, whereas the lay Civil Servant looks for something which will work'. Hence 'the sphere of the specialist should be mainly advisory rather than executive', for

> The specialist is rightly so enthusiastic about his own particular work that he is in danger of lacking that sense of proportion and that recognition of political, financial, and practical limitations which every administrator must learn to possess.

Or, as a commentator in the *Daily Express* put the same point in the late 1960s, we should beware

the present trend towards the production of experts as against men of all-round wisdom. I would far rather be ruled by men who were familiar with the tragedies of Sophocles, who had a grounding in the wisdom of Socrates and Plato and then topped it up by a wide reading of Shakespeare, Hobbes, Locke and Stuart Mill, than by one who was an expert electronics engineer or a first-class nuclear physicist. By acquiring all this expertise in the most modern sciences, a man is bound to cut himself off from the wisdom of the ages.[7]

The belief that men who are to advise ministers should have wide experience, a sense of proportion and a general grounding in the wisdom of the ages has frequently been used since the 1920s both to defend the insertion of a screen of administrators between specialists and ministers, and to justify the fairly general exclusion of officials who started as specialists from promotion to the higher administrative posts. That this exclusion was prevalent was argued by the IPCS in evidence to the Tomlin Royal Commission on the Civil Service in 1931. Although it was stated officially that no barrier existed to prevent the promotion of specialists to high controlling positions in the civil service, the IPCS maintained that

the door to effective preferment is in fact almost as effectively closed to Professional, Scientific and Technical Officers possessing administrative talent as if they were excluded by statutory enactments.[28]

The commission, however, concluded that the claims of specialists for promotion were usually considered, but that it was 'inevitable that most Administrative posts should be filled by officers with Administrative rather than specialist experience'. They had been assured by the head of the service that it would be 'ridiculous' to suggest that in filling higher posts specialists were *ipso facto* overlooked.[29]

Yet the charge continued to be laid over the years. In 1976, four years after changes in the structure of the top levels of the service had been introduced (see the discussion of the Fulton report below), in part to improve the promotion prospects of scientists and other specialists, the IPCS was to claim in evidence to an inquiry into the civil service by the Expenditure Committee that nothing had materially changed.[30] It published the accompanying table (table 3.1) in support of this claim and went on to argue that administrative officials got faster promotion than specialists and hence, not surprisingly, were in the running for the top posts at an earlier age. Whereas, said the IPCS, 24·4 per cent of assistant secretaries were aged under forty-five on 1 January 1976 (assistant secretary being the rank just below the top jobs in question), only 4·5 per cent of scientific civil servants at the comparable grade were under forty-five.

Table 3.1
Comparison of professional backgrounds of staff at
Under-secretary and above

Group	1 January 1970		1 January 1976	
	No.	%	No.	%
Administrative	405	62·5	481	58·9
Economist/Legal/Statistician	80	12·3	122	14·9
Scientific and Department Variants	67	10·3	83	10·2
Professional and Technical and Department Variants	44	6·8	53	6·5
Medical Officers	16	2·5	33	4·0
Others	36	5·6	45	5·5
Total	648	100·0	817	100·0

Source. IPCS memorandum to Expenditure Committee, 1976–77 (HC 535, vol. 2, p. 547).

At the same inquiry the then head of the civil service, Sir Douglas Allen, himself a specialist economist by background, acknowledged that 'in the past the generalist administrator probably did rather better than the scientist' in terms of career prospects, but felt that this was now changing.[31] He also suggested that one reason for the relatively poor showing of specialists at the top administrative levels was the reluctance of many of them to move away from their hard-won expertise, a conclusion for which some empirical evidence exists[32] but which seems never to have been systematically investigated. If it were found that the more able scientists were unwilling to seek administrative posts, that would not be the end of the debate, however, for it would then need to be asked how far this attitude stemmed from expectations laid down during their higher education and the early part of their scientific careers. As Baker has put it, occasionally 'an exasperated administrator will complain that specialists are narrow, soulless technocrats' who will never understand the subtle and far-reaching considerations of high-level administrative work. But, he suggests, 'it could be argued on the contrary that they will always be so obsessed if they are not allowed powers of decision in the wider field'.[33]

A comparison: the French case

Despite the regularity with which it is cited as a counter-example to Britain in the debate about specialists and generalists, the French case continues to prove illuminating about what can be done with a different educational approach and with different expectations about the work which specialists should do. In making the comparison one must, however, acknowledge the full force of Ridley's warning that the different contexts in which officials work in the two countries must be taken into account. As he observes, 'While much has changed in Britain since the days of the "nightwatchman" state, France has a far older tradition of state intervention in all spheres of national life. Its civil service was established against a background of active government, responsible for the development of public services.'[34] The central government is still responsible for the management of a far wider range of services than in Britain. As Ridley again notes:

> The Ministries of the Interior, Education, and Public Works (by whatever changing name) have field administrations parallel to those, more familiar in Britain, of the financial and postal administrations. British ministries, by comparison, are more concerned with policy-making in areas where executive responsibility is left to other bodies or, negative side of the coin, with regulatory and supervisory activities – with 'office work' rather than technical operations in the field. The French civil service is thus much larger and, though France is thought of as a centralised state, the great majority work in a complex network of 'external services' of central government departments. Many senior officials, with considerable delegated powers, serve in the provinces. As they are responsible for the management of specialised services, they are themselves specialists. The position is not unlike that of the local government services in Britain (in fact responsible for many of these

activities) with their professionally qualified chief officers.[35]

Hence while it may be true, as Self notes, that 'Between one-third and one-half of the 120 directorships of divisions, which constitute the key posts in French ministries, are held by members of the technical corps among whom engineers predominate',[36] one could not directly compare this with the British case because British central government does not manage so many technical field services as its French counterpart.

Nevertheless, in so far as French post-war modernisation owes something to government, and does not owe that debt to the structure and responsibilities of government but to the people within it, it is worth inquiring further about the role of specialists within the French civil service.[37] One of the clearest differences from Britain begins during the final stages of education. Prospective members of the senior generalist classes will probably have read law or politics at university before entry, through a stiff competitive examination, to the École Nationale d'Administration (ENA) for three years' postgraduate training as administrators. The training is both practical (the first year is spent within the administration, normally in the provinces) and theoretical, and the examinations determine which 15–20 per cent of the students will join one of the elite *grands corps* (such as the finance inspectorate) from which they may expect to attain the highest posts in the service, and which of them will become mere civil administrators. Thus even the generalists in France have a specialised training, usually in law, followed by administrative training.

Technical specialists enter the service differently. The best of them enter the École Polytechnique, again after a competitive examination which picks the best 150 from some 2,000 candidates, and the top 20 or 25 per cent of the graduates are offered posts in one of the technical corps of the civil service. The education at the Polytechnique (unlike that at the ENA) is at undergraduate level, with the emphasis on general scientific culture and mathematics. The best students then go on to two years' postgraduate specialised training at one of the schools attached to the technical corps. Typically, the best students enter the Corps des Mines or the Corps des Ponts et Chaussées and take post graduate courses in engineering or civil engineering at the École des Mines or the École Nationale des Ponts et Chaussées.

To get a better idea of the work of an elite technical corps, let us follow Ridley's description of the Corps des Ponts et Chaussées, the civil engineers, founded in 1716 and responsible for the 'public works' concerns of government long before there were ministries of that name. The corps provides the main field services of whatever ministry is responsible for public works and transport, and so it has direct or supervisory responsibility for roads and road traffic, rail transport, waterways, docks and harbours, urban water supply and drainage, school and hospital building. It also supervises the production and distribution of electricity on behalf of the Ministry of Industry and acts at county level on behalf of local government. Members of the corps perform technical, scientific, administrative, economic and social functions. Field work is only partly technical; much is managerial, financial and even political (in their relations with local politicians and other local interests). They can spend part of their career in policy-making sections of the ministry and can aspire to the highest posts there. They may be transferred into ministries throughout the government service in both their administrative and their technical capacities, and can easily transfer to the highest managerial positions in public or private enterprise, often on extended leave from their government post. Relations between government and industry are, in consequence, closer than in Britain. While, as Ridley and Blondel have observed, 'The administrative class of the British civil service does not include technical experts, businessmen are frequently suspicious of "bureaucrats", and technicians are said to misunderstand both', in France 'the situation is rather different. Careers are more varied. Administration is part of the technician's career. Many engineers move after some years in the corps to technical or executive posts in private enterprise.'[38] As if to emphasise this difference, a newspaper account in 1978 of the proposed take-over by Peugeot of Chrysler UK noted that Peugeot's chief executive, Jean-Paul Parayre, 'the hottest property on the French management scene', was a graduate of the Ecole Polytechnique. After service in two ministerial cabinets (a minister's personal staff of advisers) he ran the French government's engineering policy, with a seat on the board of State-owned Renault, before joining Peugeot to help in the takeover of Citroén and becoming president of the company at the age of thirty-nine.[39] Apart from the speed of promotion, this would not be regarded as an unusual career pattern in France.

Such a career evokes fear of technocracy, and certainly that subject is more discussed in France than in Britain. But, as Ridley again points out, the power given to specialists in the French State is pre-dated by the commitment of the civil service to active government: 'What has happened in France is not simply the "managerial revolution" – a take-over by experts. The administrative elite are the heirs of Colbert and Napoleon: it is not because they are technocrats that they have obtained power; they have become technocrats in order to exercise the power that has always been considered rightly theirs.'[40]

One lesson which he then draws is that Britain could not simply copy the French by changing the structure of its civil service. Cultural attitudes are important, for while the influence of specialists depends objectively on the structure of the civil service, subjectively it depends on its values, and in so far as these are part of a tradition built up over the centuries they are unlikely to be readily transferable between countries. But, he adds, 'the educational system and wider career patterns also play a role, probably more important', and here at least one might expect to find some lessons from the French experience.

Fulton and after

French experience in avoiding a sharp dichotomy between specialists and generalists, by expecting specialists to undertake administrative work and by providing even the generalists with a professional training in administration, was clearly one of the influences on the Committee on the Civil Service, set up under the chairmanship of Lord Fulton, Vice-chancellor of Sussex University, in 1966. The committee's report was completed in 1968 and began: 'The Home Civil Service today is still fundamentally the product of the nineteenth-century philosophy of the Northcote–Trevelyan Report. The tasks it faces are those of the second half of the twentieth century. This is what we have found; it is what we seek to remedy.'[41]

Not surprisingly, after such a start, the report criticised the predominance of 'amateurs' in the service. It also criticised the system of classes, the fact that specialists were not given enough responsibility, and the fact that too few officials were skilled managers. To remedy these and other shortcomings, the committee made 158 recommendations. The most important of these, for present purposes, were that a classless service should be created, that administrators should specialise, particularly in their early years of service, in specific subjects such as economic affairs or social affairs, that specialists should be allowed to carry more responsibility and should have an equal chance with administrators of reaching the top, that a Civil Service College should be created to provide, among other things, administrative training for specialists and post-entry training for newly recruited administrators, and that a Civil Service Department should be set up to take over from the Treasury responsibility for the central management of the service.[42]

Much has happened since the Fulton report, particularly since the reinforcement of some of its proposals by Lord Rothschild in 1971, though debate still rages as to how much has fundamentally changed.[43] The Civil Service Department and the Civil Service College were set up, the latter providing in-service courses for all types of officials. Amongst these was the Senior Professional Administrative Training Scheme (SPATS), designed to provide administrative training and two years' experience as Principals for scientists and other specialists. Changes were also made in the structure of the service, but these were not as thoroughgoing as Fulton had recommended. In particular, and in accordance with a Treasury recommendation to Fulton, unification of classes has taken place at the top, forming the so-called 'open structure' for the three grades of permanent, deputy and under-secretary, comprising some 800 staff. Posts at these levels are said to be filled by the people most suitable for them, regardless of academic background or mode of entry to the service. Below them, three major mergers have taken place since 1972, abolishing a number of classes and creating three new occupational groups, the administration group (including the former administrative, executive and clerical classes), the science group (including the former scientific officer, experimental officer and scientific assistant classes), and the professional and technology group (including, among others, engineers). Finally, some 4,000 posts have been listed as 'opportunity posts', meaning that they have been specifically designated by departments as being open to all or to a range of groups and classes.

The official explanation for this shortfall in terms of the Fulton proposals was that, after consultation with the staff associations, it had been felt that such problems as pay and recruitment within a unified service could not easily be solved.[44] Furthermore, 'Restructuring entails a great deal of effort and upheaval which is well worth while where a structural barrier stands in the way of the optimum deployment of a large number of people but much less so where few people need or wish to cross from one group to another'.[45] Commenting on this version of the law of diminishing returns, Painter, drawing on Self, argues that the shortfall was predictable, given that the very officials who incurred the wrath of the Fulton committee were handed responsibility for implementing the proposals. 'The fact that the unification shuddered to a standstill at that point in the hierarchy previously recommended to Fulton by the Treasury is revelatory. To those familiar with the creed of "incrementalism", the strategy of the least possible modification of existing practice to meet changing circumstances is all too apparent.'[46] The response of the IPCS to these developments as they impinge on the specialist–generalist debate has already been noted. One may add their comment that 'All the trends are in the right direction, but they have not yet gone far enough. There are still very few people at the top of the civil service with specialist qualifications.'[47]

The government itself has accepted that there have been difficulties with some of the measures which have been taken to try to increase the flow of specialists into administrative work.[48] In a review of the post-Rothschild reforms, published in 1979, it was noted that the number of scientists taking SPATS training had declined from twenty-four in 1972 to four in 1978. Secondly, although there had been an increase since 1972 in the number of 'opportunity posts' open to all or a range of groups and classes, there had been a recent decline in the number and quality of scientists applying for these posts.

The failure of these schemes was attributed to the traditional reluctance of scientists to work outside their specialism, to the fact that with promotion opportunities less certain because of programme cuts in some areas, even fewer scientists have wanted to risk a major career change, and to the findings that the SPATS trainees had felt isolated from the scientific community, thought that they were regarded merely as short-stay administrators and felt that their special skills were insufficiently valued. The failure of another scheme – the introduction of a special competition for specialists to achieve permanent transfer to the Administration Group at Principal level, which had attracted only sixteen scientists in 1977–78 – was attributed to differences in the 'personal priorities' of scientists and administrators, and to the possibility that the likelihood of having, if successful, to work in London had been a deterrent. Not content to leave matters as they stood, a 'wide-ranging and radical review of the structure and management of the Scientific Civil Service' had been set in train in the spring of 1979 under Dr M. W. Holdgate, Director General of Research at the Departments of Environment and Transport. The report of the working group was expected to be published, probably early in 1980.

Two other developments in the direction sought by the IPCS should, however, be mentioned here. First, following the Rothschild report of 1971, some moves were made to increase the authority and influence of scientific advisers within ministries. These will be discussed in chapter five. Second, both before and since the Fulton report, some departments have been experimenting with ways of using specialists so as to give full rein to their administrative skills. This has taken the organisational form of the 'integrated' or 'mixed' hierarchy.

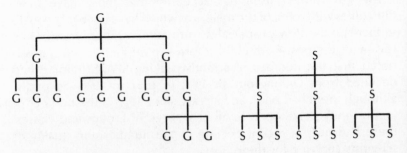

Fig. 3.1 **Traditional organisation of government department.** G generalist; S specialist.

As Regan has written, 'The traditional organisation of government departments embodies ... two principles: the separation of professional and non-professional staff into distinct organisational units, and the placing of the primary responsibility for each department's work on the general administrative divisions.'[49] One could illustrate this as in fig. 3.1. The hierarchies of generalists and specialists are kept separate, and the latter are subordinate to the former.

Since the 1960s, however, some ministries have adopted organisations which could be illustrated as in fig. 3.2. From 1964 the Ministry of Transport began to use both the 'single head' and the 'joint heads' versions of integrated hierarchies of specialists and generalists. They did so partly in order to try to overcome problems in recruiting good engineers to the ministry, but also to strengthen the role of the ministry vis-à-vis the local authorities in the formulation of transport policy. In 1966 Regan judged the arrangement to be working well, with good relations established between administrators and professionals. All administrators had access to at least one engineer within their own group, division or branch, and though he could not prove it Regan thought that this improved the quality of policy; it certainly made getting advice easier and freer from constraints. On the other hand, the integrated hierarchy could complicate lines of communication (this would be particularly so with joint heads), and entailed a slight tendency to duplication of work. There was the possibility too that specialists and generalists might each go too far in trying not to display a bias in favour of their own 'kind'. Finally, the problems of a professional working to a generalist superior seemed trickier than the converse; where, for instance, was an engineer to go for engineering advice if his superior was an administrator?

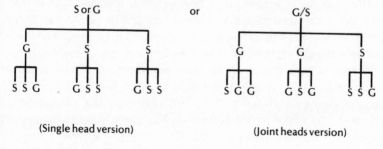

(Single head version)   (Joint heads version)

Fig. 3.2 **Integrated hierarchies.** G generalist; S specialist.

Despite these problems, the experiment continued on a broader field within the Department of the Environment (which was set up by merging the Ministries of Transport, Public Building and Works,

Housing and Local Government, in 1970). By 1976 thirty-nine of the ninety-six members of the department's 'Open Structure' – posts at under-secretary and above – were filled by officers who had entered the service in a specialist or professional grade.[50]

Mixed hierarchies also began to be used in the Ministry of Technology from 1965, a practice which continued in the Department of Trade and Industry from 1970.[51] The IPCS, however, continued to argue that, despite improvements, specialists still had insufficient access to posts of responsibility even in the Department of the Environment, and certainly closer examination of the thirty-nine Open Structure posts held by specialists in that department shows that while twelve of these posts carried general administrative or policy responsibilities, twenty-five were filled by officials who were still engaged in the same area of specialist work and occupying the same type of post as they would have done before the creation of the Open Structure.[52] It would seem, therefore, that while progress has been made towards the mixing of specialists and generalists, Regan was a little over-optimistic in his claim in 1966 that 'Recent experiments ... perhaps herald far-reaching changes in the principles on which the structure of the British Civil Service has rested ... since Northcote–Trevelyan'. Furthermore, while he is right to note that these changes entail a one-way transfer of responsibility from administrators to professionals, there is, as he also noted, little serious risk as yet of the administrators being squeezed out from their key overall position in the civil service.[53]

The struggle, as Weber put it, between the 'specialist type of man' and the 'cultivated man'[54] has some way still to run in the British civil service and leads to two final thoughts. First, one may hope that, as the struggle continues, it will yield more encouragement for scientists within Whitehall to seek administrative experience at sufficiently early an age to be able to capitalise on it later. The second point is related to this and concerns the education of scientists, to which some reference has already been made and which will be returned to in the final chapter. Briefly, it should surprise no one that the British system of education, with its emphasis upon narrow specialisation from the age of sixteen, turns out scientists and engineers who, if they enter the civil service, give little thought to the attractions of administrative work until it is too late to make the transition. While the civil service should consider whether the barriers between the different Groups can be reduced, it should also consider whether the schools and universities do enough to prepare future scientists and engineers for careers other than in research and development. Perhaps, to mix the Weberian categories, we need more cultivated specialists.

Notes

[1] Key books on post-industrial society and on technocracy are Daniel Bell, *The Coming of Post-industrial Society* (New York: Basic Books, 1973) and J. Meynaud, *Technocracy* (London: Methuen, 1968). Good reviews of the relevant literature are to be found in K. Kumar, *Prophecy and Progress: The Sociology of Industrial and Post-industrial Society* (Harmondsworth: Penguin Books, 1978); Roger Williams, *Politics and Technology* (London: Macmillan, 1971); and David Elliott and Ruth Elliott, *The Control of Technology* (London: Wykeham, 1976).

[2] On Saint-Simon, see G. Ionescu, *The Political Thought of Saint-Simon* (London: Oxford University Press, 1976); G. G. Iggers, *The Doctrine of Saint-Simon* (New York: Shecken, 1972, second edition); and Kumar, *op. cit.*, chapter 1.

[3] Kumar, *op. cit.*, pp. 42–3.

[4] The following passages on Weber are based on Kumar, *op. cit.*, pp. 102–7.

[5] *Ibid.*, pp. 43–4, for example.

[6] Max Weber, 'Bureaucracy', in H. Gerth and C. Wright Mills (eds.), *From Max Weber: Essays in Sociology* (London: Routledge and Kegan Paul, 1948; my reference to Routledge Paperback edition, 1970), p. 232.

[7] This and the subsequent paragraph is based on Andrew Dunsire, *Administration: The Word and the Science* (London: Martin Robertson, 1973), pp. 18–28.

[8] For a good illustration of this point, see G. K. Fry, *Statesmen in Disguise: The Changing Role of the Administrative Class in the British Home Civil Service 1853–1966* (London: Macmillan, 1969), pp. 43–4.

[9] P. Randman, 'Government Science in Britain 1875–1921' (Manchester University: unpublished MSc dissertation, 1977), pp. 57–68.

[10] 1947 figures from E. N. Gladden, *The Civil Service: its Problems and Future* (London: Staples Press, 1948, second edition), appendix 1; 1968 figures from Department of Trade and Industry, *Persons with Qualifications in Engineering, Technology and Science 1959 to 1968* (London: HMSO, 1971); 1978 figures from Civil Service Department, *Civil Service Statistics 1978* (London: HMSO, 1978).

[11] J. Poole and E. Kay Andrews (eds.), *The Government of Science in Britain* (London: Weidenfeld and Nicolson, 1972), p. 292.

[12] See Eric Hutchinson, 'Scientists as an Inferior Class: The Early Years of the DSIR', *Minerva*, **8** (No. 3, 1970), pp. 396–411.

[13] J. D. Bernal, *The Social Function of Science* (London: Routledge and Kegan Paul, 1939; my reference to M.I.T. Press edition, 1967), p. 107.

[14] *Report of the Committee on the Staffs of Government Scientific Establishments* (chairman: Professor H. C. H. Carpenter) (London: HM Treasury, 1930), p. 37; cited in Poole and Andrews, *op. cit.*, p. 296.

[15] *Second Report from the Select Committee on Science and Technology, Session 1968–69, Defence Research, Report, Minutes of Evidence, Appendices and Index* (London: HMSO, HC 213, 1969).

[16] *Report of the Task Force on Interchange of Scientists*, Hermann Bondi (London: Civil Service Department, 1974), para. 43.

[17] Stuart S. Blume and Elizabeth Chennells, 'Professional Civil Servants: A Study in the Sociology of Public Administration', *Public Administration*, **53** (summer 1975), pp. 111–31, at p. 124.

[18] *The Report of the Barlow Committee on Scientific Staff* (1943), para. 5, published as an annexe to *The Scientific Civil Service Reorganisation and Recruitment during the Reconstruction Period* (London: HMSO, Cmd 6679, 1945).

[19] For further details see Geoffrey K. Fry, 'Civil Service Salaries in the Post-Priestley Era 1956–1972', *Public Administration*, **52** (autumn 1974), pp. 319–33.

[20] See *The Times*, 29 March, 10 May and 16 May 1974.

[21] See 'Government scientists on the warpath', *New Scientist*, 12 July 1979, pp. 88–9.

[22] *Royal Commission on the Civil Service* (Priestley), *British Parliamentary Papers 1955–56* (London: HMSO, 1956), vol. II, Evidence, question 3411; cited in Fry, *op. cit.* (1969), p. 210.

[23] F. A. A. Menzler, in *The British Civil Servant*, ed. W. A. Robson (London: Allen and Unwin, 1937); cited in Poole and Andrews, *op. cit.*, p. 299.

[24] Sir Henry Tizard, Haldane Memorial Lecture, 'A Scientist in and out of the Civil Service', delivered at Birkbeck College, London, 1955; cited in Poole and Andrews, *op. cit.*, p. 100.

[25] For a useful international review of this question, see F. F. Ridley (ed.), *Specialists and Generalists: a comparative study of the professional civil servant at home and abroad by a group of university teachers* (London: George Allen and Unwin, 1968). This contains a chapter on Great Britain by T. H. Profitt, then Deputy Secretary General of the IPCS.

[26] This, and subsequent quotations by Floud, are taken from Dunsire, *op. cit.*, pp. 29–30.

[27] Wilfrid Sendall, cited in John Garrett, *The Management of Government* (Harmondsworth: Penguin Books, 1972), pp. 48–9.

[28] *Report of the Royal Commission on the Civil Service* (Tomlin), (London: HMSO, Cmd 3909, 1931), Evidence, appendix II, part 2, para. 36;

cited in Fry, *op. cit.* (1969), p. 202.

[29] Fry, *op. cit.* (1969), p. 204.

[30] 'Reforming the Civil Service', memorandum submitted by the Institution of Professional Civil Servants, in *Eleventh Report from the Expenditure Committee, Session 1976–77, The Civil Service* (London: HMSO, HC 535, 1977), vol. II, pp. 529–67, especially pp. 546–9.

[31] *Ibid.*, vol. II, question 49 on p. 60.

[32] Blume and Chennells, *op. cit.*, p. 128; see also the evidence of the then permanent secretary, Department of Environment, in *Eleventh Report*, etc., *loc. cit.* (note 30), vol. II, p. 305, question 727.

[33] R. J. S. Baker, *Administrative Theory and Public Administration* (London: Hutchinson, 1972), p. 158.

[34] F. F. Ridley, *The Study of Government: Political Science and Public Administration* (London: George Allen and Unwin, 1975), pp. 122–3.

[35] *Ibid.*, p. 123.

[36] Peter Self, *Administrative Theories and Politics* (London: George Allen and Unwin, 1972), p. 197.

[37] What follows is based on Ridley (1975), *op. cit.*, pp. 124–7; and F. Ridley and J. Blondel, *Public Administration in France* (London: Routledge and Kegan Paul, 1964), chapters 2 and 9.

[38] Ridley and Blondel, *op. cit.*, p. 212.

[39] *The Sunday Times*, 13 August 1978.

[40] Ridley (1975), *op. cit.*, p. 130.

[41] *Report of the Committee on the Civil Service 1966–68* (Lord Fulton), (London: HMSO, Cmnd 3638, 1968), para. 1.

[42] *Ibid.*, para. 15–18, and pp. 104–6.

[43] For developments since the Fulton report see 'The Response to the Fulton Report', memorandum by the Civil Service Department in *Eleventh Report from the Expenditure Committee, op. cit.*, vol. II, pp. 1–49, and C. Painter, 'The Civil Service: Post-Fulton Malaise', *Public Administration, 53* (winter 1975), pp. 427–41.

[44] Sir Douglas Allen's evidence in *Eleventh Report from the Expenditure Committee, op. cit.*, vol. II, p. 60.

[45] Civil Service Department, 'The Response to the Fulton Report', *loc. cit.*, p. 19.

[46] Painter, *op. cit.*, p. 431.

[47] Cited in Painter, *op. cit.*, p. 432.

[48] See *Review of the Framework for Government Research and Development (Cmnd. 5046)*, (London: HMSO, Cmnd 7499, 1979), paras. 27–33. For further details of the difficulties with SPATS, see J. Walker, *Survey of Successful SPATS Candidates* (London: Civil Service Department, 1979); and for further information on the review of the Scientific Civil Service, see Civil Service Department, press release, 27 April 1979.

[49] D. E. Regan, 'The Expert and the Administrator: Recent Changes at the

Ministry of Transport', *Public Administration*, **44** (summer 1966), pp. 149–67, at p. 150. On this subject, see also Garrett, *op. cit.*, pp. 70–9.

[50] 'Memorandum by the Department of the Environment', in *Eleventh Report from the Expenditure Committee, op. cit.*, vol. II, p. 280.

[51] See, for instance, Sir Richard Clarke, 'Mintech in Retrospect – I', *Omega*, **1** (No. 1, 1973), p. 38; and Regan, *op. cit.*, p. 152.

[52] IPCS evidence in *Eleventh Report of the Expenditure Committee, op. cit.*, vol. II, p. 333, questions 878–81; and vol. III, appendix 27, 'The Open Structure in the Department of the Environment', supplementary memorandum from the Department of the Environment.

[53] Regan, *op. cit.*, pp. 149 and 163. Profitt, referring to Regan's paper, went much further. He argued that professionals in the Ministry of Transport criticised the 1964 changes as being simply a reorganisation enforced on the generalists because of the increasing technical complexity of their work: 'Their citicism is that it has integrated administrators and professionals on the basis of the rigid class structure of the ... Civil Service with its separation of roles, and that it has failed to deal with the central problem whether there are really two different roles requiring two differently educated and trained people to carry them out.' (Profitt, *op. cit.*, p. 50.)

[54] Weber, *op. cit.*, p. 243.

IV

ADVISORY ELITES AND PROBLEMS OF SCIENTIFIC ADVICE

Scientists can acquire influence in the corridors of Whitehall without necessarily spending a lifetime as 'regular' civil servants. They can instead be invited to serve on one of the many advisory or executive bodies which operate on the periphery of the civil service machine, and which are sometimes called QUANGOs – 'quasi-non-governmental organisations'. They may also be invited to serve temporarily as individual advisers to ministers, possibly combining with that role some management responsibility for government-sponsored research and development. The characteristics of both sorts of adviser and the general problems of acting as a scientific adviser in government form the subjects of this chapter.

Advisory committees

It is a characteristic of advanced societies, according to Apter, that the link between government and the wider society is forged by élites.[1] These he takes to be small groups which represent the views of their constituencies to government, and vice versa. It is its representational function or brokerage activity which, for Apter, characterises an élite, rather than the more traditional idea of élites as prestige groups deriving status from their exercise of power. If one may mix Apter's model into the systems approach[2] to political activity, which speaks of political systems receiving inputs from, and transmitting outputs to, their environment, then one may suggest that élites can be seen as operating on the boundary of the political system. On the input side, élites translate and channel the general mood and specific claims of the social environment into forms which the system can accommodate as it sets about specifying social goals. As Apter says, 'Untranslated claims (like unheard sound) do not exist for political purposes'.[3] On the output side, élites translate policies into terms which their constituencies can accommodate.

This formulation is a generalised version of what has long been said about the role of consultative or advisory bodies in British politics. Consultation with the representatives of organised social groups has become so integral to the fabric of British politics that, as one authority has said, 'if an organised group does not exist, the government helps invent it'.[4] Another has observed that the formal recognition of a group rests 'not on the references to the need for consultation in statutes, but rather on the advisory committee. The advisory committee is the means by which the pressure group has been given a place in the formal structure of government'.[5] And a third has concluded that the main significance of advisory committees lies 'in the link they provide between the governmental system proper and the organisations in the community outside',[6] a link which acts in the directions both of policy formulation and of policy implementation. On these arguments, advisory groups exist for reasons additional to the simple need of government for advice; conversely, the advisory function involves political complexities over and above the simple transmittal of advice.

Scientists from industry, the universities and other non-governmental organisations may be invited into Whitehall to serve on a plethora of advisory committees, royal commissions and committees of inquiry. Examples of these are the Advisory Board for the Research Councils, the Advisory Council on Energy Conservation, the Genetic Manipulation Advisory Group, the Royal Commission on Environmental Pollution and the Standing Commission on Energy and the Environment. They may also be invited to serve in organisations which have at least some, and perhaps a great deal, of authority to take executive action within their area of responsibility. Examples of these include the research councils, the Atomic Energy Authority and the National Research Development Corporation. Finally, and as already indicated, there are a number of posts, such as departmental chief scientists, head of the Central Policy Review Staff, and executive head of a research council, to which a scientist from outside the civil service may be appointed on a full-time but temporary basis.

Backgrounds of scientific advisers

There has never been a full inquiry into the routes through which scientific advisers arrive at their positions of influence. Some data are, however, available for the research councils in the 1950s, and for the Advisory Council on Scientific Policy (ACSP), Council for Scientific Policy (CSP) and Advisory Board for the Research Councils (ABRC).

Guttsman's study[7] of the seventy-four members of the Agricultural and Medical Research Councils and the Department of Scientific and Industrial Research between 1950 and 1955 showed that nearly one-third of the sample had attended a public school and that 27 per cent had degrees from Cambridge University. Only two men derived from the industrial working class, while fifteen represented industry and commerce at top managerial or board level. Twenty-five members of the sample were also members of another of Guttsman's 'élite groups', such as the peerage, the academic élite, the BBC, government departmental committees or advisory committees, boards of nationalised companies, or high-level membership of very large companies; eight were members of two such groups and ten of three.

Blume's study[8] of the members of the ACSP between 1947 and 1955, and 1956 and 1963, and of the CSP from 1964 to 1971, in which he included only the *scientists* who were appointed in their personal capacities (and not *ex officio*) found that in terms of age, scientific eminence and educational (especially doctoral) background, these scientific advisors were 'a remarkably cohesive élite, constantly renewed in their own image'. Their average age had remained at fifty-two to fifty-three years, even though that of the scientific population as a whole had fallen between 1947 and 1971. The percentage who were fellows of the Royal Society had risen from 74 in 1947–55 to 80 in 1956–63 and 85 in 1964–71. For all three samples, between 29 and 50 per cent had taken first degrees at Cambridge, and between 42 and 46 per cent PhDs. Cambridge, Oxford and London accounted for between 52 and 73 per cent of first degrees, and between 75 and 100 per cent of PhDs. The same three universities were the employers of 51–63 per cent of the

Table 4.1
Biographical details of members of ACSP, CSP and ABRC (%)

	ACSP		CSP	ABRC	
	Indep-endent	Indep. + ex officio		Indep-endent	Indep. + ex officio
1. Status at start of service					
(a) FRS	71	67	73	50	48
(b) Knight or peer	54	56	19	25	17
2. Background					
(a) Attended public school	29	28	27	37	26
(b) Proportion who attended the following universities for a first or higher degree:					
Cambridge	34	35	46	31	33
Oxford	9	11	5	12	17
London	20	22	27	50	45
Manchester	14	13	3	0	0
(c) Disciplinary area:					
Physical science	46	44	35	44	40
Life science	23	24	35	37	40
Engineering	26	22	19	6	7
Social Sciences/Arts	0	6	11	13	12
3. Occupation at start of service					
(a) Academic	63	41	65	81	31
Distributed between following universities (percentages of (a)):					
Cambridge	23		17	38	
Oxford	14		13	15	
London	23		33	31	
Manchester	14		4	0	
Edinburgh	4		8	8	
Other	23		25	8	
(b) Government service	0	35	5	0	62
(c) Other (including industry)	37	24	30	19	7
4. Age at start of service					
(a) Proportion aged 50 or less	49	41	40	44	38
(b) Average age (in years) at start of service	52	52	52	53	53
Total numbers in each column	35	54	37	16	42

scientists in the three samples.

A fuller study of the origins of *all* the members of the ACSP and CSP, and of the ABRC until June 1978, has been made by the present author.[9] Perhaps the first point to note is that the ACSP was an entirely male preserve. If we include Treasury officials as well as all other members and its two chairmen, we find that sixty-four men served on the ACSP during its lifetime (1947–64).[10] Of the thirty-seven members of the CSP, one was a woman (a social scientist) and of the forty-two members (until June 1978) of the ABRC, again one was a woman (another social scientist).

Details of status, background, occupation and age of members and chairmen of the ACSP (excluding Treasury representatives), CSP and ABRC are given in table 4.1. It is important to note here that, owing to the small size of the sample, the data relating to the independent members of the ABRC must be regarded cautiously.

Notes to table 4.1

1. The analysis is based on the total membership of the ACSP (except Treasury officials) and of the CSP, and on the membership of the ABRC up to 30 June 1978. In the case of the ABRC, assessors (three in number) have been included (neglecting one who served for only a few months).
2. 'Membership' includes chairmen.
3. For the definition of public school, see note 11 to this chapter.
4. The universities listed under 2(*b*) and 3(*a*) are the main ones attended by or employing all three groups of advisers as a whole. London medical schools have been included under London University.
5. In item 2(*c*), physical science includes mathematics and geology, and life science includes medical subjects. There are inevitably some grey areas in a classification such as this, and the figures should be treated as broad indications only.
6. Two industrial members of the ACSP had no degree: hence the low total of the ACSP percentages in item 2(*c*).
7. All figures have been rounded.

A number of points emerge from the table. First, and in apparent contradiction of Blume's results, the proportion of appointees who were fellows of the Royal Society or were knights or peers has fallen considerably in recent years, though remaining at a high level. The difference between this conclusion and Blume's seems to derive from the fact that his data refer to smaller and differently constructed samples from those used here. Thus the CSP sample used here includes all CSP members over the entire life of the council. Furthermore, in an attempt to assess the significance of the fellowship of the Royal Society for appointments to these bodies, the data collected for table 4.1 refer to fellowships already held at the time of appointment. Although it emerges from the table that election to the Royal Society is an important channel in the appointment of these advisers, what is not shown is that the process can also work in reverse: for instance, two men who were appointed to the ABRC in January 1977 were elected fellows of the Royal Society in March of that year, and six members of the ACSP became fellows during or after their service on the council.

While the prominence of fellows of the Royal Society and of knights and peers has declined in recent years, that of education at a public school (on a narrow definition of public school)[11] has not. The findings on this point reported here are fairly close to those obtained by Guttsman's study of the research councils in the 1950s, suggesting that they might be broadly typical of the science policy élite as a whole. The importance of attendance at Cambridge University also emerges from Guttsman's and Blume's studies and from the data given here, with the replacement of Cambridge by London University (including the London medical schools) as the most popular training ground for top scientific advisers of the post-1972 era also being clear. The predominance of the same two universities as employers of the academic members of the three advisory committees can also be seen.

Two other noteworthy details are the decline in the proportion of engineers on the advisory committees and the remarkable constancy of the average age of their members.

Despite the variations across the years, it remains the case that the resultant groupings are in some respects not typical of the scientific population as a whole, and that they have a good deal in common by way of background. This point can be emphasised by drawing upon some additional data relating to the ACSP.[12] The proportion of independent academics on the ACSP who were fellows of the Royal Society was higher than for all university scientists; and professors in science, technology and medical subjects from Oxford, Cambridge and Manchester (but not London) were present in greater numbers than their absolute strengths in the population of professors as a whole would suggest. (Contrarily, however, for the industrialists the pattern was of a somewhat low average age for persons of such eminence, and a much lower probability of having been to a public school combined with a much higher probability of being a graduate than for all senior managers and directors.) Of the twenty-five ACSP members with a degree from Cambridge, eighteen had been to just five colleges.

Fragmentary though these data are, they do at least permit some generalisations to be made about the channels through which a scientist might have, or have had, a rather greater than average chance of reaching a position of significance within ARC, MRC, DSIR, ACSP, CSP and ABRC. To some extent they confirm Harold Laski's remark that it is important to pick one's parents wisely, although, it is fair to add, this may be less true in science than in other fields. Certainly Guttsman considered his sample of research council members to be somewhat more 'plebeian' than its counterparts in the BBC, Arts Council and British Council.[13]

When one turns, however, to the relatively few men (there are no women in this group) who have made names for themselves as top-level scientific advisers the data become even more fragmentary and the only safe generalisations that can be made are that all these advisers had high reputations as scientists or science administrators, and most of them were fellows of the Royal Society before being appointed to their posts in Whitehall, an interesting exception on the latter count being Professor John Ashworth, who was appointed chief scientific adviser to the Cabinet in 1976. A brief review of the careers of a handful of such key advisers serves to illustrate the diversity of their routes to the top.

F. A. Lindemann, later Viscount Cherwell, was born in 1886, the son of an American mother and a German father who had taken British nationality in his youth.[14] The family was extremely wealthy, and was related to the Continental aristocracy. Lindemann was educated in Scotland and Germany, and took a PhD in physics under Nernst in Berlin in 1910. There he met Born, Einstein and

Tizard.

In 1915 he joined the Royal Aircraft Factory, Farnborough, as a temporary technical assistant and became involved in the new science of aerodynamics. (Contrary to the impression which its name conveys, the 'Factory' was the chief centre of experimental aviation in Britain.) Lindemann learnt to fly and himself tested his theory for the correction of aircraft spin. After the war he was elected to the chair in physics (or experimental philosophy as it was then called) at Oxford, thereafter being widely known by the nickname 'The Prof', and became a fellow of the Royal Society at the age of thirty-three.

Lindemann's social life involved a procession from one stately home to another travelling in his Rolls-Royce with chauffeur and valet. In 1921, at the house of the Duke of Westminister, he first met Winston Churchill. Their friendship grew, and in the 1930s began to involve Lindemann in public affairs. The principal subject on which he assisted Churchill was that of air defence. Lindemann stood, unsuccessfully, for Parliament in 1935 in order to publicise his concern about the state of Britain's defences against attack by bombers. With Churchill, and independently of him, he pressed the government not to rest content with Baldwin's assertion of 1932 that 'the bomber will always get through' but to develop defensive devices, such as aerial mines.

In a move which may have been designed to silence the embarrassing attacks on defence policy which the government was suffering at the hands of Lindemann and Churchill, both were appointed to committees dealing with the subject. Lindemann joined the Air Ministry's Committee for the Scientific Survey of Air Defence under Tizard's chairmanship, while Churchill joined the superior Air Defence Research Sub-committee of the Committee of Imperial Defence, under the chairmanship of the Secretary for Air. Lindemann and Churchill became increasingly impatient with what they regarded as the slow progress made by the Tizard Committee with organising the testing of methods of air defence other than radar, and the resulting acrimony between Tizard and Lindemann is well known. On some, but not all, accounts this was the cause of the famous resignation of all the members of the Tizard committee other than Lindemann and the reconstitution of the committee without him.[15]

When war began, Lindemann became Churchill's personal

adviser, first at the Admiralty and later at Downing Street. His work was directed at least as much to non-scientific as to scientific questions, his value to Churchill being not only his ability to bring a fresh quantitative or analytical approach to affairs of state, but also his capacity for compression. He is said by his biographer to have been able to present the results of inquiries of weeks in a minute of ten lines. His biographer also notes, in relation to the undoubted influence which Lindemann had on Churchill, that the war was for him 'an extraordinary period of power without responsibility, power greater than that exercised by any scientist in history'.[16]

Lindemann received a peerage in 1941, and became a member of the Privy Council in 1942, with a seat in the Cabinet as Paymaster General. He became a member of the Shadow Cabinet in 1945, returning to office in 1951 and being instrumental then in moving the atomic energy programme out of the Ministry of Supply and into the Atomic Energy Authority. His rise to these successive positions of influence is in marked contrast to that of his pre-war adversary, Henry Tizard.

Tizard was born in 1885 in Kent.[17] His father was a naval captain, later Admiralty Hydrographer and fellow of the Royal Society. Tizard's family were not well off, and he entered Westminster School on a scholarship. Another scholarship took him to Oxford and a degree in chemistry, and from there he went to Nernst's laboratory in Berlin, where he and Lindemann became close friends. Research and lecturing posts at the Royal Institution and Oxford followed, and with the outbreak of war Tizard was commissioned in the Royal Garrison Artillery, transferring in 1915 to the Royal Flying Corps. Here he worked on bomb-aiming devices, learning to fly in the process, and later turned to developing methods for testing the performance of new aircraft and weapons.

In 1919 Tizard returned to Oxford and played a major part in Lindemann's appointment there, but moved within little more than a year to DSIR, where he was initially responsible for co-ordinating work of interest to the armed services. In 1926 he became a fellow of the Royal Society, and in 1927 he became secretary of DSIR, but left in 1929 to become Rector of Imperial College. Since 1920 he had been a member of the government's Aeronautical Research Committee, becoming chairman in 1933, and playing an important part in the promotion of the jet engine. From 1935 he was chairman of the Committee for the Scientific Survey of Air Defence, which nursed radar into existence in time for the Battle of Britain, and from 1937 (in which year he was knighted) he was chairman of a parallel committee on air offence, becoming scientific adviser to the Chief of Air Staff on the outbreak of hostilities.

After the bitter battle with Lindemann on the Tizard committee, a battle fought not only over the relative priorities of different projects but also over the degree of political activism which was appropriate to their promotion, and with Lindemann's accession to Downing Street in 1940, Tizard resigned his Air Ministry post, though not before hastening the birth of the atomic bomb project. He continued, however, to play a role in scientific affairs. In September 1940 he was sent to America to hand over the cavity magnetron (of vital importance to the development of radar) and other British inventions. On his return, he found himself, in the words of his biographer, in the position of 'unofficial adviser to many of the advisers'.[18] He was a friend and close colleague (as Foreign Secretary of the Royal Society from 1940 to 1945) of the members of the newly-founded Scientific Advisory Committee to the War Cabinet. And he became unofficial adviser to Lord Beaverbrook at the Ministry of Aircraft Production, a 'post' which maintained his *entrée* to the Air Force and to defence affairs in general.

In 1943 Tizard resigned the rectorship of Imperial College (which he had continued to hold throughout his war work) to become President of Magdalen College, Oxford. He continued to be involved in war work, particularly with planning the 'dam-busters' raid, although the involvement decreased from mid–1943, reflecting Tizard's view that he had insufficient access to the centres of authority to be of great use. In 1946, however, he returned to the centre of events as chief scientific adviser to the Minister of Defence and as chairman of both the Defence Research Policy Committee and the Advisory Council on Scientific Policy. These posts, the last formal advisory posts which he held, he resigned in 1952. The resignation was not due to Lindemann's return to power, but had in fact been planned since late 1949.[19]

If Lindemann achieved his influence as an adviser from his friendship with a key political and national leader, and Tizard his from his long experience as an administrator of science with wide contacts in the worlds of science, the armed services and Whitehall, the career of Patrick Blackett represents a third type, that of a brilliant scientist who, without ceasing to practise science, remained throughout his career in contact with science policy and moved influentially to the centre of the stage from time to time.

Blackett was born in 1897, the son of a stockbroker. After preparatory school he won a place at Osborne Naval College, going on to Dartmouth College and naval service in the first world war. In 1919 he was sent on a six-month course in general studies at Cambridge University, and three weeks later resigned from the navy to become an undergraduate. He took his degree in physics in 1921 and became a research student under Rutherford. Academic posts in Cambridge (with a year in Germany) followed, and he was elected a fellow of the Royal Society in 1933. From 1933 to 1937 he was Professor of Physics at Birkbeck College, London, moving to the chair of physics at Manchester from 1937 to 1953, and to the chair of physics at Imperial College from 1953 to 1974. He was awarded the Nobel Prize for Physics in 1948, was President of the Royal Society from 1965 to 1970, was invested with the Order of Merit in 1967 and was created a life peer in 1969.

Blackett's significant governmental work began in 1935 when he was appointed to the Tizard Committee on the Scientific Survey of Air Defence. In 1939 he joined the Royal Aircraft Establishment to work on the development of bomb-sights, and in 1940 he became scientific adviser to the head of Anti-aircraft Command where, among other things, he worked on the operational use of gun-laying radar. In 1941 he moved to Coastal Command as scientific adviser to the Commander-in-chief and as head of a team of scientists (which included C. H. Waddington) who were to apply operational research to such problems as the optimum setting of depth charges and the appropriate colour paint for camouflaging anti-submarine aircraft. Nine months later he transferred to the Admiralty and set up yet another operational research team, becoming the Admiralty's Chief Adviser on Operational Research.

From 1940 Blackett had also become one of the handful of people concerned with the development of atomic weapons. He became a member of the so-called Maud Committee, which played a vital part in getting the bomb project under way, and after the war he became a member of the very high-level and secret Advisory Committee on Atomic Energy, under the chairmanship of Sir John Anderson. His views on atomic energy had been sceptical since

1941, when he had dissented from a Maud Committee report which had concluded that Britain could build an atomic bomb by 1943 at a cost of £5 million. On the Anderson committee he became a strong and, in British science advisory circles, unique critic of the development of atomic weapons. Although Tizard was to argue from 1949 that Britain should not attempt to make her own bombs but should rely for any strategic atomic air offensive on the United States and thus save precious resources,[21] Blackett in 1947 and 1948 had gone much further. He had been strongly critical of American policy towards nuclear weapons, arguing that Hiroshima and Nagasaki had been bombed for political, not military reasons, and fearing that the Americans might yet fight a preventive war with the Soviet Union. He urged upon deaf ears a policy of atomic neutralism for Britain, and was apparently quite alone in Whitehall in advocating this policy.[22]

Whether it was his strong (and published) views on atomic weapons, or his left-wing inclinations (President of the Association of Scientific Workers, 1943–46; member of the Trades Union Science Advisory Committee, 1945–57), Blackett seems not to have held any significant governmental advisory posts from 1947 to 1964 save his membership, at the initial appointment of Harold Wilson, of the NRDC from 1949 to 1964. Whether this would have been so had there been any Labour governments between 1952 and 1964 cannot be said. Blackett's return to prominence in 1964, however, followed from his close involvement with the formation of Labour's policy towards science and technology, particularly from 1963 and Harold Wilson's accession to the leadership. Carrying forward ideas which he had been developing for several years, Blackett was influential in the establishment of the Ministry of Technology, and became its scientific adviser and, some said, 'Deputy Minister'.[23] Had he so chosen, however, he could have gone to the House of Lords and become a minister in the first Wilson administration.[24]

Whereas Blackett went out of favour in the late 1940s, and did not re-emerge in a governmental post until 1964, another man whose reputation as an adviser was also born during the war went on from strength to strength during the '50s, climaxing, like Blackett's, with the Wilson administration, but continuing unabated into the succeeding Conservative government under Edward Heath. Solly Zuckerman was born in 1904 in South Africa, the son of South African-born children of Eastern European Jewish emigrés.[25] After taking a degree at the University of Cape Town he became a medical student at University College Hospital, London, on a scholarship from Cape Town, and quickly found his way into London society. Between 1923 and 1934 he held various research posts in anatomy at universities in Britain, South Africa and the United States, and at the Zoological Society of London. In 1931 he was instrumental in setting up the influential Tots and Quots dining club.[26] Between 1934 and 1945 he was Lecturer in Anatomy at the University of Oxford, and from 1943 to 1968 Professor of Anatomy at the University of Birmingham. He became a fellow of the Royal Society in 1943. During the war he became involved in studies of the effects of bombs and conducted pioneering research in this field. It led on to work (with his friend J. D. Bernal) under Mountbatten in Combined Operations, culminating in his work in the Mediterranean and elsewhere on strategic bombing, which eventually involved Zuckerman in an intra-governmental conflict right up to prime ministerial level.

The issue was the use to be made of strategic bombers in the preparation for Operation Overlord, the Allied invasion of France. Zuckerman, through the commanding officers of the Allied Expeditionary Air Force, had been advocating a policy of destruction of the railway network of Western Europe, thus bringing German industry to a halt. This proposal required, however, a significant diversion of effort from the major existing commitment of the American and British strategic air commands, namely the destruction of the German fighter forces and the industry sustaining them. Zuckerman's plan threatened the independence of those strategic air commands, since, if it were accepted, it would bring them under the control of those responsible for Overlord. The fierce controversy which ensued has been vividly described by Zuckerman, and provides an interesting gloss on the tactics available for use by advisers in politics. Zuckerman was asked to accompany his Air Force chiefs to a late-night meeting of the War Cabinet's Defence Committee, and describes how the meeting, under the chairmanship of Churchill, began.

It started quietly enough, and in good humour, with the P.M. reading from what looked like a narrow sheet of script, which it soon transpired was a brief written by the Prof. It began something like this. The meeting had been called to discuss the A.E.A.F. proposals for the use of strategic bombers in the preparation for *Overlord*, and everyone was aware that [the Commander-in-chief of the AEAF] knew nothing about bombing or about the merits of the plan. The whole thing was 'the brain child of a biologist who happened to be passing through the Mediterranean' . . . [The Chief of the Air Staff] then interrupted to say that that particular observation was grossly unfair . . . At this point the Prof moved his hand as though to pull the brief from the P.M. There were smiles on some faces as Churchill looked up, seemingly aware for the first time that the said biologist was in the room.[27]

Zuckerman's postwar career in scientific advice covered a wide range of activities. He was a member of the Barlow Committee on Future Scientific Policy, which, in 1946, recommended the establishment of the Advisory Council on Scientific Policy. In 1947 he became a member of that council, becoming deputy chairman in 1948 and remaining such until the council's demise in 1964. He was chairman of the Advisory Council's Committee on Scientific Manpower from 1950 to 1964, chairman of the interdepartmental Natural Resources (Technical) Committee from 1951 to 1964, member of the ARC from 1949 to 1959, member of the sub-committee of the ACSP which recommended the establishment of the NERC, and chairman of an ACSP offshoot, the Committee on Toxic Substances in Consumer Goods. In addition, he was a member of the General Advisory Council of the BBC from 1957 to 1962, was a member, later chairman, of a committee appointed by the Minister for Science to report on the organisation and management of government research and development, and was for a time British representative to the NATO Scientific Committee.

He resumed his involvement with defence research in 1960, being appointed chairman of the Defence Research Policy Committee and chief scientific adviser to the Secretary of State for Defence (while remaining deputy chairman of the ACSP). In 1964, while still chief scientific adviser in the Ministry of Defence, he became chief scientific adviser to the government, giving up his defence post only in 1966. He left his new post in 1971, but had by then (in 1970) been appointed to the Royal Commission on Environmental Pollution, on which he continued to serve until 1974. Zuckerman was knighted in 1956, awarded the Order of Merit in 1968 and created a life peer in 1971.

Tizard and Zuckerman must be regarded as the two giants on the British scientific advisory scene in view of the range and duration of their service at the highest levels within government. It may, however, be useful to conclude this section by recounting briefly some features of the biographies of some other advisers who are still active in British government. Consider first Dr Duncan Davies, who, after leaving Trinity College, Oxford, began working for ICI Dyestuffs in 1945, rising to become general manager of ICI Research in 1969.[28] Dr Davies was appointed to the Swann Working Group of the Council for Scientific Policy, which sat from 1964 to 1966 and produced a well known report on the move into employment of science graduates. From 1969 to 1973 he was a member of the Science Research Council, becoming chairman of the Joint Committee of the Science and Social Science Research Councils from 1973 to 1978. In 1977 he left ICI to become Chief Scientist (a title he later had changed to Chief Scientist and Engineer) at the Department of Industry, and at the same time he became an ex officio member of the Science Research Council and of the Advisory Board for the Research Councils. Unusually for a chief scientist, Davies was not a fellow of the Royal Society at the time of his appointment.

Another of the current set of departmental chief scientists, and one who has achieved the rare distinction of holding such a post in two departments, is Professor Sir Hermann Bondi.[29] Professor Bondi was born and educated in Vienna, going later to Trinity College, Cambridge. He spent the years 1942 to 1945 as an experimental officer in the Admiralty before taking up a Trinity fellowship. In 1954 he moved to the chair of mathematics at Kings' College, London. Between 1967 and 1971 he took leave of absence to become director-general of the European Space Research Organisation. From 1971 to 1977 he was chief scientist at the Ministry of Defence. Here, among other things, he acquired an interest in nuclear proliferation which carried over (as Britain's chief negotiator at the International Fuel Cycle Evaluation) into his new appointment, from late 1977, as chief scientist in the Department of Energy. Professor Bondi became a fellow of the Royal Society in 1953 and was knighted in 1973.

A third key adviser is Professor Sir Frederick Stewart, whose governmental career differs from the cases discussed above in having been largely confined to the research council system.[30] Professor Stewart was educated in Scotland and did postgraduate research at Cambridge. After two years with ICI he became a lecturer in geology at Durham University in 1943, moving in 1956 to the chair of geology at Edinburgh. He became a fellow of the Royal Society in 1954. From 1967 to 1970 Professor Stewart was a member of the geology and geophysics committee of the Natural Environment Research Council, and from 1967 to 1971 a member of the Council for Scientific Policy. From 1971 to 1973 he was chairman of the Natural Environment Research Council, and from 1973 until 1979 he was chairman of the Advisory Board for the Research Councils. In that capacity he also became an ex officio member of the Advisory Council for Applied Research and Development. Professor Stewart was knighted in 1974.

Finally, mention must be made of Lord Brian Flowers, whose governmental work has ranged very widely indeed.[31] Lord Flowers was born in 1924 and educated at a grammar school in Swansea, then at Cambridge University. He worked on the Anglo-Canadian Atomic Energy Project from 1944 to 1946, moving then to the Atomic Energy Research Establishment, Harwell. He was lecturer in mathematical physics at Birmingham University from 1950 to 1952 before returning to Harwell for a further six years. From 1958 to 1972 he was professor of physics at Manchester University, becoming a fellow of the Royal Society in 1961. Professor Flowers was a member of the Advisory Council on Scientific Policy from 1962 to 1964, and of the Board of the National Institute for Research in Nuclear Science from 1962 to 1965. He became a member of the Council for Scientific Policy from 1965 to 1967, and chairman of the Computer Board for Universities and Research Councils from 1966 to 1970. From 1967 to 1973 he was chairman of the Science Research Council, becoming an ex officio member of the Advisory Board for the Research Councils from 1972–73 and also becoming a member of the interdepartmental task force on the interchange of scientists between the civil service and industry, the universities and the research councils, under Sir Hermann Bondi, which sat from 1972 to 1974. Away from the research council–university nexus, Sir Brian (who was knighted in 1969) became a member of the Atomic Energy Authority in 1971, and chairman of the Royal Commission on Environmental Pollution from 1973 to 1976. Since leaving the SRC in 1973 to become Rector of Imperial College, he has also been appointed president of the European Science Foundation (from 1974), member of the Energy Commission (from 1977) and chairman of the Commission of Energy and the Environment (from 1978). He has not been afraid to adopt controversial positions when occupying these posts. In 1968, while chairman of the SRC, he expressed publicly his regret that the government had rejected a proposal for the SRC to finance a British contribution to the planned CERN 300 GeV particle accelerator.[32] In 1976 the Royal Commission on Environmental Pollution, under his chairmanship, published its well known report on nuclear power and the environment which raised the first authoritative doubts in Britain about the wisdom of too large a commitment to nuclear power.[33] Sir Brian, it should be remembered, was also a member of the Atomic Energy Authority at the time. He became a life peer in 1979.

It is difficult to draw generalisations from such a small sample of advisers as those discussed here, but the importance of being a fellow of the Royal Society seems clear enough. The significance of Cambridge as a jumping-off point for high advisory posts, indicated by the more systematic data presented earlier, also receives suggestive confirmation here but should not be over-emphasised. The educational, career and social backgrounds from which people have reached the relatively few senior scientific advisory positions in government may perhaps admit of more variety than for those appointed to somewhat less eminent positions. Thus Tizard, Lindemann and Zuckerman were not educated at Cambridge, nor was Sir Alan Cottrell (Zuckerman's successor in the Ministry of Defence and the Cabinet Office), though he did move to the Ministry of Defence from the chair of metallurgy at Cambridge. On the other hand, both heads of the Central Policy Review Staff to date, Lord Rothschild (a biologist) and Sir Kenneth Berrill (an economist), went to the same Cambridge college (Trinity) as Sir Hermann Bondi. To make this observation is not to suggest that such factors as social and educational background have entered consciously into the selection process, nor that the calibre and public-spiritedness of the people selected is anything but extremely high. It is, however, to suggest that there exist channels within the British scientific community which, in similar measure to those in other parts of British society, give those who enter them a rather higher than average chance of reaching the top. But to avoid misunderstanding it must be emphasised that this is a subject on which much more work must be done, and that the educational and social variables are only two among many which, one presumes, influence an individual's chances of reaching a top advisory position. Of key importance is that individual's perceived ability to be of use within government, and it is to the problems of acting as a scientific adviser within government that we now turn.

Problems of scientific advice

A convenient way to begin to address the problems faced by scientists when acting as advisers to governments is to consider what resources and skills they bring to their task. Brooks[34] lists seven roles which scientists may play as advisers, and from these we may infer seven corresponding categories of resources and skills. The first is the expert knowledge which the scientist has of his or her subject. Second is the scientist's general 'connoisseurship' of science and scientific ways of thinking, which allows him to grasp scientific matters outside his particular field. Third is his acquaintance with other scientists and with scientific institutions, which enables him to suggest candidates for advisory and other governmental posts and to predict the effects of government policies upon scientific institutions. Fourth is the prestige enjoyed by scientists, which public officials often use in order to obtain backing for their policy proposals. Fifth is the possession by some scientists of specialist skills in policy research, a phenomenon which Brooks traces to the development of operations research during the second world war. Sixth, Brooks notes that scientists are often sought for policy advice 'merely because the scientific community provides a convenient and efficient process for selecting able and intelligent people', and finally, scientists are brought into policy-making because, and here he cites C. P. Snow's argument, 'science is more oriented toward the future than most other disciplines, and scientists are animated by a belief that problems are soluble'.

Some of those categories require amplification or criticism. The first three are unexceptionable, belief in the second and third being illustrated by the willingness of governments at certain times to appoint one man as 'chief scientific adviser' even though there is no reason to suppose an anatomist (Zuckerman) or a metallurgist (Cottrell) to be especially competent over more than a restricted area of scientific activity. Brooks's fifth point, that scientists may possess policy research skills, particularly in the form of operations research, is well attested from wartime records and also, as he himself notes, from the post-war development of think tanks and other groups who apply policy research techniques in such fields as arms control and disarmament.

The other items on Brooks's list are, however, more questionable. He supports his sixth point, which referred to the general ability and intelligence of scientists, by recalling Macaulay's desire 'to recruit university graduates in the classics not because they had been studying the classics, but because the classics attracted the best minds, who could adapt themselves to anything'. Substitute nuclear physics for classics, says Brooks, and one has the basis for the selection of certain kinds of advisory committees. Furthermore, 'It is also probably true that physicists have a way of simplifying problems which is especially useful to harassed administrators'. Lindemann offers a good example of a physicist with that facility, his capacity for compression having been of great value to Churchill.

Brooks is aware of the corresponding danger, the ever-present temptation to oversimplify, but it is not clear that he is aware of two further objections to his argument: first, why should physicists be the only scientists thought to have useful powers of simplification, and second, does not the implication that the physicist is the modern equivalent of the classicist result in just as one-sided an approach to the specialist–generalist question in public administration as the traditional emphasis upon the classicist ever did? He is not alone, however, in holding the analytical capacity of the scientist in such high esteem. While serving as chief scientific adviser to the Ministry of Defence, Sir Frederick Brundrett once told an audience of administrative civil servants that the scientist 'has the habit of analysing phenomena into superficial and fundamental factors, into . . . transient and permanent . . . He has perhaps a better capacity than many others to escape from the emotional content . . . of catchwords because . . . by and large the scientist is a very cold fish.'[35] It would be interesting to know his audience's response.

There are also difficulties with Brooks's seventh point, the future-orientation of scientists which supposedly makes them useful to policy-makers. The difficulty with this view is that it is far from clear that scientists do, as C. P. Snow put it, 'have it within them to know what a future-directed society feels like'.[36] Thus, Steiner's examination of the roles played by scientists and politicians in the atomic energy policy of the United States in 1945–46 concludes that, while their contribution was enormous, the scientists were wrong in their predictions about 'the dominant strategic issues of the ensuing years, the prospect of agreement [over nuclear arms control], the place of atomic bombs in weapons systems and in national power, the rate and course of proliferation' and other matters.[37] While, therefore, as Brooks observes, the natural optimism of the scientist may be an asset in tackling intractable policy problems, it is not self-evident that he has any special insight into the future.

Finally, some comments are needed on Brooks's fourth point, that public administrators may use the prestige of the scientist to further their own policy proposals. While this use of scientists is not necessarily to be deplored, says Brooks, it is subject to abuse, as when an administrator 'packs' a committee to obtain the advice he wants. The general conclusion which, however, emerges from the use by the administrator or politician of the prestige of the scientist — and this point is not made by Brooks — is that the advice which is the ostensible reason for the involvement of the scientist in government may be used in ways which are beyond the control of the adviser. This proposition must now be developed.

Consider first the extreme possibility that scientific advice may be exploited in a highly cynical fashion. In his study of the use made of expert advice in the controversy over the supersonic transport (SST) in the USA, Clark[38] boils down the procedure for exploitation to a few principles, which include:

1. Choose the right expert.
2. Invoke more experts than your opponents.
3. Use numbers dramatically: do not, for instance, say that the expected noise from a supersonic transport will be twice that of a Boeing 707; say it will be equivalent to fifty jumbo jets taking off simultaneously.
4. Emphasise the extreme case: do not discuss what will *probably* happen if stratospheric ozone is reduced but what *could* happen.

That example comes from an open debate in a legislative assembly where one would expect passion to run relatively high and rationality relatively low. Even within the executive side of government, however, it is reasonable to expect that expert advice will be used in ways which are beyond the control of the adviser. This conclusion follows from a consideration of the circumstances of the recipient of the advice.

The primary constraint upon the decision-maker, as Bryson noted some years ago, is that 'Exercising power is drastically interfered with by the need to hold it'.[39] In trying to ensure their survival, decision-makers, as Williams has noted, have available to them, or are confronted by, two other kinds of information in addition to specialist advice, namely, non-specialist advice (administrative and political), and the communication of pressures, subsuming under that term the effects of ideology, mandates, promises, debts, and so on.[40] Remembering that decision-makers have their own biases, one arrives at Williams's argument that:

> For any given decision the limits of choice are then effectively defined by the relevant pressures, advice and decision-maker bias, the decision-maker being more a leader, less a broker, to the extent that he determines to resist these constraints.[41]

If political survival is the *sine qua non*, and if the constraints upon the decision-maker are as just described, then it must be concluded first that expert advice is only one of a number of inputs to the thinking of a decision-maker, its prominence varying according to issue, circumstance, decision-maker and adviser, and second that the expert advice will often be viewed by the decision-maker through eyes which are focused upon his own survival. The sharpness with which the advice is seen, and the use to which it is put, are thus largely beyond the control of the adviser, and that conclusion can be reached even without raising the spectre of deliberate distortion or manipulation of advice by the decision-maker.

The need for political skills

To guard against deliberate manipulation or, more generally, to try to maintain a degree of control over the use to which their advice is put, it would seem to follow that scientists in government must have at their disposal certain skills which are more political than scientific in nature. There are additional reasons to those given above for making this statement.

The first of these additional reasons concerns the question of how to present data. This is difficult enough even when the disputants in an issue agree on the essential facts. In discussing, for instance, the significance of agreed figures for the lives saved if a nuclear test ban were introduced, does one present the results as a simple statement of the number of deaths which could otherwise be expected from radio-active fall-out, or does one present them as the ratio of the sums, for a given population, of expected life-shortening due to fall-out compared with expected life-shortening due to cigarette smoking? To do the former is to risk being dubbed an alarmist, while to do the latter (the ratio in fact being much less than 1) is to risk being charged with complacency or deviousness. When one leaves the world of agreed data and enters the realm of what Weinberg has called 'trans-science'[42] (questions which can be asked of science but not answered by it, because the answer is either in practice or in principle unavailable), then the need for careful judgment, and the room for disagreement, grows. Many contemporary issues concerning, for instance, radiological protection, energy forecasting, and the safety of nuclear reactors, food additives and vaccines fall into the trans-scientific category. In all such cases the need for experts to think carefully about how to present their arguments and, particularly, how to make their assumptions explicit is paramount.

Another reason why experts in government need skills which are more political than scientific is that the issues with which they deal are seldom wholly technical. Although Wood[42] has argued that the scientist in politics gains influence not by 'conscious adaptation to the political world ... but by continuing [his] own sharply differentiated behaviour pattern', and that he is part of an 'apolitical élite, triumphing in the political arena to the extent to which it disavows political objectives and refuses to behave according to conventional political practice', this is a minority view among commentators. Thus Gilpin argues that scientific advisers must at least understand the nature of politics, because

> The advice of experts to the policy-maker ... is seldom if ever solely
> technical ... careful analysis of its substance will reveal it to be political
> in nature ... The necessity for such a combination of technical and
> political judgement gives to the scientist-adviser his special status.[44]

A similar conclusion is implicit in Nelkin's criticism of the idea of 'Science Courts' as a means of clarifying the technical basis of major policy problems. As she argues:

> Experience shows that as the policy importance of an issue increases, the significance of straightforward technical questions (compared with political and social issues) diminishes. Issues that are clearly factual ... are either relatively non-controversial or are dealt with adequately by existing non-adversary procedures. Controversial policy questions are unlikely to be resolved primarily on the basis of scientific/technological data.[45]

Indeed, in another context Nelkin has argued that while expert advice can help to clarify technical constraints, it is also likely to increase conflict, especially when expertise is available to those communities affected by a plan.[46] Mazur, likewise, has pointed to the confusion which a technical controversy can create.[47]

If any further argument on this point is needed, consider the treatment of one additional aspect of this subject by Don K. Price.[48] Price quotes Einstein's remark, given as encouragement to those scientists who seek to find order in the universe, that 'God is subtle, but he is not malicious'. But in an international negotiation, Price continues, 'no matter how high a scientific content the subject matter may have, the contribution that science can make is a limited one because the Russians may be malicious'. The same problem arises in domestic politics and can be put in general terms thus:

> the physical scientist is used to working with data that may be difficult but not malevolent – that is, the data have no will of their own to exercise against the experimenter – whereas in politics the data not only have wills of their own, but sometimes oppose the experimenter not because they dislike what he is doing but because they dislike him.

Qualities of advisers

What, then, are the qualities, other than technical proficiency, which the expert must possess or acquire in order to survive and be useful in government? Clearly, political sensitivity is one, meaning by this that the adviser must understand how the political system works, must be aware of the key political concerns of, and constraints upon, his minister, and must be able to judge the likely responses across the political spectrum to any course of action which he advocates, including here such details as the timing and the form of words of any public statements.

Perhaps the next most important requirement for effective science advising is to spend a considerable amount of time in close proximity to the decision-maker. In a study of US science advisers, Eiduson concluded that 'most important' was 'being present at the critical time'.[49] It would follow from this that full-time advisers would have much greater opportunity to gain the attention of decision-makers at key moments and would, therefore, be more influential than part-time advisers, although, as a corollary, they tend to be able to spend less time working as scientists than part-time advisers. R. V. Jones, a leading British scientific adviser of the second World War, has observed that the timing of contributions to a debate can be crucial; he reports having seen committees 'even up to cabinet level, almost stampeded by isolated pieces of "stop-press" information'.[50] One can add here that a sense of timing can refer not only to the tactical introduction of material at critical points in a debate, but also to the understanding of the routine of budgetary cycles, with the consequent appreciation of when it is, and is not, possible to affect budgetary decisions.

Related to the question of access to decision-makers is the matter of what to do with the limited time available when the adviser does gain access. Jones emphasises the importance of being able to put the issues across in the simplest of language, and considers that the decision-maker may wisely suspect any adviser who relies on jargon.[51] Benveniste makes the same point more fully, referring to the decision-maker, with Machiavellian allusion, as the Prince:

> To educate the Prince requires special skills. Since access time is a precious commodity, a half-hour presentation may have to accomplish what a graduate student takes months to achieve. Clarity of presentation and condensation is essential. The learning process cannot be overt, because the Prince may be impatient if lectured at. The presentation has to be practical, and the technical dimension and political context cannot be dismissed. If the policy has to be explained to relevant publics, the expert suggests how this might be achieved. He knows the Prince cares less about why than he does about how to bring about the new venture.[52]

To the requirements that the adviser be politically sensitive, that he be on the spot at the right time and that he present his advice clearly and concisely may be added a fourth, that he has done his homework. By this is meant not only that he has made a routine examination of the problem in question, but also that he has sought advice himself from all relevant quarters. Nichols, quoting with approval the observation that 'scarce as truth is, the supply is greater than the demand', has commented that when a government programme does not work out, we often learn 'that there were persons who knew, and stated in detail, why it probably would not, but they were not consulted or, if they were consulted, they were not heeded'.[53] To say this is not to argue that all eventualities can be foreseen but simply that it behoves the adviser, who will often not be an authority himself on the subject in question, to be sure that he has ranged widely enough in taking soundings from others. In particular, he will wish to avoid the occasion, embarrassing to himself, confusing and irritating to the decision-maker, of having contradictory scientific arguments, of which he was unaware, raised at a critical meeting. He will probably wish to resolve technical disagreements prior to any meeting at which decision-makers will be present.

A fifth characteristic of much influential advice is that the expert seeks the approval not only of the decision-maker but of those who are to implement the decision and those who are to benefit from it. Like the prior resolution of technical differences, this tactic, *in extremis*, can suggest that the adviser is seeking to usurp the role of the decision-maker. The formation by the expert of what Benveniste calls coalitions with implementers and beneficiaries[54] can easily create the impression that the adviser is seeking to pre-empt the choice before the decision-maker. Yet, if practised with respect for the proper lines of authority within government, this 'coalition-formation' can be essential, firstly, to the success of authorised policies and, secondly, to the general effectiveness of the adviser himself. An example of the first case is Tizard's active canvassing of radar with operational units of the RAF even before it was certain that the technology could be made to work.[55] Tizard's concern was that unless the ultimate users were persuaded of its merit and began soon enough to develop operational procedures that took account of radar, no amount of high-level decision-making in Whitehall would yield the full benefit to be gained from the new technology. As an example of the second case, consider Lord Zuckerman's account of the alleged failure of the scientific advisory groups set up in a number of departments in 1947 and 1948, following a recommendation from the Advisory

Council on Scientific Policy. According to Lord Zuckerman, the scientists 'contributed little, if anything, to the central policies of their Departments. In my view the reason for this is that they were not effectively integrated into those lower, leave alone higher, administrative levels where policy begins to be formulated. The job of the scientists was to back up departmental policy, once this was decided.'[56]

Finally, the successful adviser, if he is to retain his integrity as both scientist and adviser, must take care to avoid in himself, and to watch for in others, a number of simple human failings. These include, as Jones has noted,[57] the temptation to engage in *argumentum ad hominem* (as illustrated earlier in the description of Lindemann's attack upon Zuckerman at the wartime Defence Committee), the temptation to 'slant' the advice so that whatever the outcome the adviser will have been 'right', and the temptation, in seeking to serve one's master well, of sycophantic analysis – of producing advice which will be acceptable to the decision-maker even though the adviser has doubts about it. Jones gives as an example of 'slanting safe' the question of how to advise, in 1943, whether Britain was threatened by a long-range rocket attack. Unable to assess the evidence, the adviser may be tempted to say that there is a threat: if one materialises, he is proved right; if not, he can always blame the non-materialisation on counter-measures taken as a result of his advice. But to advise that there is no threat, and to be wrong, would be to ruin one's reputation for ever. Sycophantic analysis, on Jones's conception, can include the temptation, when faced with a master whom you know will not accept what you regard as the right advice, to give advice which will be acceptable and which will make the decision-maker tend in the right direction. All these failings are condemned by Jones.

The scientist who enters government is invariably good at some branch of science, but is selected from among the ranks of good scientists for reasons which go beyond mere scientific competence. Skill in communication, in judgment, in getting on with people, and in political (which need not imply *party* political) survival are all important. As a summary of what scientific advisers must bear in mind, and as the distilled wisdom of over three decades of high-level scientific advisory activity on his own part, the following paragraphs from Lord Zuckerman provide a fitting conclusion to this chapter:

What I have learnt over the years is that it is not the primary function of scientific advisers at the centre of Government to teach their masters about science. They usually have more urgent matters with which to deal. I also learnt that scientific advisers were unwise when they became mere propagandists for more resources for science. . . .

The main contribution of scientists is their particular approach – their scientific approach – as an aid to judgment in the formulation of government policy. But they cannot do this *in vacuo*. Scientists in Government first have to appreciate the political problems, and they must realize that scientific and technical matters are only one input into the complex of considerations which have to be taken into account when policy decisions are made. As they cannot be omniscient about science, they must also know where to seek advice, and they must also know when to reject it – because much scientific advice in Government derives from vested interest.

Above all, it is essential to bear in mind the political context within which decisions on policy are taken. For example . . . no technical arguments about Concorde would have the political force with Government to match the warnings of Trades Union leaders that the project should not be abandoned. . . . For this and many other reasons, scientists who are advisers have to be modest. But at the same time they should never trim their advice for political reasons or vary it in accord with the opinions of a political master.[58]

The combination of political sensitivity with the dispassionateness implied in the last sentence requires rare strength of character, which is perhaps the final quality that one would hope for in an adviser.

Notes

[1] D. E. Apter, *Choice and the Politics of Allocation* (New Haven, Conn.: Yale University Press, 1970), chapter 4.

[2] See D. Easton, *A Systems Analysis of Political Life* (New York: John Wiley and Sons, 1965).

[3] Apter, *op. cit.*, p. 112.

[4] A. Potter, *Organised Groups in British National Politics* (London: Faber and Faber, 1961), p. 32.

[5] J. D. Stewart, *British Pressure Groups: Their role in relation to the House of Commons* (Oxford: Clarendon Press, 1958), p. 8.

[6] Political and Economic Planning, *Advisory Committees in British Government* (London: George Allen and Unwin, 1960), p. 105. On this subject, see also K. C. Wheare, *Government by Committee* (London: Oxford University Press, 1955), and S. E. Finer, *Anonymous Empire*

(London, Pall Mall Press, 1966).

[7] W. L. Guttsman, *The British Political Elite* (London: MacGibbon and Kee, 1965), pp. 345–9 and 366.

[8] S. S. Blume, *Toward a Political Sociology of Science* (New York and London: The Free Press, and Collier Macmillan, 1974), pp. 199–201.

[9] Some of the information given below is from P. J. Gummett, 'British Science Policy and the Advisory Council on Scientific Policy' (Manchester University, unpublished PhD thesis, 1973), chapter 3, and also from P. Gummett and R. Williams, 'Assessing the Council for Scientific Policy', *Nature*, **240** (8 December 1972), pp. 329–32.

[10] Gummett, *op. cit.* (1973), contains a full list. Alternatively, see the annual reports of the council.

[11] The definition of public school used here is that of the Newsom report: *The Public Schools Commission, First Report*, vol. 1 (London: HMSO, 1968), appendix 2. Using the less restrictive definition of inclusion of a school in the *Public and Preparatory Schools Yearbook 1971*, 45 per cent of all members of the ACSP (31 per cent of independent members) could be said to have attended public schools.

[12] Comparative data in this paragraph come from the Robbins report, *Higher Education* (London: HMSO, Cmnd 2154, 1963, Part III, annex J, table J.I; A. H. Halsey and M. A. Trow, *The British Academics* (London: Faber and Faber, 1971), table 7.6; UGC, *Returns from Universities and University Colleges in Receipt of Treasury Grant, Academic Year 1958–59* (London: HMSO, Cmnd 1160, 1960), table 9; Acton Society Trust, *Management Succession* (London: Acton Society Trust, 1956), table 1; and G. H. Copeman, *Leaders of British Industry* (London: Gee, 1955). See Gummett, *op. cit.* (1973), chapter 3, for a fuller treatment.

[13] Guttsman, *op. cit.*, p. 345.

[14] Details of the life of Lindemann are taken from the Earl of Birkenhead, *The Prof in Two Worlds: The official life of Professor F. A. Lindemann, Viscount Cherwell* (London: Collins, 1961).

[15] One dissenting view is that of R. V. Jones, cited in Sir Bernard Lovell, *P. M. S. Blackett, a biographical memoir* (London: The Royal Society, 1976) – reprinted from *Biographical Memoirs of the Royal Society* – at p. 52. For further argument on the issue see Lovell, *op. cit.*, pp. 51–2 (giving the view of Blackett, a member of the committee); Birkenhead, *op. cit.*, chapter 6; C. P. Snow, *Science and Government* (London: Oxford University Press, 1961); and R. W. Clark, *Tizard* (London: Methuen, 1965), chapter 6.

[16] Birkenhead, *op. cit.*, p. 211.

[17] Details of the life of Tizard are taken from Clark, *op. cit.*

[18] *Ibid.*, p. 275.

[19] *Ibid.*, p. 401.

[20] Details of the life of Blackett are taken from Lovell, *op. cit.*

[21] M. Gowing, *Independence and Deterrence: Britain and Atomic Energy, 1945–1952*, vol. 1 (London: Macmillan, 1974), p. 229.

[22] *Ibid.*, p. 183.

[23] Lovell, *op. cit.*, pp. 76–81; and A. G. Mencher, *Lessons for American Policy-Making from the British Labor Governments's 1964–70 Experience in Applying Technology to Economic Objectives* (Washington, D.C.: National Science Foundation, 1975), Part 1, appendix 2, pp. 2–3.

[24] Lovell, *op. cit.*, p. 80. Lovell's source was Harold Wilson.

[25] Most of the details given here of the life of Lord Zuckerman are taken from Lord Zuckerman, *From Apes to Warlords: The autobiography (1904–1946) of Solly Zuckerman* (London: Hamish Hamilton, 1978), with additional material from *Who's Who* and the Annual Reports of the Advisory Council on Scientific Policy.

[26] *Ibid.*, appendix 1.

[27] *Ibid.*, p. 248.

[28] Details of the life of Dr Davies are from *Who's Who* and an interview with D. Dickson in *The Times Higher Education Supplement* (1 April 1977).

[29] On Sir Hermann Bondi, see the profile by C. Sherwell in *Nature*, **270** (17 November 1977), p. 201.

[30] See *Who's Who*.

[31] *Ibid.*

[32] See the report of Professor Flower's speech to the CERN Council in *Nature*, **219** (6 July 1968), p. 15.

[33] Royal Commission on Environmental Pollution, *Sixth Report, Nuclear Power and the Environment* (London: HMSO, Cmnd 6618, 1976).

[34] H. Brooks, 'The Scientific Adviser', pp. 73–96 in R. Gilpin and C. Wright (eds.), *Scientists and National Policy-Making* (New York: Columbia University Press, 1964), at pp. 77–9.

[35] Sir Frederick Brundrett, 'Government and Science', *Public Administration*, **34** (autumn 1956), pp. 245–56.

[36] C. P. Snow, *op. cit.*; my reference from paperback edition published by New American Library, p. 73.

[37] A. Steiner, 'Scientists, Statesmen, and Politicians: The Competing Influences on American Atomic Energy Policy 1945–46', *Minerva*, **XII** (No. 4, winter 1974), pp. 469–509, at p. 507. For Lord Zuckerman's doubts on this point, see Sir Solly Zuckerman, 'Scientists in the Arena', in A. de Reuck *et al.* (eds.), *Decision Making in National Science Policy* (London: J. and A. Churchill, 1968), pp. 5–25, at p. 6.

[38] I. D. Clark, 'Expert Advice in the Controversy about Supersonic Transport in the United States', *Minerva*, **XII** (No. 4, winter 1974), pp. 416–32, at pp. 426–30.

[39] L. Bryson, 'Notes on a Theory of Advice', *Political Science Quarterly*, **66** (September 1951), pp. 321–39, at p. 332.

[40] R. Williams, 'The Political Context of Scientific Advice', paper presented to the ninth IPSA World Conference, Montreal, 1973, p. 2.

[41] *Ibid.*, p. 3.

[42] A. M. Weinberg, 'Science and Trans-Science', *Minerva*, **X** (No. 2, April

1972), pp. 209–22.

[43] R. C. Wood, 'Scientists and Politics: The Rise of an Apolitical Elite', in Gilpin and Wright (eds.), *op. cit.*, pp. 41–72, at p. 44.

[44] R. Gilpin, *American Scientists and Nuclear Weapons Policy* (Princeton, N.J.: Princeton University Press, 1962), pp. 15–16.

[45] D. Nelkin, 'Thoughts on the Proposed Science Court', *Harvard University Newsletter on Science, Technology and Human Values*, No. 18 (January 1977), pp. 20–31, at p. 22.

[46] D. Nelkin, 'The Political Impact of Technical Expertise', *Social Studies of Science*, **5** (1975), pp. 35–54, at p. 51.

[47] A. Mazur, 'Disputes Between Experts', *Minerva*, **XI** (No. 2, April 1973), pp. 243–62, at p. 261.

[48] D. K. Price, *The Scientific Estate* (Harvard: Belknap Press, 1965; my reference to London: Oxford University Press paperback, 1968), pp. 141–2.

[49] B. T. Eiduson, 'Scientists as Advisers and Consultants in Washington', *Bulletin of the Atomic Scientists*, **22** (October 1966), pp. 26–31.

[50] R. V. Jones, 'Temptations and Risks of the Scientific Adviser', *Minerva*, **X** (No. 3, summer 1972), pp. 441–51, at p. 449.

[51] *Ibid.*, p. 448.

[52] G. Benveniste, *The Politics of Expertise* (Berkeley: Glendessary Press, 1972; my reference to London: Croom Helm, 1973 edition), p. 121.

[53] R. W. Nichols, 'Some Practical Problems of Scientist-Advisers', *Minerva*, **X** (No. 4, October 1972), pp. 603–13, at p. 606.

[54] Benveniste, *op. cit.*, pp. 130–5.

[55] R. W. Clark, *op. cit.*, chapter 7.

[56] Lord Zuckerman, 'Scientific advice during and since World War II', *Proc. R. Soc. Lond. A.*, **342** (1975), pp. 465–80, at p. 475.

[57] Jones, *op. cit.*, pp. 450, 444 and 445.

[58] Zuckerman (1975), *op. cit.*, pp. 478–9.

V

SCIENCE IN GOVERNMENT DEPARTMENTS

Governments support research and development for three main reasons. First, it is internationally regarded as a governmental responsibility to provide for the education and training of young scientists and hence to support post graduate research, generally in institutions of higher education. Second, governments often take it upon themselves to support certain fields and types of research for which they consider there is a national need, but which are unlikely to be performed without their support. Thus they support basic research in the higher education sector, and also support basic and applied research in a range of other institutions. These include industrial firms, institutions which perform research to governmental specification but are managed non-governmentally (such as the federally funded contract research centres in the USA), institutions which exist on the fringes of the public sector and enjoy a high degree of autonomy over their programmes (such as the research councils in the UK), co-operative government–industry research associations (which support particular industrial sectors such as the wool or the shoe industry) and, finally, research establishments which are wholly owned and run by government departments. The third reason why governments support research and development is that they require their own sources of technical information and advice. These sources can embrace all the institutions listed above, but with the emphasis generally upon those under fairly direct governmental control, such as government research establishments.

Marked differences can occur between countries in the use made of the various institutions through which governments can support research and development. With respect to work required under the second (national need) and third (governmental need) reasons, one aspect of these differences can be illustrated with the examples of the USA and the UK. Whereas in the United States, after the last war, a deliberate policy choice was made to have research done under those headings performed as far as possible by non-governmental bodies working under contract to the federal government, in Britain the development of intramural government research establishments was emphasised. The differences between the two systems should not be overdrawn, and table 5.1 may provide useful perspective, but the table also shows the relative emphasis upon contracting, in the USA, and on the use of government research establishments, in the UK.

Table 5.1
Main sources of funds (S) and sectors of performance (P) for research and development, 1969 (percentages of total national expenditure)

	Business		Government		Higher education	
	S	P	S	P	S	P
USA	38	70	58	14	3·4	13
UK	44	65	51	25	0·6	8

Source. *Science Policy*, September–October 1972, cited in Keith Pavitt and Michael Worboys, *Science, Technology and the Modern Industrial State* (Leeds: Siscon, 1975), p. 11.

A note on the contract mechanism in the United States

The contract mechanism developed, therefore, as a result of the policy choice made in the United States in the 1940s, reinforced by a political culture which opposed the expansion of governmental institutions, to maintain and expand the nation's research and development resources through contracting, rather than through the establishment of intramural government laboratories. The advantages sought by this approach were considerable. Government would have access to the whole range of scientific and technological expertise available in the country, including those individuals who would be loath to leave the private sector to work in government research establishments. Consequently there would be access to a wide range of approaches to problem-solving, and cross-fertilisation between competing institutions could be enhanced. Furthermore, flexible use of scientific resources would be possible, since the responsibility for responding to programme changes would fall on non-governmental institutions.

There was, of course, nothing new about governments placing contracts for goods and services.[1] But the effects of the application of the contract mechanism to research and development in the United States in the 1940s were sufficient for Price, in the early 1950s, to be writing of 'Federalism by Contract', an early version of the 'Contract State' thesis.[2]

Price identified five types of relationship between government agencies and the private institutions which were undertaking contract research and development.[3] First was the fairly straightforward case where contracts were placed for research leading to equipment improvement or some similar specific objective. Second, 'master contracts' were being placed with some organisations, allowing a continuing relationship between agency and contractor to be maintained with the minimum of formality. Third, there were cases where special tactical and strategic studies, traditionally the exclusive province of the military, were being performed by private contractors. Fourth, to meet certain military requirements which entailed the establishment of new, large-scale laboratories, together with the associated scientific *and* managerial competence, some universities were proving willing to take on such assignments in special, off-campus laboratories. Finally, new private bodies such as the Rand Corporation were being established specifically to undertake federal contracts. In total these developments constituted 'a new and rather unsystematic system of improvised federalism, the significance of which it will take years to appraise'.

At least two new industries grew to maturity, sustained by federal contracts for research and development. In the case of one of these, nuclear power, Orlans has noted that the Atomic Energy Commission operated almost entirely by contract, partly because most of the key industrialists and scientists opposed governmental operation of major installations, but also so as to strengthen the industrial sector and keep non-governmental groups well informed about the evolving technology.[4] In the other case, electronic components, Freeman has shown the importance of federal contracts in establishing the US industry as a world leader.[5]

The contract mechanism is not without its difficulties. According to a former chairman of the Atomic Energy Commission, these can include problems with information flow between government and the contractors; the fact that contractors usually have their own organisational practices and may resist some of the controls and procedural requirements which the government may seek to impose; and that valuable experience and technological advances may be initially in the hands of a few contractors.[6]

Despite these problems, however, successive US governments have preferred the contract mechanism to alternative approaches to government-sponsored research and development. From its origins the mechanism quickly evolved into an extremely flexible policy instrument, although one capable of generating mutual dependence between an agency and its contractors. By the mid-1960s Price was writing of the 'fusion of public and private power',[7] a theme which has since often been explored with reference to military contracts.[8] The general position as regards science and technology was summarised as follows by Danhof in 1968:

> The contractual system is . . . more than a device to get work done for a government agency. An agency's program is built upon contributions from many sources, public and private. There are numerous channels through which interested and knowledgeable groups may suggest courses of action . . . A formal contract is merely a step in a process of interaction between private and public groups with an interest in a scientific or technical area . . . In both the formulation and the execution of its program the agency is heavily, and sometimes wholly, dependent upon the initiative of outside institutions in developing the expertise necessary to prepare the proposals and do the work.[9]

Had the objectives sought through the contract mechanism been pursued by traditional methods, Danhof concludes, there would inevitably have occurred in the United States, despite strong ideological objections, a vast expansion of governmental establishments. Such a form of organisation, he argues, 'would have isolated in some large degree the government's operations from those of private institutions'. Administrative tidiness would have been a poor substitute for the 'greater stimulus' provided by an 'open competitive system'.[10]

The British approach

In Britain, however, greater emphasis was placed after the last war on the development by successive governments of intramural research establishments. The reasons for this are not clear but probably centred on three considerations: the centripetal tendencies of British government in general; the existence since the turn of the century of a tradition of creating government research establishments; and third, perhaps, the structure of British industry. This last certainly introduced a difference between the US and the UK atomic energy programmes. Unlike the United States, Britain did not, in the late 1940s, have sufficient large companies capable of undertaking major contracts in the atomic energy programme; it was for this pragmatic reason, and not on ideological grounds, that the British (Labour) government itself undertook so much of the necessary work in the early post-war years.[11] The questions of industrial structure, and the relations between government research establishments and industrial research were, as we shall see, to become important in the 1960s.

Apart from the foundation of the Royal Observatory (1675), the Geological Survey (1832) and the Laboratory of the Government Chemist (1843), the first of the major British government research establishments was the National Physical Laboratory, established in 1899. As Moseley has put it, the establishment of the Laboratory signalled a new relationship between the government and science:

> While the principle of giving financial support to technical education had, by the late nineteenth century, ceased to be a matter of contention, the provision of funds and institutions in which research workers could undertake scientific work which it was thought industry was incapable of conducting marked a departure from previous practice.[12]

Initially defined as 'a public institution for standardizing and verifying instruments, for testing materials and for the determination of physical constants', the Laboratory was encouraged by its original controllers, the Royal Society, to develop rather more broadly, branching by 1910 into metallurgy, aerodynamics and ship hydrodynamics.

With the establishment of the Department of Scientific and Industrial Research, protracted negotiations over the future control of the Laboratory began, ending in 1918 with its transfer to the new department.[13] In the course of time, work which had begun at the National Physical Laboratory became the basis of new research establishments, some of which were immediately located within DSIR, others going to other departments and perhaps returning later to DSIR. The Radio Research Station, National Engineering Laboratory, Hydraulics Research Station, Road Research Laboratory and Building Research Station were all to some extent spawned by the National Physical Laboratory. In addition, the Geological Survey and, later, laboratories concerned with fire prevention, fish preservation and transport, forest products, pest infestation and water pollution also became attached to or were set up by DSIR.[14]

Much work of great practical use has been done by these laboratories.[15] Research by the Road Research Laboratory in the 1940s and 1950s produced improvements in the wear, reliability and skidding resistance of surface dressings. Other work done at that laboratory produced standard designs for construction of different categories of roads. An example of the work of the then Fire Research Station in the 1960s is its development of a new system of protecting electrical equipment in explosive atmospheres. Other work done at the station included the specification of safety requirements for portable oil heaters which is estimated to have reduced by over a thousand a year the number of serious oil heater fires in Britain. In the field of aerodynamics, the National Physical Laboratory has provided detailed advice and experimental facilities for design and constructional engineers concerned with the design of bridges and other structures. It has also devised a cheap and simple 'stack stabiliser', in the form of three metal strips arranged in a spiral round the tops of tall chimney stacks, which prevents the aerodynamic excitation of dangerous oscillations of these stacks in high winds. Finally, the National Engineering Laboratory has developed a range of innovations of industrial importance. These include hydrostatic transmissions for use in dumper trucks, the standardisation of languages for numerically controlled machine tools, a range of grinding machines with air-bearing wheelheads, and various types of fans and pumps.

In the defence field there are some twenty-three research establishments with various histories, functions and sizes. Among the largest are the Atomic Weapons Research Establishment at Aldermaston, which was formerly part of the Atomic Energy Authority; the Royal Aircraft Establishment, Farnborough, which is the largest research establishment in Western Europe and is involved in many aspects of research and development into civil and military aviation and space activities, including aerodynamics, avionics, communications, computation, navigation, optics and structures; the Royal Signals and Radar Establishment; the Materials Quality Assurance Directorate; the Admiralty Marine Technology Establishment; and the Meteorological Office. Smaller, but probably as familiar-sounding as any of the above, are the Chemical Defence Establishment at Porton Down, which dates from 1916; the National Gas Turbine Establishment, concerned principally with the development and testing of military and civil aircraft engines and marine engines for naval use; and the Royal Armament R and D Establishment, Sevenoaks, which designs, develops and evaluates conventional weapons for all three services.[16] Since 1970 these establishments have formed part of the Procurement Executive of the Ministry of Defence.[17]

The complete range of government research establishments at the time of writing comprises some fifty or so establishments (depending on the definition used), half of which are in the defence field, the remainder being distributed between agriculture, fisheries and food, health and safety, industry, energy, environment, the Home Office, and overseas development.

Changing roles

The roles of the government research establishments have never been entirely clear-cut, have been subject to change over time, and have also often been the subject of criticism by outsiders. Thus the National Physical Laboratory was heavily attacked in 1905 by commercial testing agencies and the Institute of Chemistry over its right to undertake, in return for fees, work such as the analysis of steel samples, which could be carried out by private analysts.[18] The criticism is somewhat ironic in view of attempts in the 1960s and 1970s to make the Laboratory more commercially-minded (although over its research, not its testing facilities, which were already run commercially) and less like, to use an epithet sometimes applied to it by irreverent civil servants, the 'Free University of Teddington'. In that regard it is interesting that in 1939 J. D. Bernal argued that:

> For political as well as economic reasons there is ... on the part of Governments an extreme reluctance to take any active part in research

on the application of science. If a Government laboratory arrives at any result which could have commercial value, it is not in a position to exploit it, rather it is definitely prevented from either selling the process to an industrial firm or operating it on its own account. The general principle is laid down that in no circumstances, outside military requirements in war time, should Government Departments compete in production with industrial enterprise. The inevitable result is that the attitude of Government institutions towards applications of research is almost entirely negative.[19]

The reply of the Institution of Professional Civil Servants to a similar claim made by a trade association nearly three decades later was to admit that many of the staff in government research establishments did not work within commercial terms of reference; that, however, was because they were in general not required to do so, but where, as at the Hydraulics Research Station, there had long been a requirement to work on a commercial basis, government scientists had proved perfectly able to do so.[20]

The question of the degree to which government research establishments have in recent years been required to develop more of a commerical, or, more broadly, customer orientation will be returned to shortly, but first a little more must be said about the way in which the roles of these establishments have until relatively recently been set. The key point to make is that until the 1970s the establishments enjoyed a considerable degree of autonomy from whichever was their supervising authority. Thus, in a statement about the aims and functions of its research stations, made in 1960, the DSIR noted that:

> Basic research in the stations ... must be directed to the general advancement of technology and applied science. We recognise, however, that each station should have the freedom to follow up new ideas that fall within its field of interest, and so to include in its programme some research which is not directed towards any immediate need of industry or Government.[21]

In 1961 the report of the Committee of Enquiry into the Management and Control of Research and Development, while recognising that ultimate control rested with the council of DSIR, also observed that 'The pattern and scale of effort having been agreed by the Council, the Director of a station is given a large measure of freedom to determine the details of his programme and to support or stop subsidiary items'.[22] Furthermore, the committee also noted that proposals to open up some new field of research usually came from the research establishments or from their advisory boards, and less frequently from the council or headquarters staff of DSIR. Finally, as late as 1972, the Chief Scientist at the Department of Industry was to describe the situation at the time as one in which each director was 'very much captain of his own ship' and had 'a great deal of independence'; under the then current arrangements the programme was 'more or less invented within the [establishments] and then endorsed by a process of advisory committees and ultimately by myself'.[23] Moves within Whitehall to change this state of affairs began in the 1960s, and can conveniently be approached by examining the history of certain developments at the Atomic Energy Research Establishment, Harwell.

Redeployment and diversification at Harwell

The Harwell laboratory was set up in 1946 as part of Britain's nuclear weapons programme.[24] Increasingly, however, Harwell became responsible for research and development on civil nuclear power, growing to 6,000 staff by 1956.[25] After the Suez crisis the reactor programme expanded, and most of the Reactor Division of the Atomic Energy Authority was transferred from Harwell to Winfrith in 1958–60. A Research Group of the Authority was formally established in 1961, comprising the laboratories at Harwell, Culham (fusion work) and Amersham (radio-isotopes). Weapons, Reactor, Production and Engineering groups were also established. This reorganisation, however, coincided with the end of the period of rapid growth for Harwell, and the start of a period of fixed, and later declining staff.

By 1965, with the start of the programme for the second generation of nuclear power stations, it was clear that a watershed had been reached. Nuclear power was now well established as a means of generating electricity, and although much research would continue to be needed for the third generation of reactors, the scale of effort would be reduced to about one-third of the then current level. It was felt within Harwell that to reduce the laboratory by such a large amount would completely destroy its viability, and therefore two objectives were set by the staff. As Dr Marshall, Harwell's director from 1968 to late 1975, explained:

We needed to reduce the size of the laboratory and therefore our call
on atomic energy funds but at a rate which was modest enough to retain
the morale and coherence of our research teams and we needed to
introduce an additional mission to give renewed vigour and
opportunities in the future.[26]

With an eye to such problems, the Science and Technology Act
(1965) made provision for the Authority to undertake research 'in
such matters not connected with atomic energy as may, after
consultation with the Authority, be required by the Minister of
Technology', the Authority by now being accountable to that
minister. Within months of the Act being passed the Authority
noted that a wide variety of non-nuclear projects was under
consideration, including one on desalination at Harwell.

At the same time Harwell was considering what its new mission
should be. According to Dr Marshall, there were no great
difficulties here. Referring to 'the constant complaint that British
scientists regularly produce good scientific ideas which led fairly
rapidly to an improvement in the balance of payments of other
countries but not of our own', he continued, 'we decided that an
additional Harwell mission to help industry with research and
innovation was one which was important, attractive to our staff and
likely to win Government backing'.[27]

Once the decision had been made, and the ministerial
permission obtained, to proceed with the industrial programme (as
it came to be called), progress was swift. Between 1966–67 and
1974–75, and within a declining staff total, the proportion of
Harwell's staff employed on work for industry and for government
outside the atomic energy programme grew from 5 to 50 per cent.
Over the same period, earnings from the industrial programme
grew to about half of Harwell's total income (the remainder coming
chiefly from the Atomic Energy Authority's reactor programme).
Of the income from the industrial programme, about 40 per cent
came from industrial customers by the mid-'70s, the rest coming
from governmental sources for work deemed to be of industrial
importance. The proportion of income on the industrial
programme earned for routine services, as opposed to research
and development, fell from about 60 per cent in 1966–67 to about 20
per cent in 1974–75.[28]

The commercial projects undertaken by Harwell have ranged
from those fully paid for by a firm to joint developments with both

sides committing money and effort under an agreement to share any benefits. There has been a noticeable tendency for firms to place their first contracts with Harwell on a joint development basis, becoming sufficiently confident of technical success by the second or third contract to opt to accept all the financial risk (and all the benefits) themselves.[29]

In developing its capacity to conduct commercial work, Harwell has had many difficulties to overcome in getting close enough to firms to be able to see problems through their eyes, in avoiding conflict with work being done in other laboratories, and in convincing customers that it could work within commercial constraints. Some help with the second and third of these difficulties came from its decision to restrict its industrial work to areas in which it was already technically excellent, thus avoiding the need simultaneously to learn new science and business practices. The task of getting close to firms can only have gained from Harwell's decision, in sharp contrast with the usual practice in government research establishments whereby knowledge is made available to all comers, to co-operate in very many cases with single companies and in secret. This 'Principle of Maximum Unfairness', as it was dubbed, has been justified on the grounds that companies will be more likely to place contracts with government laboratories under conditions which do not split the market in the early stages of development, thereby giving the firm a chance to establish a lead over its competitors.

In redeploying staff on the scale that Harwell has, much depends on their quality. Here Dr Marshall has observed that while such commercial experience as it had at its disposal has been valuable to Harwell, the most important factor governing success has been the cultivation of the entrepreneurial skills of which, in his view, a good scientist is capable, given the right environment and encouragement. At Harwell part of that environment has been created by the lead of the senior staff themselves. The creation of the right conditions for the success of the industrial programme has also depended upon the work of Harwell's Marketing and Sales Department. As at the only other government civil research establishment with a well developed marketing function, the National Engineering Laboratory, Harwell's Marketing Department does not seek to dominate the marketing process but adopts instead a philosophy of decentralisation. According to Dr Clarke, then

Marketing Director and now Director of Harwell's Energy Programme, care must be taken not to dampen the innovative spirit of the individual scientist by having marketing information thrust upon him from someone whom he does not know as a colleague. 'This would be highly undesirable. Successful innovation is founded, not in a committee process, but on the motivations and energies of entrepreneurs. The marketing input must inform the judgement of the entrepreneur, not replace it.'[30]

Accordingly, Harwell has instituted a training scheme under which scientists and engineers learn to operate professionally in the marketing function and then return to their research work. The basic idea, to quote Dr Clarke again, 'is to give the technical innovators, the same access to, and the same type of relationship with, the marketing function that they have *vis-à-vis* the technical function'.

Writing in 1974, when this educational programme had been going for only two years, Dr Clarke felt able to claim that it was already bearing fruit. The scientists and engineers were increasingly building marketing knowledge into their work, with the interesting consequence that some customers were including marketing components in their contracts for research at Harwell.

The customer–contractor principle and the industrial research establishments

Harwell is perhaps the most dramatic example of the diversification and increasing customer-orientation which characterised all the civil government research establishments, or at least characterised official and political thinking about their role, from the late 1960s and early 1970s, and which had roots stretching back into the 1950s.

Government support for research and development, both extra- and intra-mural, had grown throughout the 1950s. The number of government research establishments reached a peak of about sixty. Doubts, however, began to be expressed in the late 1950s and early 1960s about the role of the more industrially-oriented of these establishments, particularly the so-called Industrial Research Establishments of the Department of Scientific and Industrial Research.[31] These doubts arose in the context of more general questions about the organisation and value of government civil research, it having been widely observed that despite a relatively high level of expenditure on R&D the economy in general, and the state of manufacturing industry in particular, left much to be desired.[32]

The Trend report in 1963 proposed the transfer of the industrial research establishments to a new organisation operating with the autonomy of a research council,[33] but this proposal was overtaken by the Labour victory at the general election in 1964. For several years previously an influential group of scientists and Labour politicians had been developing plans to make more purposive use of science and technology in the service of economic development. It was in this context that Harold Wilson made his well known reference to harnessing 'Socialism to science, and science to Socialism', and to the new Britain that was to be 'forged in the white heat of the scientific revolution'.[34]

After the Labour victory, as has been seen, a Ministry of Technology was set up with responsibility for the industrial research establishments, the AEA, and the NRDC, and with sponsorship responsibilities for the machine tools, computers, electronics and telecommunications industries. The ministry was given the general responsibility of guiding and stimulating a major national effort to bring advanced technology and new processes into British industry,[35] and it soon became clear that this objective could not be achieved by the ministry in its original form. The take-over of the Ministry of Aviation in 1967, with its massive procurement programme in the advanced technology sectors (especially aerospace and electronics), greatly strengthened the capacity of the Ministry of Technology to raise the technological standards of manufacturing industry.

The question of how to relate the work of the industrial research establishments to the overall purpose of the ministry continued, however, to prove extremely difficult. As Sir Richard Clarke, the permanent secretary, observed: 'It was reasonable enough to believe that a relationship existed between R&D, innovation and industrial performance; but this did not tell the Ministry where it should push'.[36] By 1967, however, the idea had entered the ministry that the contract mechanism might offer at least a partial solution. But the way in which that mechanism was to be used differed markedly from practice in the United States and requires careful examination.

It is not fully clear how this idea gained currency within the ministry, but one important source was Professor Patrick Blackett,[37] who had been closely involved in the Labour Party's science policy discussions prior to the 1964 election, and became a senior adviser to the Minister of Technology. In February 1967 Blackett was to argue that Britain might have 'taken the wrong road' immediately after the war by putting too high a proportion of her research and development into government research establishments, and not involving industry more intimately.[38]

By late 1967 this argument had taken root, but with a surprising outcome: the Minister of Technology stated that he wished to break down the barriers between research and industrial production; he therefore announced, not that he would be curtailing his own research establishments and putting research programmes out into industry, but that his establishments would be encouraged to undertake confidential contract research for industrial firms.[39]

It is plausible to suggest that the ministry may have been encouraged in this line of thought by the developments which had been taking place at Harwell. It may also have owed something to thinking within the Institution of Professional Civil Servants, which by early 1968 was discussing such ideas as that government research establishments should take the initiative in selling their ideas to firms, that they should perform research for industry, that payment might be made for their research services on a royalty basis, and that discrimination between firms might be necessary in order to ensure the commercial development of government research ideas.[40]

The chain of cause and effect here is, however, hard to untangle. What is clear is that by 1970 the weight attached to the modified contract mechanism had increased. In January 1970 the ministry issued a discussion document outlining a proposal that a British Research and Development Corporation be set up, outside the civil service, to run the civil laboratories of the Atomic Energy Authority and of the ministry itself.[41] The proposed corporation was to be financed partly by a general grant from the government, partly by specific government contracts, and the rest (about a third of its income) from the sale of services, royalty income, joint ventures and other contract work from industry. As Sir Richard Clarke later put it:

> The size and health of the organisation was intended to depend upon its
> ability to provide economically and commercially for industry's needs;
> and it [the proposal] was an attempt to introduce a market test into
> predominantly government-financed research establishments ... if
> BRDC could not sell its services, its scale of operation would have to be
> cut down.[42]

The idea of a 'market test' for civilian industrially-related research
(at least for that which fell outside the aerospace and nuclear
sectors) became central to thinking about research policy within
the Ministry of Technology and its successors, the Department of
Trade and Industry (1970–74) and the Department of Industry. It
was further expounded in the 1970 document, in words which
presaged the Rothschild report of 1971:

> no Government department can decide centrally what research
> programmes are best designed to serve the needs of industry. As a
> general rule, only the 'customer' knows what he wants, and by his
> readiness to pay for it, makes the 'supplier' aware of his requirements.[43]

The proposal was, however, lost amidst the changes introduced
by the Conservative victors in the election of October 1970. The
Ministry of Technology was transformed into the Department of
Trade and Industry and, as part of a wide-ranging review of the
work of government departments, a review began of the work of
the department's research establishments. The review focused on
programmes, projects and strategic aims, rather than on
institutional reorganisation,[44] and was able to build on similar work
begun in 1969 within the Ministry of Technology. As a result of this
review, it was possible by early 1972 for Dr (later Sir) Ieuan
Maddock, the Chief Scientist, to claim that the department was
moving 'to a different concept of determining the programme and
monitoring it. We have, indeed, moved quite a long way toward the
customer–contractor relationship.'[45]

The language, by this stage, was that of the Rothschild report[46] of
November 1971, which had advocated wider application of the
'customer–contractor' principle to government-sponsored
applied research and development, together with the appointment
within each department of a chief scientist (to provide scientific
advice and to formulate research policy) and a controller of R&D
(to be responsible for the execution of the departmental research

programme). As regards government research establishments, the thrust of the proposals was to reduce somewhat the control over their own programmes which they had long enjoyed. Henceforth government laboratories were going to have to apply to their ministers for funds for programmes in areas that the minister (or his officials) had defined. It was only in this sense that the laboratories would 'tender for contracts'.

In accordance with the Rothschild proposals, but owing more to the way the department's own thinking had been developing than to Rothschild, a new structure for the formulation of research policy within DTI was established. This structure, the department claimed, was 'aimed at identifying and involving all the end users'. As laid out in March 1972 (and as subsequently implemented) the structure was to involve

> a series of broadly based [Research] Requirements Boards which ... would be given ... direct 'customer' responsibility for commissioning work within the R&D fields allotted to them, and which would be expected to play the leading role in determining the balance of R&D programmes within these fields.[47]

In other words, committees called requirements boards were to be established with responsibility for fields such as standards and metrology, chemical and mineral processes, and engineering materials. These boards were to be responsible for deciding what work in their respective areas should be financed by the department, and the terms on which it should be financed.

As for the 'end users', the department argued that it had very little direct use itself for R&D. Its function was to assist the development of industry, and it was industry that should be the end user of government-sponsored industrially-oriented research. The department could act only as a 'proxy customer' for research, thus putting it in a different position from, say, the Department of the Environment, or the Ministry of Agriculture, Fisheries and Food, which regarded themselves as the direct user of much of the research which they financed. Hence, whereas the post-Rothschild executive (but not advisory) machinery for formulating research and development policy within those latter two ministries comprises only government officials (see below), about half the members of each requirements board in the Department of Industry are industrialists, the remainder being academics and officials.[48]

The identification and involvement of end users has not, however, stopped with the composition of the requirements boards. Indeed, the industrialists on the board would be unlikely themselves to be the direct beneficiaries of governmentally sponsored research which they had approved; one could confidently expect questions in Parliament were this not so. The argument for their inclusion on the boards is, however, that they will have a better appreciation of industrial requirements than civil servants could be expected to have.

Among the measures taken to try to improve that appreciation have been the publicising of the work of the boards, visits by their members to companies, and requests to companies to comment on the boards' programmes. In addition, research into the diffusion of innovations has been supported, and in one case a proposal has been supported to allow several factories within one industrial sector to act as 'shop windows', demonstrating the productivity levels that could be achieved with up-to-date technology.

Perhaps the most important of these measures, however, has been the frequent imposition, as a condition of governmental finance, of the requirement that the project in question be partly supported by an industrial customer. In other words, a government laboratory will often be told by a requirements board that it will get support for a particular project only if, say, 30 per cent of the necessary funds can be obtained from industry. This condition is said not only to serve as a guarantee that a genuine industrial demand for the project exists, but also to foster a new kind of relationship between government laboratories and private firms (one which, at Harwell, pre-dated the requirements boards). Previously, the results of work done at government laboratories, if published at all, were published freely in the technical press. Realising that this practice would be unlikely to appeal to companies which were paying for research and development, other laboratories have begun to apply the Harwell 'Principle of Maximum Unfairness'. This change in practice epitomises the developing commercial-mindedness which has been the most striking feature of the bid by the industrial research establishments, since the late 1960s, to serve more directly the needs of industry.

Environment and Agriculture

If a greater measure of commercial-mindedness has been the chief characteristic of change in the industrial research establishments since the late 1960s, the research establishments of other government departments have been expected, since Rothschild, to display analogous changes in terms of greater responsiveness to the needs of their departmental customers. These are worth discussing briefly with reference to the Department of the Environment (DOE) and the Ministry of Agriculture, Fisheries and Food (MAFF), so as to show a little more of the variety of requirements which can be placed upon government research establishments, and the variety of administrative responses which is possible under the rubric of so apparently uniform a set of recommendations as those of the Rothschild report.[49]

DOE was formed in November 1970 by the amalgamation of, chiefly, the ministries of Housing and Local Government, Public Buildings and Works, and Transport. Although the new department simultaneously 'hived off' certain major executive functions, such as the Property Services Agency, it nevertheless qualified for description as a 'giant' department,[50] the principal characteristic of which, after sheer size, is the attempt to produce greater integration and coherence of policy between its components. At the time of the Rothschild report, DOE spent about £15 million per annum on R&D, compared with £259 million by the Ministry of Defence, £205 million by the Department of Trade and Industry, £109 million by the Department of Education and Science, and £13 million by MAFF. The main areas of DOE research interest in 1972–73, in expenditure terms, were land use planning, strategic transport planning, urban and interurban transport, road safety, the design and construction of roads and buildings, building regulations and water supply and treatment. Since then the main change has been an increase in the proportion of total resources devoted to planning and transport.[51] Until 1974 the greater part of these programmes was conducted within DOE's own establishments, but in line with the department's expressed view[52] that 'the growth of the extramural proportion of the research programme [is] a vital element in its development' the proportion of funds spent extramurally (in universities, research associations and industry – including British Rail) had grown from some 40 per cent in 1972 to nearly 60 per cent in 1974–75, and this despite increasing intramural expenditure.[53]

DOE's intramural R&D expenditure was largely concentrated in two establishments, the Transport and Road Research Laboratory (TRRL) and the Building Research Establishment (BRE). TRRL, or the Road Research Laboratory as it was then called, was part of the Department of Scientific and Industrial Research (DSIR) until 1965, when it was transferred to the Ministry of Transport, whence it naturally became part of DOE in 1970. BRE comprises three laboratories, chief of which is the Building Research Station (BRS). This also was a DSIR establishment, transferring via the Ministry of Technology and the Ministry of Public Buildings and Works to DOE. In January 1971 four research establishments which were part of DTI (and before that of the Ministry of Technology and of DSIR) were transferred to DOE. These were the Fire Research Station, the Forest Products Research Laboratory, the Hydraulics Research Station and the Water Pollution Research Laboratory, the first two of which were integrated with BRS in January 1972 to form the Building Research Establishment. At the same time, to indicate, as the DOE put it, that 'its activities are wider than its former name suggested',[54] the Road Research Laboratory was renamed the Transport and Road Research Laboratory. Two years later, in April 1974, the Water Pollution Research Laboratory (the only national laboratory engaged in the study of water pollution problems, and in its field one of the largest in the world) was transferred to a new Water Research Centre, outside the civil service. This left only TRRL, BRE and the Hydraulics Research Station (HRS) available for DOE's intramural work, and also drew to a close a period of considerable change in the departmental location of a number of laboratories.

With the establishment of the giant Department of the Environment, it was decided to set up a unified research organisation to provide co-ordinated research support for the activities of the whole department. The research arm of the department at this time embraced nearly 2,000 non-industrial staff, mainly scientists and engineers, and amounted to a significant element of total departmental expenditure. The new research organisation came into operation in July 1971, headed by a Director General of Research (DGR) of deputy secretary rank.[55]

Within the Directorate General a Directorate of Research Requirements (DRR) was set up to perform part of what Rothschild called the 'Chief Scientist' function. It was divided into three main sections (Building and Construction, Planning and Transportation, Environmental Pollution and Resources), conforming to the three main programme areas of interest to DOE. The functions of DRR were: to assist customers in formulating their research needs and translating these into programmes; to advise the Director General on the required scale and balance of the research programme; and to coordinate the activities of DOE's fifteen internal Research Requirements Committees.

These last were committees chaired by the relevant under-secretaries, with membership from DOE's policy and executive divisions, together with representatives of the appropriate contractor and of DRR. Their areas of responsibility included urban planning and land use strategy, road safety and vehicles, building design, and road design and construction. Each committee was said to provide

> a forum in which a continuing dialogue can take place between the customer and the contractor, and by means of which a research programme can be developed which both meets a defined policy need and represents a technically feasible field of investigation. The programmes which are thus agreed by the Committees reflect the full customer requirements in their areas.[56]

It will be observed that the 'customer' for R&D in DOE is, in effect, the appropriate policy directorate.

Hierarchically related to the Research Requirements Committees were three Programme Review Committees, covering the three main DOE programme areas of Planning and Transportation, Building and Construction, and Environmental Pollution and Resources. The committees, which comprised deputy secretaries together with appropriate laboratory directors, under the chairmanship of the DGR, met about twice yearly and were responsible with the DGR for reviewing the programmes in each area. They examined the programmes in the light of the reports of the Research Requirements Committees, the advice of the DRR on the scale and balance of the programme, and the available financial and manpower resources. With the DGR, they effectively decided which programmes should be undertaken and with which resources. It should not, incidentally, be overlooked that the provision for representation of the research establishments on the Research Requirements Committees and the Programme Review Committees allowed the establishments an active part at all levels in the formulation of their programmes.

In coming to its conclusions about these programmes, the department also received advice from three external advisory bodies: the Construction and Housing Research Advisory Council; the Planning and Transport Research Advisory Council; and a sub-committee of the Royal Commission on Environmental Pollution.

Finally, and with respect to Rothschild's 'Controller, R&D' function, it should be noted that during 1973 a Research Management Division was formed in the Directorate General of Research. The new division had responsibilities for the management of programmes conducted within DOE establishments or by other contractors.

Following the decision by James Callaghan in 1976 to transfer the transport functions of the Department of the Environment to the newly created Department of Transport, it was decided to retain one overall research organisation to serve both departments. Certain changes were, however, made.[57] The Director General for Research is now supported by two central directorates. The Directorate of Research Operations has general responsibility for the formulation and management of extramural work and for co-ordinating the preparation of estimates (the 'Controller' role), while the Directorate of Science and Research Policy is concerned with the development of overall research strategy (the 'Chief Scientist' role). The number of Research Requirements Committees has been reduced to seven, and the Programme Review Committees to two, one for each department. Furthermore, in language similar to that used since 1972 by the Department of Industry (and its precursor), it is now being argued within the Departments of Environment and Transport that their policy directorates, are, in the case of much of the research which they support, 'proxy' customers for the real users in local government and the construction and water industries. Accordingly the departments have been examining how to improve their machinery for obtaining external advice on their research programmes, but without, it seems, moving as far as the Department of Industry in this respect.

Turning now to research into agriculture, fisheries and food, it must first be explained that the departmental arrangements in Britain for administering agriculture, horticulture, fisheries and food are complex, and the complexity is reflected in the distribution of responsibility for R&D in those areas. The principal agencies, each with their own set of research establishments, which must be taken into account are:

1. The Ministry of Agriculture, Fisheries and Food.
2. The Department of Agriculture and Fisheries for Scotland (DAFS),
3. The Agricultural Research Council (ARC).

Their contributions to the national research effort in this field for 1971–72, together with (in round numbers) the position in 1975–76, are shown in table 5.2.

Table 5.2
R&D expenditure of ARC, and MAFF/DAFS, 1971–72 and 1975–76 (£ million)

	1971–72	1975–76
ARC	18·7	13
MAFF	6·2	29
DAFS	6·5	12
Total	31·4	54

Source. 1971–72 figures adapted from *A Framework for Government Research and Development*, Cmnd 4814, 1971, tables 2 and 3, pp. 8 and 9. 1975–76 figures from MAFF.

While this chapter has sought to exclude discussion of the research councils, the centrality of ARC to government expenditure in its field leads me to make an exception in its case. For purposes of simplification I shall not, however, have much to say about DAFS, which, as its name suggests, is responsible for Scottish interest in agriculture and fisheries (but not food, over which MAFF presides throughout the UK). The ARC is responsible for the provision of scientific advice to DAFS in relation to the eight Scottish grant-aided research institutes.

MAFF has long had a responsibility for R&D in the fields of

agriculture, fisheries and food, in respect of work done in its own establishments, and until 1965 it grant-aided certain independent agricultural research institutes through the ARC, which, however, like the other research councils, was responsible to the Privy Council and not to any executive ministry.[58] At that time there were two chief scientific advisers in the ministry, one responsible for food and the other for agriculture. With the Science and Technology Act, 1965, which transferred full responsibility for ARC to the Secretary of State for Education and Science, the Ministry of Agriculture ceased to have any responsibility towards ARC, although it continued to be represented on its council. The post of Chief Scientific Adviser (Agriculture) lapsed. The ministry continued, however, to be responsible for agricultural development and advice, these functions being performed through its advisory services, now amalgamated into the Agricultural Development and Advisory Service (ADAS). Within ADAS there is a nation-wide network of twenty-two experimental husbandry farms and horticulture stations as well as eight regional laboratories for diagnostic and experimental work.

In addition to providing these advisory services, the ministry continued after 1965, as before, to conduct in its own establishments programmes of research designed largely to support its statutory and advisory responsibilities. The principal establishments concerned were the Central Veterinary Laboratory, the Pest Infestation Control Laboratory (from 1971), the Plant Pathology Laboratory and the Fisheries Laboratories. Food research was supported by grant-aiding four industrial research associations and by the small MAFF food laboratories.

Following the Rothschild report and the subsequent acceptance by the government of both the customer–contractor principle and the proposal to transfer to MAFF a substantial part of the funds previously allocated to ARC, changes in MAFF's internal machinery became essential. In transferring this money (£7·2 million in 1973–74, rising to £14·8 million in 1975–76)[59] from ARC to MAFF, the government's expectation was that it would be returned to ARC in the form of payment for work performed by ARC as contractor to MAFF. From MAFF's point of view, the new situation required it to be responsible for disbursing through ARC's twenty-two research institutes and ten university research units in England and Wales more money than it spent in its own establishments.

During the few years immediately preceding the Rothschild proposals, MAFF, on its own admission, had

> felt the lack of an effective scientific voice able to make a contribution to the framing of policy at the top level. The loss of the close contact which existed pre-1965 with ... the ARC had also ... created an undesirable gap.[60]

The same MAFF document of early 1972 went on to observe that, with the government's endorsement of the customer–contractor principle (in its introduction to the Rothschild report), it was necessary to devise machinery whereby MAFF could effectively play its customer role in formulating ARC's research programmes. Soon afterwards, a chief scientist was appointed at deputy secretary level,

> responsible to the Permanent Secretary for framing the Ministry's R&D programme for agriculture and food, whether in-house or external; for commissioning the work and allocating funds to it; and for keeping it under review. He is also responsible for providing general scientific advice to the Minister over the broad range of Ministry policy.[61]

The chief scientist is assisted by two deputy chief scientists, one concerned with food science and technology, the other with agricultural and horticultural science and production. They in turn are supported by seven Scientific Liaison Staff, these being senior principal scientific officers seconded from MAFF or ARC or other government research establishments for a three-year term, who are responsible for surveying all the R&D in progress in one of six areas (food science, fisheries, animal husbandry, horticulture, arable crops and plant science, and agricultural engineering and buildings). Administrative support for this organisation is provided by an R&D Requirements Division which acts as the co-ordinating and accounting point for the R&D activity financed by the Ministry.

New consultative machinery was set up in the form of an advisory organisation called the Joint Consultative Organisation (JCO). This replaced many of the separate advisory bodies which had previously served ARC and the agricultural departments, and comprised members of the farming and food industries, scientists, economists and members of the departments' professional, technical and administrative services.[62] Its advice on priorities for all State-aided R&D in food and agriculture in England, Wales and Scotland goes equally to MAFF, DAFS and ARC, and it works principally through five advisory boards, each supported by specialist committees. The whole JCO involves some 300 people.

To assist the chief scientist in focusing the customer view and in making the final decision about what R&D in agriculture and food should be commissioned, MAFF has also created an R&D Requirements Board. The board is regarded as part of MAFF's internal decision -making machinery and, accordingly, it comprises the four deputy secretaries of MAFF (including the Director General of ADAS), the budget officer and the chief economist, together with the secretary of ARC and an under-secretary of DAFS, the latter two being present for co-ordination. It is chaired by the chief scientist.

In addition to receiving the recommendations of the JCO Advisory Boards, the R&D Requirements Board also receives the recommendations of the Fisheries R&D Board and three MAFF Laboratory Programme Committees. These latter committees, one per laboratory, have been created because the MAFF central laboratories (the Central Veterinary, Plant Pathology, and Pest Infestation Control laboratories), besides being engaged on R&D, also perform a substantial amount of routine work concerned with the ministry's statutory and executive functions which is not regarded as R&D. It was therefore though important for each such laboratory to have a committee charged with general advice on *all* the laboratory's work.

Until 1973, Fisheries R&D was administered separately from R&D on food and agriculture, the result, apparently, of a long-standing arrangement within MAFF whereby fisheries matters generally were treated somewhat separately from the other elements of the ministry's purview. Since then, however, the R&D work of the Fisheries laboratories has become the responsibility of the chief scientist, acting on the advice, through the R&D Requirements Board, of a Fisheries R&D Board, comprising industry members from the trawling and inshore fisheries sectors, the directors of the Fisheries laboratories, independent scientists and the MAFF Deputy Chief Scientist (Food). The secretary of NERC is also a member. The board fulfils a function parallel to that of the JCO Boards for Agriculture and Food.

The procedure by which the MAFF R&D programme is decided and commissioned is thus somewhat complex. Advisory groups of the JCO and Fisheries R&D Boards play a substantial role in discussion of needs and priorities, in which both laboratory scientists and administrative divisions, and, of course, the Chief Scientist's Group, all take part. The results of these deliberations are then passed to the chief scientist, who makes the final decisions in consultation with the R&D Requirements Board. Clearly the judgment of the chief scientist, his two deputies and the seven scientific liaison staff on what they might regard as gaps (or excesses) in the proposed programmes are significant at this stage.

Adopting now the perspective of the research organisations which are on the receiving end of this headquarters machinery, perhaps the most interesting laboratory-level developments post-Rothschild within MAFF have been not to do with MAFF's own laboratories but with its assumption of considerable responsibility for expenditure through the ARC. In considering the effect on ARC of the transition from a largely autonomous research council within the Department of Education and Science to a body dependent for half its income upon commissions from MAFF, it is important to note that certain changes were likely within ARC even had the Rothschild report not been written.

Within ARC itself note had been taken[63] by the early 1970s of the change-over from a period of rapid expansion to one of static (then – and later declining) budgets; of the change in the public attitude to science and technology; and of the realisation that the organisational system for dealing with agricultural research had not kept pace with the increase in personnel and resources during the growth phase. In 1971 the council set up a Planning Section to advise it on strategy and, in the words of the head of that section,

> What we found was a well-administered and conscientiously run system, but one in which there was little central planning, and in which budgeting was incremental. The system could certainly give precise information regarding the budget for a particular institute, but it would be in classical terms of staff costs, equipment, chemicals, animals, library.[64]

When it came to aggregating expenditure on related projects (e.g. all work on potatoes) being performed at different institutes, the system was unhelpful. Consequently, a matrix Project System began to be planned to allow aggregation of costs by institute, by field of work, and along other dimensions, and one of the chief effects of the Rothschild report was to accelerate this, and related managerial changes.

Some of the more interesting recent developments in DOE laboratories, particularly in the two larger ones, TRRL and BRE, were also under way before Rothschild and were a function of DOE's 'giant department' status. The fusion into one department of responsibilities which had previously been held by the ministries of Housing and Local Government, Public Building and Works, and Transport led to considerable expansion of the areas of interest of the former Building Research Station of MPBW (an expansion which was accentuated by the fusion of BRS with two smaller laboratories to form BRE), and of the former Road Research Laboratory of MOT. The wider range of departmental responsibilities led to an expansion in laboratory staff at an annual rate of 2–3 per cent, to a change in personnel in so far as, increasingly, 'soft' as well as 'hard' scientists began to be recruited to allow a more complete analysis to be made of research problems, and to changes in the types of problems examined by the laboratories.

On the last point, TRRL has established a Transport Group which examines[65] the types of transport systems which it might be desirable to have, and the possible ways of mitigating the adverse effects of road transport, and it does these things in ways which include much more than engineering analysis. Its studies have, for instance, included aspects of possible urban traffic restraint policies, including parking control, supplementary licensing, road pricing and physical planning, and have also included operational aspects of land–sea/land–air modal interchanges. In addition to such traditional projects as work on condensation in buildings, and on the structural use of timber, BRE's programme[66] now likewise contains elements with a much reduced proportion of engineering content, such as a study intended to assist local authorities to assess the needs for urban renewal, and another designed to assist planners in assessing factors that influence people's judgment of, and reaction to, the urban environment.

Some reflections

As regards DTI and, to a lesser extent, DOE, the Rothschild report simply catalysed changes that were already taking place. Its effects on MAFF have been more noticeable, it being, in particular, the case that MAFF is the only ministry among those discussed here to have strictly followed the Rothschild division of functions between, on the one hand, a chief scientist and staff (to advise the 'customers'), and on the other a controller, R&D (to oversee the execution of the research programmes), with no line relationship between them. The MAFF Chief Scientist is of the same rank as the Director General of ADAS and the Secretary of ARC, the latter two being the Rothschildian 'controllers', and therefore the arrangement exactly meets Rothschild's conditions.

Within DOI (then DTI) and DOE there were already in post at the time of Rothschild's report senior scientific officials with the titles Chief Scientist and Director General of Research respectively. For reasons presumably to do with the maintenance of existing and accepted patterns of official hierarchy, it has remained the case post-Rothschild that these officers retain full responsibility for all activity to do with advice and the formulation and execution of R&D programmes within their departments, but beneath them in the hierarchy some division of functions has occurred. The 'Chief Scientist' function can be said within DOI to be performed by the Requirements Boards together with the Research Requirements Division, and within DOE by the Research Requirements Committees, the Directorate of Science and Research Policy and the Programme Review Committees. Similarly, within DOI the 'Controller, R&D' function is performed by the Research Contractors Division; and within DOE by the Directorate of Research Operations.

With regard to contracting, since the second world war the operation of the contract mechanism with respect to science and technology has been aimed principally at the procurement of goods and research which were wanted by governments for their own use. The relationships which have ensued between government agencies and private contractors have played their part in the much-remarked fusion of the public and private sectors, particularly in the defence field, but also in high technology more generally, where long lead times, high capital expenditure, the perceived need to maintain a national capacity to produce 'strategic' goods and the uncertainties of the technology itself have been among the factors educing this interdependence.

Contracting for goods has probably been as common a practice of British as of American government, but the application of the contract mechanism to scientific R&D has, in the main, been more highly developed in the United States, although it should not be overlooked that one of the Department of Industry's research establishments, the Computer Aided Design Centre, is largely staffed by industrial employees working under contract to the government.

The Rothschild report introduced the language of customer–contractor relationships to British science policy circles and, together with developments that were already under way in some ministries, led to significant changes in the Whitehall machinery for formulating and executing research policy. The language of the Rothschild report should not, however, be allowed to obscure the fact that, although British government research establishments have, since 1972, had to learn to 'tender' for 'contracts' or 'commissions' from their ministries, the actual practice of the contract mechanism has been rather different from what an American observer might expect. First, as if to illustrate Hague's argument that the difference between a grant and a contract is largely a matter of institutional context, expectations and practices,[67] the post-Rothschild 'contracts' or 'commissions' placed by ministries with their own laboratories can perhaps best be understood as the formal output of a new, more stringent, but, with the exception of the Department of Industry, intramural programme evaluation procedure.

A second difference from American practice is that within the Department of Industry, the contract mechanisam has been expanded to accommodate the introduction of non-governmental actors into positions of importance in the commissioning of research at government research establishments. This has occurred through the appointment of a majority of industrialists and academics to the research requirements boards, and through the provision that work done at those establishments should often be partly financed (and may even be wholly financed) by industry. Worthy though these developments may be, particularly in the light of the evidence cited in chapter two that British industry spent less in real terms on R&D in 1975 than in 1967, they seem remote from Blackett's position of 1967. They have done nothing directly to reduce the proportion of the national research effort which is conducted in government laboratories, although there are signs that some of the requirements boards are themselves anxious to move in that direction: in 1976 one board complained that it had received no research proposals from industrial companies, while a second spent 40 per cent of its funds in industry, and a third spent almost all its funds in industrial research associations or similar bodies.[68]

The post-Rothschild application of the customer–contractor principle derives, in most of the departments of government, from a desire for enhanced public accountability in respect of research and development policy. That, however, is only partly true for the Department of Industry, where prior moves to introduce such a principle derived from both a belief in the need to gear the industrial research establishments more closely to industry's needs, and the problem of what to do with Harwell (and other laboratories) as they began to run out of work. This serves to illustrate that if, in an attempt to promote industrial technology through research and development, governments choose to set up their own research establishments, they do more than merely create laboratories. Specifically, they create for themselves two serious problems. The first is that of determining how best to employ those research establishments so as to assist industry. The second is what to do with those laboratories when the need for them appears to diminish. By that time they have probably become well established features on the governmental scene, and their rundown is not easily achieved. That flexibility in the use of scientific resources which was explicitly sought in the United States through the introduction of the contract mechanism is not achieved any more easily in the Britain of the customer–contractor principle than it was before.

Notes

[1] See, for instance, Colin Turpin, Government Contracting (Harmondsworth: Penguin, 1972), p. 260.

[2] Don K. Price, Government and Science (New York: New York University Press, 1954), chapter 3.

[3] Ibid., pp. 68–73.

[4] Harold Orlans, Contracting for Atoms (Washington, D.C.: Brookings Institution, 1967), pp. 5–8.

[5] Christopher Freeman, The Economics of Industrial Innovation (Harmondsworth: Penguin, 1974), pp. 146–52. Many other industries have

benefited significantly from the contract mechanism, and recent work by Reppy has shown that the benefit has been even greater than had been commonly realised, large sums of Department of Defense money ($1 billion in 1975) having been registered in the national statistics of R&D as deriving from companies, not government. See Judith Reppy, 'Defense Department payments for "company-financed" R&D', *Research Policy*, **6** (1977), pp. 396–410.

[6] Orlans, *op. cit.*, p. 9.

[7] Don K. Price, *The Scientific Estate* (Harvard: Belknap Press, 1965), especially, chapter 2.

[8] See S. Rosen (ed.), *Testing the Theory of the Military–Industrial Complex* (Lexington: Heath, 1973); Sam C. Sarkesian (ed.). *The Military–Industrial Complex: A Reassessment* (Beverly Hills: Sage, 1972); Carroll W. Pursell (ed.), *The Military Industrial Complex* (New York: Harper and Row, 1972); and Martin Edmonds, 'Accountability and the Military–Industrial Complex', in B. L. R. Smith (ed.), *The New Political Economy: The Public Use of the Private Sector* (London: Macmillan, 1975), pp. 149–80.

[9] Clarence H. Danhof, *Government Contracting and Technological Change* (Washington, D.C.: Brookings Institution, 1968), p. 5.

[10] *Ibid.*, p. 451.

[11] M. Gowing, *Independence and Deterrence: Britain and Atomic Energy 1945–1952*, vol. 2 (London: Macmillan, 1974), pp. 155–61.

[12] Russell Moseley, 'The Origins and Early Years of the National Physical Laboratory: A Chapter in the Pre-history of British Science Policy', *Minerva*, **16** (1978), pp. 222–50, at p. 222. See also Sir Gordon Sutherland, 'The National Physical Laboratory', in Sir John Cockcroft (ed.), *The Organisation of Research Establishments* (London: Cambridge University Press, 1965).

[13] E. Hutchinson, 'Scientists and Civil Servants: The Struggle over the National Physical Laboratory in 1918', *Minerva*, **7** (1969), pp. 373–98.

[14] On DSIR see Sir Harry Melville. *The Department of Scientific and Industrial Research* (London: George Allen and Unwin, New Whitehall Series, 1962); R. M. MacLeod and Kay Andrews, 'The Origins of DSIR: Reflections on Ideas and Men, 1915–1916', *Public Administration*, **48** (1970), pp. 23–48; Ian Varcoe, 'Scientists, government and organized research: the early history of the DSIR, 1914–16', *Minerva*, **8** (1970), pp. 192–217; and Ian Varcoe, *Organizing for Science in Britain: a case-study* (London: Oxford University Press, 1974).

[15] The details which follow are taken from Institution of Professional Civil Servants, *Exploiting Technology* (London: Institution of Professional Civil Servants, 1968), pp. 11–12; but see also the annual reports of the laboratories themselves.

[16] A convenient list and brief description of all governmental defence and civil research establishments can be found in the Civil Service Commission's recruitment booklet entitled *Scientists: Posts in*

Government Service. The Ministry of Defence issues a more detailed booklet entitled *Careers for Science Graduates*, and many research establishments (defence and civil) issue their own booklets giving quite full details of size, work, etc.

[17] See *Government Organisation for Defence Procurement and Civil Aerospace* (London: HMSO, Cmnd 4641, 1971), and *Review of the Framework for Government Research and Development (Cmnd 5046)* (London: HMSO, Cmnd 7499, 1979), appendix A.

[18] Moseley, *op. cit.*, pp. 242–3.

[19] J. D. Bernal, *The Social Function of Science* (London: Routledge, 1939), p. 148.

[20] J. Lyons, *The Role of Public Research and Development in Exploiting Technology* (London: Institution of Professional Civil Servants, 1969), p. 19.

[21] Department of Scientific and Industrial Research, *Report for the Year 1959* (London: HMSO, Cmnd 1049, 1960), p. 11; cited in J. B. Poole and K. Andrews (eds.), *The Government of Science in Britain* (London: Weidenfeld and Nicolson, 1972), p. 219.

[22] Office of the Minister for Science, *The Management and Control of Research and Development* (London: Office of the Minister for Science, 1961), para. 116; cited in Poole and Andrews, *op. cit.*, p. 223.

[23] Select Committee on Science and Technology, session 1971–72, *Research and Development: Minutes of Evidence and Appendices* (London: HMSO, HC 375, 1972), p. 458, questions 3 and 4, and p. 465, question 49.

[24] Gowing, *op. cit.*, chapter 18.

[25] F. A. Vick, 'The Atomic Energy Research Establishment, Harwell', in Cockcroft (ed.), *op. cit.*

[26] W. Marshall, 'Interaction between Government and industry: lessons from Harwell's experience', *Atom*, No. 210 (1974), p. 75.

[27] *Ibid.*

[28] *Ibid.*, p. 78.

[29] Select Committee on Science and Technology, *op. cit.*, p. 573, question 176.

[30] F. Clarke, 'Three golden rules of contracting', *New Scientist*, **62** (supplement; 1974), p. 12.

[31] These laboratories were: Building Research Station, Fire Research Station, Forest Products Research Laboratory, Hydraulics Research Station, Laboratory of the Government Chemist, National Engineering Laboratory, National Physical Laboratory, Road Research Laboratory, Torry Research Station, Warren Spring Laboratory and Water Pollution Research Laboratory.

[32] Norman J. Vig, *Science and Technology in British Politics* (Oxford: Pergamon Press, 1968), chapter 2 and *passim*.

[33] *Committee of Enquiry into the Organisation of Civil Science* (London: HMSO, 1963, Cmnd 2171), paras. 89–90.

[34] Vig, *op. cit.*, especially pp. 34 and 83; and Sir Richard Clarke, 'Mintech in Retrospect', *Omega*, 1 (1973), pp. 25–38 and 137–63, at p. 26.

[35] House of Commons, *Debates*, **702** (26 November 1963), col. 216 (written answer).

[36] Clarke, *op. cit.*, p. 139.

[37] A. G. Mencher, *Lessons for American Policy-Making from the British Labor Government's 1964–70 Experience in Applying Technology to Economic Objectives* (Washington, D.C.: National Science Foundation, 1975), appendix 2.

[38] Report of address by Lord Blackett to the Parliamentary and Scientific Committee, *Nature*, vol. 213 (No. 5078, 1967), p. 747.

[39] The Rt. Hon. Anthony Wedgwood Benn, *The Government's Policy for Technology*, lecture given at Imperial College of Science and Technology, 17 October 1967 (London: Ministry of Technology, 1967); see also Ieuan Maddock, Selected Papers, available in the Library, London Graduate School of Business Studies.

[40] Institution of Professional Civil Servants, *op. cit.*, paras. 94, 95, 101, 103.

[41] Ministry of Technology, *Industrial Research and Development in Government Laboratories: A New Organisation for the Seventies* (London: HMSO, 1970).

[42] Sir Richard Clarke, *New Trends in Government* (London: HMSO, Civil Service College Studies, 1971), pp. 95 and 95n.

[43] Ministry of Technology, *op. cit.*, p. 11.

[44] Select Committee on Science and Technology, Session 1970–71, *Research and Development Activities of the Department of Trade and Industry* (London: HMSO; 1971, HC 525), question 14.

[45] Select Committee on Science and Technology, Session 1971–72, *op. cit.*, p. 329 and pp. 459–61, questions 11–18 and 23–7.

[46] Lord Rothschild, 'The Organisation and Management of Government R&D', in *A Framework for Government Research and Development* (London: HMSO, Cmnd 4814, 1971).

[47] Select Committee on Science and Technology, Session 1971–72, *op. cit.*, p. 329.

[48] See Michael Gibbons and Philip Gummett, 'Recent Changes in the Administration of Government Research and Development in Britain', *Public Administration*, **54** (1976), pp. 247–66; and Philip Gummett and Michael Gibbons, 'Government Research for Industry: Recent British Developments', *Research Policy*, **7** (1978), pp. 268–90, on which the next three paragraphs are also based. For a few more up-to-date details of machinery within the Department of Industry for the formulation and execution of R&D policy, see *Review of the Framework for Government Research and Development (Cmnd 5046)* (London: HMSO, Cmnd 7499, 1979), appendix B.

[49] Details of post-Rothschild machinery in all other government departments can be found in the appendices to Cmnd 7499, *loc. cit.*

[50] See Sir Richard Clarke, *op. cit.* (1971), chapter 1.

[51] Department of the Environment, *Report on Research and Development 1974* (London: HMSO, 1974), table 1.

[52] Select Committee on Science and Technology, Session 1971–72, *op. cit.*, p. 344.

[53] Department of the Environment, *op. cit.*, table 4.

[54] Select Committee on Science and Technology, Session 1971–72, *op. cit.*, p. 344.

[55] *Ibid.*, p. 343.

[56] Department of the Environment, *op. cit.*, p. 56.

[57] The details of the changes given below are from Cmnd 7499, *loc. cit.*, appendix D.

[58] See MAFF Memorandum in Select Committee on Science and Technology, Session 1971–72, *op. cit.*, pp. 326–8.

[59] MAFF, *Report on Research and Development 1973*, HMSO, 1973, para. 16.

[60] Select Committee on Science and Technology, session 1971–72, *op. cit.*, p. 327.

[61] MAFF, *op. cit.*, (note 59), para. 22.

[62] *Ibid.*, para. 23. See also Cmnd 7499, *loc. cit.*, appendix G.

[63] T. L. V. Ulbricht, 'Contract Agricultural Research and its Effect on Management', paper presented at the Conference on Resource Allocation and Productivity in International Agricultural Research, Airlie, Virginia, USA, January 1975, mimeo., p. 2.

[64] *Ibid.*

[65] See A. Silverleaf, 'The Work of the Transport and Road Research Laboratory', paper presented at 100th conference of the Institution of Municipal Engineers, 14 June 1973, pp. 4–5.

[66] See Building Research Establishment, *Research Programme 1973–74* (BRE, 1973), and also J. B. Dick, 'BRS and its role', paper presented to the Building Research Station Golden Jubilee Congress, 9 June 1971.

[67] D. C. Hague, in D. C. Hague et. al. (eds.), *Public Policy and Private Interests: The Institutions of Compromise* (London: Macmillan, 1975), pp. 4–6.

[68] Research and Development Requirements Boards, *Reports 1975–76* (London: Department of Industry, 1976), pp. 10, 29, 37.

VI
THE RESEARCH COUNCIL SYSTEM

In the Supply Estimates for 1978–9, 13 per cent (or £229 million) of all government funds for research and development were shown as allocated to the Science Budget of the Department of Education and Science. This money was to be spent mainly by the five research councils (introduced in chapter two), with small sums also going to the Natural History Museum (£1·8 million) and the Royal Society (£1·5 million). Taking into account funds which the research councils would also receive for postgraduate training and for research commissions placed by government departments under the post-Rothschild arrangements, the total funds available to the councils in 1978–79 were expected to be some £308 million, distributed between councils and activity areas as shown in table 6.1. Thus, although the research councils no longer feature as prominently in the institutional arrangements for the governmental support of research and development as DSIR did in the 1920s, nevertheless they are still clearly very important agencies, especially as regards the support of research which lies towards the basic end of the spectrum of research and development activities.

This chapter examines the overall functioning of the research council system, and looks particularly at how the councils spend their money and how they get their money in the first place. It then reviews certain of the major policy problems with which the research council system has had to contend, specifically, the problem of priorities – particularly in relation to 'big science' and to the SRC's policy of selectivity and concentration – and the problem of scientific manpower. Finally, it considers the question of ministerial involvement with the research councils, especially with respect to the Rothschild debate and subsequent developments.

Table 6.1
Research council expenditure, 1978–79, by activity area and source of funding (£m at 1978 Survey prices)

		Science Budget	Expenditure financed from commissions[a]	Total
Agricultural	Projects of special priority	3·4	–	3·4
Research	Animals	6·6	8·8	15·4
Council	Arable crops and forages	5·5	6·9	12·4
	Horticulture	1·6	4·7	6·3
	Engineering and building	0·6	2·2	2·8
	Food science and technology	1·7	1·8	3·5
	Research grants	1·9	–	1·9
	Postgraduate awards	0·3	–	0·3
	Administration	1·0	1·3	2·3
	Total	22·6	25·7	48·3[b]
Medical	Neurosciences	6·8	2·8	9·6
Research	Cells	19·7	3·5	23·2
Council	Systems	8·0	5·3	13·3
	Tropical medicine	1·8	–	1·8
	Postgraduate awards	4·0	–	4·0
	Administration	3·2	–	3·2
	Total	43·5	11·6	55·1
Natural	The solid earth	8·6	10·8	19·4
Environment	The seas (physical)	3·2	2·4	5·6
Research	The seas (biological)	4·5	0·7	5·2
Council	Inland waters (physical)	1·1	1·6	2·7
	Inland waters (biological)	1·0	0·5	1·5
	Terrestrial environments	3·8	0·8	4·6
	The atmosphere	1·2	–	1·2
	Postgraduate awards	3·0	–	3·0
	Administration	2·0	–	2·0
	Total	28·4	16·8	45·2
Science	Engineering	17·4	–	17·4
Research	Science	25·0	–	25·0
Council	Physics 12·5			
	Biology 4·0			
	Chemistry 8·0			
	Maths 0·5			
	Astronomy, space and radio	28·8	–	28·8

	Nuclear physics	41·3	–	41·3
	Postgraduate awards	21·1	–	21·1
	Central support schemes	5·1	–	5·1
	Administration	4·9	–	4·9
	Total	143·6	–	143·6
Social	Initiative research	1·4	–	1·4
Science	Research grants	4·0	–	4·0
Research	Postgraduate awards	8·8	–	8·8
Council	Administration	1·4	–	1·4
	Total	15·6	–	15·6

a For Councils from which funds were transferred under Cmnd 5046.

b An additional £10.76 million is provided by DAFS for research it commissions at the eight Scottish Agricultural Research Institutes under the scientific oversight of the ARC.

Note. Royal Society and Natural History Museum allocations are not included in this table, nor are certain unallocated items of research councils' expenditure.

Source. Third Report of the Advisory Board for the Research Councils, 1976–1978 (London: HMSO, Cmnd 7467, 1979), p. 25.

What the research councils do

The functions of the research councils are 'to develop the sciences as such, to maintain a fundamental capacity for research, and to support higher education'.[1] Since 1973 MRC, ARC and NERC have also acted as contractors for research commissions placed by government departments. But, as will already be apparent from table 6.1, there are significant differences between the councils not only in terms of the fields of research which they support, but also in their degree of support for postgraduate training and, most obviously of all, in terms of size: the Science Research Council dwarfs the other four. These and other differences are shown more clearly in table 6.2, the table also providing a framework for a more detailed discussion of what the research councils do with their money. (The figures in table 6.2 should, however, be regarded merely as rough indicators; differences in the classification systems of the five councils make it impossible to ensure strict comparability of categories between years and between councils.)

Table 6.2
*Functional distribution of research council funds as percentage of the
total funds available to each council, 1977–78 and, in brackets, for
1972–73*

Function	Council				
	SRC	MRC	ARC	NERC	SSRC
Research grants	20 (23)	28 (30)	4 (4)	8 (7)	27 (40)
Postgraduate awards	14 (12)	6 (5)	<1 (<1)	10 (5)	58 (46)
Research units[a]	0 (0)	39 (41)	4 (6)	9 (7)	4 (4)
Own establishments, central facilities and grant-aided institutions	32 (41)	18 (18)	88 (88)	64 (75)	0 (0)
Subscriptions to international organisations	31 (21)	2 (<1)	0 (0)	0 (<1)	0 (1)
Administration and central support	3 (3)	5 (5)	4 (3)	9 (6)	10 (8)
Total (£ million)	136·8 (62·4)	54·4 (25·1)	45·7 (21·1)	27·9 (18·6)	13·9 (5·0)

Percentages are rounded; each column may not, therefore, total 100.
a In the case of NERC, research units include certain grant-aided
laboratories.
Source. Annual reports of the research councils for 1972–73 and
1977–78.

The first point to make about this table is that the pattern which it
displays has not changed much between 1972–73 and 1977–78,
except for the proportions of SSRC funds devoted to research
grants and postgraduate training, and of SRC funds devoted to its
own establishments and to international organisations. This latter
change is mainly due to the closure in 1977 and 1978 of the two
remaining British high-energy particle accelerators at the
Rutherford and Daresbury laboratories and the transfer of the
resources thus saved to the CERN project in Geneva, of which more
below. (It is, incidentally, worth noting in connection with the
relative sizes of the research councils that in 1972–73 the SRC spent

£8 million on the Rutherford Laboratory and £5 million on Daresbury; the total SSRC budget in that year was £5 million.)

Secondly, the table shows that the proportions of their budgets spent on peer-adjudicated research grants to individual scientists in the universities under the 'dual support' system, and in polytechnics, vary considerably between the five councils. (Under the 'dual support' system universities provide money from their UGC grants for the provision and running of university departments and for the salaries of academic and other staff, while the research councils make specific grants to individual scientists within those departments for selected projects.) SSRC and MRC spend the largest proportions of any council's funds on research grants, followed by SRC (which of course spends the largest absolute sum), with ARC and NERC spending relatively little in this way. Likewise, SSRC spends the largest proportion of any of the councils' budgets on postgraduate training, followed at a distance in proportional terms (but surpassed in absolute terms) by the SRC, with MRC and NERC contributing little of their budgets in this respect and ARC even less. Between them, therefore, SRC and SSRC were responsible for the most of the 7,279 awards from research councils to postgraduates reading for masters' or doctoral degrees in universities and polytechnics in 1977–78.[2]

MRC, however, allocates a large proportion of its funds to research units attached to, but not fully part of, universities, medical schools and hospitals. In a policy statement issued in 1961 the MRC gave the following as acceptable reasons for establishing a research unit.[3] First might be the need to support an 'outstanding man' for whom no other post as suitable was available. Second was the apparent emergence of a new subject (molecular biology and virology in their early days would be examples) which had not yet proved its suitability for inclusion in the university curriculum. Third was the need to set up a research team independently of a university or teaching hospital, and fourth was the existence of a public need requiring research which was either unsuitable for a university department or a hospital, or which required development on a scale which would distort their organisation (as with some toxicological research). A final reason could be the need to develop a subject that was being neglected by other organisations. Similar practice, but on a much smaller scale, has been followed by ARC, NERC and SSRC, the last-named having units for the study of race relations, industrial relations, and survey methods.

The bulk of the money spent by ARC and NERC, and large parts of the SRC and MRC budgets also, go on the support of research establishments which are wholly owned, run and staffed by the council in question, quite separately from any particular university base, although often located near a university. The reasons for this approach are the large scale and expense of the facilities in question. With the SRC establishments (namely the Daresbury, Appleton and Rutherford laboratories (the latter two to be merged, starting in late 1979), the Royal Observatories of Greenwich and Edinburgh, and the Atlas Computer Laboratory), the reason is that these facilities (which include telescopes, synchroton radiation facilities and laser facilities) are too expensive to provide at every, or even a few, universities, and so are provided centrally by the SRC, but for use by university scientists. In the case of MRC the establishments in question (the National Institute for Medical Research, and the Clinical Research Centre – basically a research hospital) are again major research centres on a scale which could not be provided at universities. With ARC the picture is of some forty research institutes either owned or grant-aided by ARC, or supervised by ARC on behalf of the Scottish Department of Agriculture and Fisheries, which may include many acres of farmland, or animal breeding centres, and where the time scale of the research may also be considerable. Among the better known of these institutes are the Rothamsted Experimental Station, the Institute for Research on Animal Diseases, the National Institute of Agricultural Engineering, and the Long Ashton Research Station. Finally, with NERC we are again dealing with long-term research programmes (such as the British Antarctic Survey and the Institutes of Geological Sciences and of Terrestrial Ecology), and with specialised and expensive equipment (such as the research vessels of the Institute of Oceanographic Sciences).

The last point to note from the table is that SRC alone among the research councils spends a considerable proportion of its budget on subscriptions to international organisations, principally to the CERN particle accelerator programme near Geneva (£22·8 million in 1978–79), but also to the European Space Agency (£8·6 million in 1978–79) and the neutron beam facility at the Institut Laue-Langevin (£6·7 million in 1978–79). MRC contributes a small sum to the European Molecular Biology Laboratory at Heidelberg (£1 million in 1978–79), and all the councils pay very much smaller subscriptions to the European Science Foundation.[4]

It being clear from this brief overview that, while there is a certain stability over time in the distribution of each council's budget, there is no uniform pattern of research council activity, it may at this stage be worth examining how the councils are organised internally. Each research council has as its chief policy-making body a 'council', composed of eminent scientists from an appropriate range of disciplines, together with appropriate departmental chief scientists, and other 'consumer' representatives (such as farmers in the case of ARC, or industrialists in the case of SRC). The members of each council are appointed by the Secretary of State for Education and Science, in consultation with the President of the Royal Society. Advising the council, or acting with authority delegated from it, are subsidiary bodies, usually called boards, which again have a mixture of scientific, governmental and other members, but with interests more closely focused upon the work to be dealt with by the particular board. Below the boards may be even more specific subject committees. Organisation charts for SRC and SSRC are given in figure 6.1.

Administering the work of the councils, boards and committees are the permanent staff of each council, whose chief executive officer in the cases of NERC, SRC and SSRC is the chairman of the council, and in the case of ARC and MRC is the secretary of the council. The chief executive is invariably a scientist of repute within one of the fields covered by the particular council and, at least in the cases where he is chairman of the council, serves only a limited term (usually of three years). The staff of the councils tend also to be specialists and are regarded as being on the 'fringe' of the Science Group of the civil service. While not regarded as fully fledged civil servants (in keeping with the relative autonomy of the councils) the staff of the research councils are (or have been) to a limited degree interchangeable with civil servants in the DES, are paid on the same scales and tend to belong to the same union (IPCS) as the Science Group (although MRC staff tend to belong to ASTMS).

To see how these elements interrelate, consider what happens when a university scientist submits a proposal to the SRC for, say, a grant for a project in chemistry. The proposal will be sent to the secretary of the Chemistry Committee of the Science Board, who

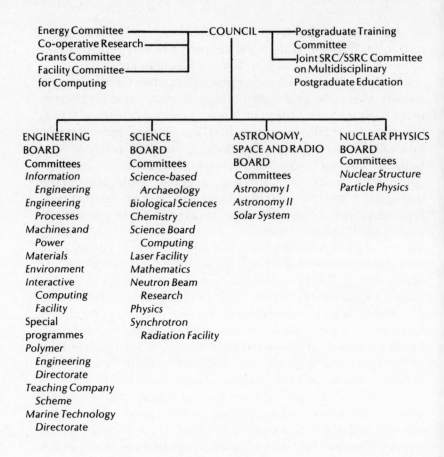

SCIENCE RESEARCH COUNCIL

Fig. 6.1 **Organisation charts for SRC and SSRC.** *Sources.* SRC, and *The Research Councils*, booklet issued by the research councils, 1975, p. 24. *Note:* the SSRC was undergoing reorganisation while this book was in press. The essential change is to be a merging of the Research Initiatives Board and the Research Grants Board.

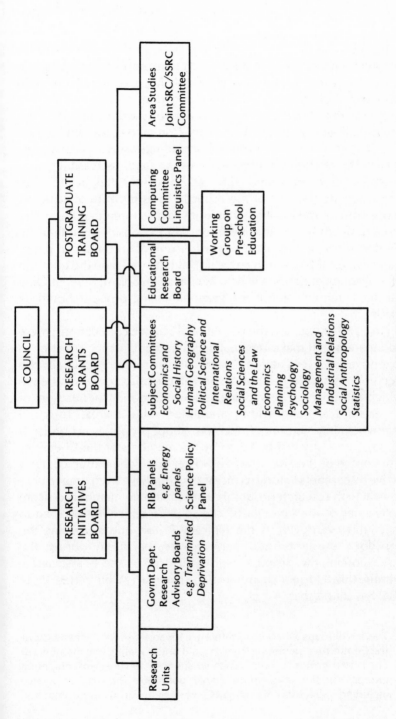

SOCIAL SCIENCE RESEARCH COUNCIL

COUNCIL

RESEARCH INITIATIVES BOARD

RESEARCH GRANTS BOARD

POSTGRADUATE TRAINING BOARD

Research Units

Govmt Dept. Research Advisory Boards e.g. Transmitted Deprivation

RIB Panels e.g. Energy panels Science Policy Panel

Subject Committees
Economics and Social History
Human Geography
Political Science and International Relations
Social Sciences and the Law
Economics
Planning
Psychology
Sociology
Management and Industrial Relations
Social Anthropology
Statistics

Educational Research Board

Working Group on Pre-school Education

Computing Committee Linguistics Panel

Area Studies Joint SRC/SSRC Committee

will check that it contains all the necessary information about the project itself, its costs, and the record of the proposer. The proposal will probably be sent to a few 'referees', that is, experts in the field, who will each be asked for an evaluation of it, and then the proposal, together with the referees' reports, will go to one of the periodic meetings of the Chemistry Committee. The committee will judge the research proposal according to such criteria as its quality, its relation to other work in the field, its feasibility, the referees' comments and the record of the applicant. Also important are the cost of the proposal in terms both of value for money and of the availability of funds to the committee. In certain circumstances it may also be important to consider whether the proposed research is likely to further one of a number of policy objectives of the research council. This last point, and the question of availability of funds, will be taken up again below, but first some further comments about the grant-allocating process should be made.

First, and unlike, say, the US National Science Foundation, where Foundation staff make the final decisions about proposals after an extensive peer evaluation, in the British research councils the decision rests with the council, or with the board or committee to which authority has been delegated by the council for decisions of a certain scale and within a defined subject area. Thus the overwhelming majority of decisions about proposals for research in, say, chemistry will be taken by the members of the Chemistry Committee of the SRC. Since, however, each committee contains active researchers among its members, they have from time to time to deal with research proposals from their own members or from colleagues of their members. The solution which has evolved to meet this eventuality is the typically British one of 'pacing the corridor': the interested party leaves the room during the discussion of the proposal with which he or she is associated. Despite this, a former chairman of the Chemistry Committee of the SRC has stated that

There is perhaps a marginal preference for applications by members of the Committee, stemming from that old British feeling that members of one's own group ... are somehow superior to those of competing groups, but this is no more than a *pourboire* for arduous service including indigestion of a dry [SRC] working lunch. Where Committee membership does confer an advantage is in understanding the grant awarding process.[5]

Despite certain criticisms which have been made of the composition of SRC committees,[6] this has never become a burning issue within the scientific community. Certainly there has never been any widespread suspicion that council or committee members have taken unfair or improper advantage of their position. It would, however, be interesting if a study were made some time of the question whether committee members, or their departments, appear to improve their chances of making successful research proposals during or immediately after service on a committee.

The availability of funds for the different fields of science

It was mentioned above that in deciding whether to support a research proposal that is judged scientifically worthwhile, a research council or subordinate body has to consider the availability of funds for the field in question. To understand what determines that availability, it is necessary to begin by examining the public expenditure process at the level of Whitehall as a whole, and I draw on the superb account of Heclo and Wildavsky for this purpose.[7]

The annual public expenditure cycle can be said to begin some time in November or December when the Treasury sends all departments a statement about the economic assumptions on which to operate in preparing their individual spending forecasts. Taking into account, therefore, such factors as the likely growth of consumer expenditure, industrial production and fixed investments, each department submits to the Treasury by the end of February preliminary expenditure projections for existing policies. From March until May, Treasury divisions discuss these figures with spending departments in order to reach some agreement on statistical assumptions, on what existing policies are, and on their probable future cost. In May an interdepartmental committee of officials called the Public Expenditure Survey Committee (PESC) writes a report projecting the cost of present policies and specifying remaining areas of disagreement. At the same time, departments engage in bilateral discussions with the

Treasury to cost any new policies which they may wish to introduce, while for its part the Treasury draws up its assessment of economic prospects in the medium term. Thus, by about June, cabinet committees and the Cabinet itself are able to begin discussions in terms of official estimates of what resources are likely to be available, what existing policies are likely to cost, and what the costs would be of new policies that departments would like to introduce. Between June and November the Cabinet takes its decisions, which are published in the annual White Paper on public expenditure during November–December.

Several features of this annual cycle require amplification. The first is that it *is* a cycle, and therefore that the projections made in a given year of the future cost of existing policies depend integrally upon the commitments which were made in previous rounds of the cycle. Associated with this is the point that existing commitments (including such elements as salaries of public employees, social security payments, contracts, treaty obligations, interest on the national debt, payments to local authorities) are the single biggest determinant of future policy in a given year, it having been estimated that the room which a government has for manoeuvre in the coming year is less than $2\frac{1}{2}$ per cent of public expenditure at the time.[8]

It was, in part, in an attempt to come to terms with this constraint that certain other features of the public expenditure process were developed in the 1960s, namely the attempts, first, directly to compare the programmes of all departments and to decide which were more or less worthy of support, and second, to ensure that the medium-term implications of spending programmes be made quite clear by requiring spending plans to show estimated costs over the next five years: there would be a high degree of confidence in the figures for the first two years, and lower confidence, but still some significance, in those for later years (at least in relatively stable economic circumstances). Within this overall framework, the really serious discussion about programmes occurs when they are first proposed: it is hard to get new elements into the existing structure of programmes, but once in, it is even harder to remove them – a phenomenon which Heclo and Wildavsky have called 'Incrementalism to the *n*th power'. Finally, with ministerial reputations within Whitehall depending as they do on each minister's capacity to defend the interests of his or her department, success in getting new programme elements through the Cabinet, and in avoiding programme cuts, is of high importance to ministers and leads to much conflict in the later stages of each year's public expenditure review.

Returning now to the specific case of the Science Budget, a smaller-scale version of the public expenditure cycle can be seen to occur within the DES, as illustrated in figure 6.2.[9] Each council, after internal discussions with boards, and boards with committees, produces a five-year 'forward look' which contains detailed spending plans for the next year, and less detailed ones for the succeeding four years. Each forward look takes as its starting point the plans which were contained in the previous year's forward look, and pays particular attention to any changes which are now being proposed, as well as to the commitments already incurred which must now be sustained. To try to ensure a measure of uniformity in the proposals from what, as has been seen, are five quite different research councils, the ABRC requires the forward looks to be organised under certain previously agreed programme headings and to be justified in terms of a standard set of criteria (discussed later). Proposed changes are discussed in terms of three assumptions for future finance which are set by the ABRC: an upper one to represent a generous increase in resources; a simple projection of the status quo; and a lower assumption representing a cut in resources. Thus, in effect, each council is asked to say what it would change if it had more money, less money, and the same money as at present. The individual forward looks are then defended by the head of each council (assisted by whatever staff he requires) before an *ad hoc* group of ABRC members. The group will include at least the chairman of the ABRC, as many independent members as can attend, and any of the *ex officio* members with an interest in the work of the council whose forward look is to be examined. The spirit of these meetings, it should be said, is not that of an inquisition; rather, it is one of assisting each council, through pointed but sympathetic questioning, to make quite clear what its priorities are. The later stages of the process involve the formulation by the independent members *only* (which include the chairman) of the ABRC's advice to the Secretary of State of the future funding of the research councils. This advice, subject to its agreement by the ABRC as a whole, goes to the Secretary of State for inclusion in the public expenditure review process. From that process, in due course, comes the Science Budget.

At the levels of both interdepartmental discussion and the research council system, therefore, the budgetary process is hierarchic and cyclic. It is hierarchic in the sense that money is allocated down a hierarchy from cabinet level to the lowest spending unit within a research council, these allocations themselves being influenced by pressure upwards through the hierarchy in the form of demands from lower levels for adequate funds to meet the volume of worthwhile claims upon them. Indeed, Nelson has coined the term 'proposal pressure' to explain the way in which the funds allocated by the SRC to its committees appears, he argues, to depend upon the volume of proposals received by each committee in preceding years.[10]

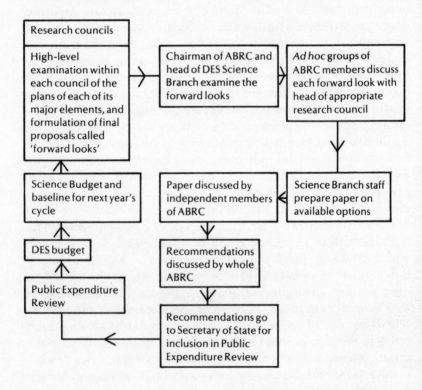

Fig. 6.2   **The budgetary process for the Science Budget.**

The process is cyclic in the sense that pressure is generated by commitments made in previous years. Within the research council system, commitments arise from the considerations that grants may endure for up to five years, that research units and research establishments cannot be managed on a year-to-year basis, and that international commitments are often bound by treaty. The last of these presents a particular problem in inflationary times: it was estimated in November 1976 that every cent by which the pound fell against the dollar added nearly £200,000 to the overseas payments of the SRC (mainly in the subscription to CERN), with consequent implications for those domestic programmes which could be cut in compensation.[11] Presumably it is with that experience in mind that the SRC has recently begun to experiment with informal exchanges of time for foreign scientists on British facilities in return for time for British scientists on foreign facilities which are not available in Britain. The effect upon the budgetary process of pressure from commitments also helps to explain why the head of a research council, faced as he may be from time to time by the ABRC with the offer of a lump sum of 'cash in hand' over and above what his council has planned for, may prefer instead to argue for a small, but enduring, change in the ABRC's 'guideline', or planned rate of growth, for his council. The achievement by the SRC's chairman, Professor (now Sir) Geoffrey Allen, in late 1978, of getting the SRC's guideline cut from minus 1·7 to minus 1·0 per cent per annum, and projected to show slight annual growth in real terms from 1982–83,[12] was of far greater value to the SRC than any immediate cash windfall in the slightly eased economic circumstances of the research councils at that time. For, with the expectation of an enduring improvement in the SRC's lot, it became possible for the council to plan commitments over a period of time in a way that a windfall would not allow.

The problem of priorities

The way in which public expenditure is allocated is intimately bound up with the problem of setting priorities, a problem which has characterised the smaller stage of policy for science no less than the larger one of government in general since at least the late 1950s. The problem of setting national priorities in scientific research became a major issue for the Advisory Council on Scientific Policy from about 1959, with increasing discussion in its reports of the cost of 'big science' projects. The problem had to an extent been avoided by the relatively generous financial support which science had come to enjoy during the 1950s, but some discussion of priorities became necessary even then. As the growth rate in the science budget fell from 13·3 per cent in 1966–67 to 4·7 per cent by 1971–72 and to minus 2·1 per cent by 1974–75[13] the problem of what these priorities should be, and how they should be set became more acute for the Council for Scientific Policy and its successor, the Advisory Board for the Research Councils.

The ACSP, of course, had no financial responsibilities. Before 1965 the research councils made individual representations to the Treasury for their funds. There was no overall Science Budget, and no body, apart from the Treasury, responsible for adjudicating between the various claims for support. The Treasury was unhappy with this arrangement, especially in view of the increasing size of the claims. It was in this context that the ACSP argued in 1961 that some re-examination of the governmental organisation for science was desirable.[14]

The Trend committee was appointed to make that examination and was, as has been noted, largely composed of current or former members of the ACSP. Among its findings was the conclusion that since the financing of the various scientific agencies fell outside the purview of the Advisory Council, that body had little means of influencing priorities. It proposed that the Minister for Science should become responsible for financing the research councils, the proposed Industrial Research and Development Authority, the National Research Development Corporation, and the Atomic Energy Authority — and that he be advised in this duty by a reconstituted Advisory Council.[15] With the exception of the proposal to transfer the National Research Development Corporation from the Board of Trade to the Ministry for Science, (a proposal which was strongly resisted by the then President of the Board of Trade, Edward Heath), these recommendations were accepted by the Conservative government.[16]

Commenting on these developments in March 1964, the chairman of the ACSP, Lord Todd (who had been a member of the Trend committee) emphasised the key role of the reconstituted Advisory Council in the determination of priorities. He observed that he did not believe 'that the making of the choices necessary to formulate national priorities in science is impossible'. While these choices might, at times, be difficult, the necessary criteria for making them existed 'even if some are not, perhaps, as explicit as we should wish'. The most important feature of the Trend proposals, to his mind, was that for the first time Britain would have 'the machinery capable of giving us the kind of integrated policy we need'. The research agencies would be so arranged as to establish priorities within their own fields, and the Advisory Council would advise the minister on broad issues of policy, 'establish rational priorities between agencies', and continuously review the manpower position.[17]

Lord Todd's belief in the prime importance, in the context of the 1960s, of establishing priorities in civil research and development was reflected in some remarks which the Advisory Council made in its final report. Noting that it had always been exercised by the question of 'the scale and balance of our national scientific effort', the council added that it could not pretend to have done more than 'achieve a measure of the magnitude of the problem, and of the great responsibilities which would rest on those who, unlike ourselves, might one day be charged with the task of cutting up the cake of our national scientific resources'. The level of government expenditure on civil science in 1964 was more than ten times its 1947 level, and could easily double over the next five years. Yet it was still not high enough, and this led the council to conclude that Britain could not engage freely in certain expensive areas of science if this would mean restraining the growth of other potentially fruitful fields. Accordingly, it would be up to the government to decide, on the best advice that could be tendered, what the national priorities should be. This, said the Advisory Council, was the most important problem which it passed on to its successors: 'The problem of priorities in science and technology lies at the heart of national science policy, and therefore of our national destiny.'[18]

One can illustrate how the ACSP itself dealt with two elements in the problem of priorities by considering its attitude towards high-energy physics and space research. Here it should first be noted that the council was by no means unsympathetic to what later came to be called 'big science'. Thus the council's first chairman, Tizard, played an important behind-the-scenes role in the early post-war support of high-energy physics through the Nuffield Foundation.[19] The ACSP's Committee on Overseas Scientific Relations also played a part, as a natural forum for the several scientific and governmental interests that were involved, in the British decision to apply to join CERN in 1951–52,[20] and the council was also actively and positively involved in discussions from 1955–56 about a proposal to establish a national research centre for nuclear physics, to be called the National Institute for Research in Nuclear Science (NIRNS). Such a centre, it was argued, would complement the facilities at CERN by providing centralised research facilities for teams from universities and other institutions on a scale which individually they could not mount.[21]

NIRNS was evidently seen by the council as providing the strong national effort which it believed was the essential counterpart to successful participation in an international venture. As the council argued in 1962, collaborative projects had to be assessed on their scientific merits, and while there might be political or economic advantages in collaboration, ultimately 'the political value of co-operation will be proportionate to the extent to which there are real scientific advantages for all the participants . . . it should not be supposed that international co-operation is a substitute for national excellence'.[22] Yet the value of NIRNS to the CERN programme was called into question by the fact that even before the 4 GeV and 7 GeV accelerators which NIRNS was to provide (at what were later called the Rutherford and Daresbury laboratories) were ready, the CERN physicists were planning to build a 300 GeV proton synchrotron (and to increase the energy range of the existing equipment by adding storage rings). Lord Hailsham, the Minister for Science, put these proposals before the ACSP in 1963, and the council began its deliberations by considering a report from a joint DSIR–NIRNS panel under the chairmanship of an ACSP member, Professor Brian Flowers. The panel supported the proposals, arguing that physics was on 'the threshhold of far-reaching developments which will come to fruition with a new theory of the nature of matter', and that non-participation in the project might have implications for the 'brain drain' which was a subject of concern at the time.[23]

While fully accepting the validity of the scientific case, the council also noted the high cost of the project and observed that it raised 'serious issues of priorities'. It continued, in phrases which occasionally echoed a speech made by Lord Todd in the House of Lords eight months earlier:

> Nuclear physics is only a part of science, although it accounts for a disproportionate amount of our total expenditure on scientific research. It is much more expensive than most other types of scientific work but, as the Council has repeatedly stressed, our expenditure on the rest of scientific research is too low. There is a widespread feeling of discontent among academic scientists at this state of affairs, and an impression that nuclear physics is already getting a very large slice of a rather small cake, despite the fact that the results to be obtained from it are likely to be of much less immediate practical importance than those from many other types of research.

On the basis of forecasts of research expenditure the council foresaw a 'serious deficiency in provision for universities', and, unless this was corrected, an increase in expenditure on nuclear physics on the scale suggested 'would be unjustifiable and would also arouse considerable resentment among scientists at large'.[24]

Despite the council's use of this proposal to highlight what, in its view, was inadequate support for science as a whole, it earned from the CERN physicists, quite unfairly, the sobriquet 'Association of Chemists for the Suppression of Physics'. The council had no desire to suppress physics – quite the reverse – but did have the responsibility to take a wider view of such issues as CERN and space research than perhaps was appreciated by some of the physicists involved.

The 300 GeV issue was still unresolved at the time of the 1964 general election, and after the election it was put back before the new machinery of science policy – the CSP, SRC and SRC Nuclear Physics Board.[25] The Nuclear Physics Board advocated British participation, largely along the lines of the earlier Flowers panel. The SRC endorsed this advice, making some reference also to the need to safeguard the other areas of science for which it was responsible. Unusually, two members of the SRC submitted a note of dissent in which they argued that it was not in the national interest to continue to spend such large sums as the proposal entailed on nuclear physics, and that many scientists would view 'with dismay' the prospect of so doing. 'Can we expect them' the two dissenters (both chemists) went on, 'calmly to accept a slowing down of their activities while we go ahead with a huge project which will directly benefit only two or three hundred academic physicists?' The country should urgently be seeking ways of investing comparable, and if possible larger, sums in projects 'which offer some prospect of material advantage to the community and which at the same time serve to train useful scientists and technologists'.

The CSP, acting largely on the advice of a working group chaired by Professor (later Sir) Michael Swann, endorsed the SRC's scientific case for the proposal, but wanted participation to be made conditional on a guaranteed rate of growth in the science budget of 9 per cent for a decade. Some attention was paid by the SRC and the CSP working group to the question of whether there would be an economic benefit if the accelerator were sited in Britain, a favourable verdict being given by the SRC and a negative one by the CSP.

The detailed economic analysis of this question, the 9 per cent growth rate for science as a whole, and the dissent within the SRC were, however, the only substantially new elements in the case advanced by the scientific community in 1965–67, compared with that made by the ACSP in 1963–64. The devaluation of the pound in November 1967, coupled, Clarke has suggested, with a lack of support for the proposal from the Cabinet's scientific adviser (and former ACSP deputy chairman), Sir Solly Zuckerman, were sufficient for the government (despite considerable behind-the-scenes activity by Sir Brian Flowers, by then chairman of SRC) to reject the proposal.[26] By 1970, however, a Conservative Secretary of State for Education and Science with an interest in science (Margaret Thatcher) on whom CERN made an 'excellent impression' during a visit there,[27] coupled with a slightly stronger economy, a new design from CERN which not only reduced the cost of the project but also resolved the locational politics by allowing construction to take place at the existing CERN site near Geneva, and the fact that the SRC was able to agree to find the extra UK money within a constant annual expenditure on nuclear physics, were sufficient conditions for British participation to be approved.

The other 'big science' subject which attracted public and parliamentary interest in the late '50s and early '60s was space research, much of the interest, of course, being due to the race between the USA and the USSR following the launching of the first sputnik in 1957. Although it approved in 1959 a British programme of experiments conducted by means of satellites, the ACSP played a part in having the satellites launched not, as the programme's proponents wanted, by converted British military rockets but, on grounds of cost, by US rockets. In commenting on this in its report of November 1959 the council noted that there was ample scope for British earth satellite experiments, but not for lunar, solar or planetary probes, nor for manned flights, the cost of which outweighed any likely scientific or technological returns. Despite its small size relative to the USA and USSR programmes, the British programme could be valuable, for 'scientific prestige is obtained through research which is important scientifically and is well planned and executed, and does not depend on the size or spectacular nature of the project'.

As with its position on high-energy physics, the council acknowledged the undoubted scientific interest and importance of space research, but it also emphasised the cost involved. The council had repeatedly emphasised the importance of maintaining an adequate level of expenditure in those fields of R&D which were vitally important

> for the welfare of our people and for the strengthening of our economic position, as well as for improvement of living standards in the less well-developed countries ... To leave these needs unsatisfied in order to shoulder the crippling cost of a large programme of space exploration on a purely national basis would be, in the Council's view, the grossest folly.[28]

Such plain speaking was not overlooked by the press. But while *Nature* thought the council displayed 'a realistic sense of priorities',[29] a newspaper columnist described the Advisory Council as 'the fifteen men who really carry the can ... who will bear the historic responsibility for this national misfortune'.[30] Whatever the merits of the case, the size and shape of the programme which was set on the advice of the ACSP fixed the matter for its successors[31] and made space research a subject to which little attention had to be paid by policy-makers, at least until the 1970s, when, as will be seen later, severe cuts in the Science Budget led to further reductions in support for big science.

Before proceeding with that development, however, it is worth going back in time to the point where the ACSP handed over to its successor, the Council for Scientific Policy, the problem of setting priorities in science. Defining the tasks of science policy as being not to direct the advance of science but

> to maintain the environment necessary for scientific discovery; to
> ensure the provision of a sufficient share of the total national resources;
> to ensure that there is balance between fields and that others are not
> avoidably neglected; to provide opportunities for inter-fertilisation
> between fields, and between the scientific programmes of nations,

the CSP saw it as its function to look into the future

> to take account of the relationships between science and other national
> activities all of which may have a competing claim for resources, and to
> provide the basis for national acceptance of the scale of resources
> which are needed for the healthy evolution of science.[32]

One of the results of looking into the future was the council's
conclusion that the rate of growth of the Science Budget in 1966
(about 13 per cent per annum) could not long continue. The
question was not whether but 'when, and at what rate, and on what
criteria, the levelling-off of the growth rate should take place'. The
council, like the ACSP, accepted the need for forward planning,
and argued as the ABRC was to argue later that planning was more
and not less necessary in times of economic uncertainty. But, added
the CSP in a characteristic turn of phrase, 'in order to plan wisely,
the mechanics of scientific growth must be analysed and
understood'.[33]

While inviting the research councils for the immediate future to
assess the effects of a declining growth rate, and to justify their
policies in terms of a set of intrinsic and extrinsic criteria, the
council also set in hand a number of studies designed to reveal the
mechanics of scientific growth and hence the criteria which should
govern the allocation of resources to science.[34]

Not until March 1970, however, did the council set up a working
group under Professor (later Sir) Frederick Stewart, charged
directly with the examination of the criteria which might be used
to determine priorities in science policy. The working group's
report,[35] published in October 1972, began with a brisk demolition
of the views associated with Michael Polanyi and others who argue
either that science is unplannable and need not be held directly
responsive to social needs, or that, while planning is needed, the
scientist should restrict his role in that exercise to judgments of
scientific merit.

The working group adopted a minimalist strategy. It made but modest claims for its results, recognising that there was nothing new in its criteria, and that they were already tacitly taken into account in most of the decisions already being taken about research support. In addition, the element of subjective judgment could not be removed from decision-making: 'The weight to be attached to the various criteria is necessarily a matter for judgment and is bound to vary from time to time'. Nevertheless, the group thought that 'there may be value in making them explicit so that new proposals and existing programmes may be more consciously assessed in their light, and that they should be more widely understood'.

The criteria fell into three groups: intrinsic, external and resource implications (see table 6.3). Oddly, although the working group can hardly have been unaware of the well known 'criteria for scientific choice' spelled out in 1963 by Dr Alvin Weinberg, Director of the US Oak Ridge National Laboratory (also reproduced in table 6.3) it did not refer to them. One difference between the two sets of criteria is that the CSP included in the intrinsic criteria (in addition to the excellence of the field and of the research workers, its cultural value, and its relationships with similar research in the field) a reference to 'pervasiveness'. This meant 'the promise of impetus to advances in other and related fields of science' and is equivalent to Weinberg's 'scientific merit', which was one of his extrinsic criteria.

The working group's external criteria included economic, social and educational benefit, national prestige and scientific reputation, and the contribution of the project to any other national goals. Quite new was its addition of the third category, resource implications, which referred to the demands which a project might make on men and on capital, and to its opportunity costs for other areas of science.

Further changes in the criteria for choice occurred in 1975, when the ABRC, under Sir Frederick Stewart (who had chaired the CSP working group on criteria) amended the categories of criteria as shown in table 6.3. It will be noted first that the intrinsic and external criteria have been merged (with the loss of one or two of them); second, that the training of scientific manpower is now regarded as a science policy criterion worthy of explicit reference; and third, that the resource implications have been subsumed within a much broader set of management criteria.

Table 6.3

Criteria for choice in science policy (some paraphrasing)

Weinberg (1963)	Council for Scientific Policy (1972)	Advisory Board for the Research Councils (1975)

(a) *Internal criteria*
1. Is the *field ready* for exploitation?
2. Are the *scientists* in the field really *competent*?
 	
(b) *External criteria*
1. What relevance has it the project to *technological development*?
2. What relevance has it to the development of the rest of science (i.e. what is its *scientific merit*)?
3. What *social merit* has it?
	(a) *Intrinsic criteria*
	1. Excellence:
	  (i) of the study field
	  (ii) of the research workers
	2. Pervasiveness, or promise of impetus to advances in other and related fields of science
	3. Cultural value
	4. Relationships with similar research in the field.
	
	(b) *External criteria*
	1. Economic benefit
	  (i) short-term
	  (ii) long-term
	2. Social benefit
	3. Educational benefit
	4. National prestige and scientific reputation
	5. Other national goals
	
	(c) *Resource implications*
	1. Demand on capital
	2. Demand on manpower
	  } includes opportunity cost.
		(a) *Scientific policy criteria*
		1. Excellence of study field
		2. Excellence of research workers
		3. Pervasiveness of the activity (with respect to other fields)
		4. Social and/or economic importance
		5. Significance for the training of scientific manpower
		6. Educational importance
		7. Significance in maintaining national scientific prestige
		
		(b) *Management criteria*
		1. Will the proposal improve the efficiency of the organisation and/or plant?
		2. Will a major item of equipment become obsolescent without this support?
		3. Is the *timing* of the activity critical?
		4. How *dependent* is it on the *Science Budget*?
		5. How available is the necessary manpower?
		6. What scope exists for redeployment of resources allocated to this activity?

Source. A. Weinberg, 'Criteria for Scientific Choice', *Minerva*, I (1963), pp. 159–71.	*Source. Third Report of the Council for Scientific Policy* (Cmnd 5117, 1972), appendix C.	*Source. Second Report of the Advisory Board for the Research Councils 1974–75* (Cmnd 6430, 1976), appendix IV.

How these criteria are applied in detail is a fascinating question which cannot, for lack of information, be discussed here. The output from the policy discussions is, however, clear enough. If, for the CSP in 1972, 'the most significant factor' affecting its work for the past five years had been the decline in the rate of growth of the science budget,[36] it was on the Advisory Board that the full force of the decline, coupled with the inflation of 1974 and after, fell. As Sir Frederick Stewart noted, the two years from January 1974 to December 1975 had been difficult ones for science policy-makers:[37]

> The science budget fell in value, in real terms, in both years, for the first time since it was established in 1965, as did the funds which Government departments made available to research councils for commissioned research. The universities also suffered significant reduction in financial support. The prospect for the coming year is expected to be one of increasing difficulty as the new system of cash limits is applied to government spending.

The Board had responded to this situation by recommending redeployment of resources away from the expensive fields of high-energy physics, astronomy and space up to 1981 so as to protect the prospects for the other sciences. This had meant

> foregoing support of work of high scientific promise, in fields where United Kingdom scientists have established excellent reputations, and where the prospects for scientific advance are at present particularly promising.

If the sentiment is familiar, so too has been the response of the proponents of big science. Thus *Nature* saw the Advisory Board's prime reason for the redeployment as being the relatively small number of research workers engaged on big science and thought this a 'depressingly bad' reason to advance, and one which suggested that 'for all the agonising, it is size that has been the criterion, not quality, nor even ... lack of obvious pay-offs to the taxpaying public'.[38]

The result of the deliberations of the ABRC was that while the 1975 guidelines for medium-term growth rates showed a reduction of about 2 per cent per annum for the total budget of the Science Research Council, the reduction for big science was twice as large. Accordingly, SRC domestic expenditure on high-energy physics and space science fell by some 33 per cent in real terms between

1973–74 and 1977–78.[39] In consequence, Britain's two high-energy particle accelerators (at the Daresbury and Rutherford laboratories) have been closed, the Skylark rocket programme is being abandoned, and the Ariel-6 astrophysical research satellite, launched in June 1979, represented the end, at least on present plans, of Britain's domestic (as opposed to European) space programme. Plans for a major new radio-telescope at Jodrell Bank, and for an electron-positron intersecting complex (EPIC) have also been abandoned since 1973–74.

Some of the resources freed as a result of redeployment from big science afforded the other research councils some relief from the worst effects of the economic constraints of the period 1973 to 1979, although the ABRC was to argue that the growth which they enjoyed went mainly on the replacement or improvement of existing equipment, and rising salary costs, leaving little, if anything, for new work. Nevertheless, all the councils have managed to expand a little in certain priority areas by reducing activity in others. This has even been true of the SRC, where the percentage of the total Science Budget spent through the Engineering Board rose from 5·6 in 1973–74 to 6·5 in 1978–79, and where special programmes have been started to try to stimulate activity in polymer engineering, marine technology and production engineering.

By late 1978, however, the research councils and the ABRC were firmly of the view that, to use a phrase which they would not have chosen, all the fat had been pared from the research councils' programmes, and especially from big science. As the ABRC noted in its third report, which was submitted to the Secretary of State, Shirley Williams, in November 1978,

> residual high-energy physics, astronomy and space budgets cannot yield up more funds without crucial items of research in these areas being abandoned ... further significant reductions in astronomy and space would lead to the closure of work on x-ray astronomy – an essential adjunct to radio and optical astronomy and a field in which the UK leads the world. There would be no new space programme. In high-energy physics SRC would have to close either the bubble chamber work or the counter physics work based on CERN: in either event it would then be impossible to sustain a level of involvement in experiments to match the UK financial contribution to CERN.

Furthermore, the problems faced by the research councils since

1973 have been compounded, as regards the support of university scientists, by pressure upon the dual support system arising from a cut in real terms of the UGC recurrent grant to universities, and the inadequate and unpredictable financing of the UGC's equipment grant. In 1978 the ABRC quoted a UGC statement that '. . . the grant for equipment . . . has not only fallen seriously short of what we judge is necessary to sustain modern teaching and research, but has varied so much from year to year that the planning of an economical cycle of replacement has become virtually impossible'. Indeed, as early as 1975 the Select Committee on Science and Technology had pointed to the collapse of the dual support system and had argued that the strains arising from the general shortage of cash in the system were exacerbated by the priority given by the UGC and the DES to the universities' teaching role.[40] In the light of all these problems the research councils will have been delighted in December 1978 to have received a promise of £47 million additional money over the next four years, obtained by the personal intervention of Mrs Williams. The budget of the new Conservative government in June 1979 seriously cut into the first tranche of that money, however, by immediately taking £5 million from the research councils in the current financial year and raising doubts about what would follow in the next full review of public expenditure.[41]

Selectivity and concentration at the SRC

The discussion above may well give the impression that the research councils are simply the victims of history and of circumstances beyond their control, and that the volume of resources available for particular fields of research ultimately depends upon the strength of the economy, the negotiating skill of the Secretary of State for Education and Science, and past commitments. To a large extent this is the impression which it is intended to create, but it must also be emphasised that, as has already been indicated, the councils have nevertheless been able in recent years to make some changes in the way in which they distribute their resources. Furthermore, they have actively sought to encourage research in particular areas which they have deemed to be of special importance. Thus the SSRC, through its Research

Initiatives Board, has explicitly encouraged proposals for grants for research to do with North Sea oil, health policy, local government, pollution, and energy studies.[42] Likewise in 1977 the Engineering Board of the SRC, apparently not without some dissent within its ranks, decreed the fields of micro-electronics, energy utilisation and medical engineering to be of especial priority.[43] In so doing both councils were following an approach to research funding which had begun to be developed in the SRC in the late 1960s.

At that time, and in the face of impending economic difficulties, the Science and Engineering Boards undertook reviews within each of their committees to identify areas where more support seemed desirable on scientific, economic or social grounds. One outcome of this analysis was the establishment of some new committees to supervise the allocation of grants in certain areas (computing science, control engineering and polymer science, for instance). Another was the publication of a document in which a policy of 'selectivity and concentration' was spelled out.[44] According to this document, certain research areas would be selected for more favourable than average support during a given period, and certain university departments would be given more favourable than average support to enable them to concentrate effort in selected areas by building up 'centres of excellence'. This concentration of resources was to take place by shifting funds from less favoured to more favoured areas, rather than by simply adding any new money to the favoured areas. Polymer science, organometallic chemistry and heterogeneous catalysis were three of the fields within the discipline of chemistry which were selected for preferential treatment.

Two observations can be made about the effects of this policy. First, the SRC has itself identified certain shortcomings, and here an observation in the council's report for 1974–75 is illuminating:

> Once an area has been selected by the Council for special support, the response has been good where there is already an active scientific community. However, it has been difficult to stimulate good proposals for work in fields which, although accepted as being of national importance, have not already proved attractive to academic research workers.[45]

Thus, for example, the field of polymer science had over the period 1969–73 yielded a satisfactory level of activity, whereas the scale of work in polymer engineering had fallen short of national needs. It is worth adding here that the SRC has made a particularly interesting response to this shortcoming by establishing a Polymer Engineering Directorate to initiate and oversee a closely co-ordinated programme of research and postgraduate training in selected universities and polytechnics.[46] The programme has the active support of industry in the form of a contribution of about one third of the administrative costs from the British Plastics Federation and the British Rubber Manufacturers' Federation, and in the form also of collaboration between those federations and the SRC in appointing the director and in managing the programme. The director has the executive authority of the head of an SRC research establishment, and is empowered to give more comprehensive support than is normal for research grants, thereby freeing a project from at least some of the constraints of the dual support system. Already a pattern of work has been established in which 80 per cent of the projects have direct industrial collaboration, and most of the others are related to programmes funded by industrial consortia and the Department of Industry at research associations or government laboratories. Although the SRC does not anticipate that such arrangements will necessarily be applicable to all fields, it has subsequently followed this basic pattern with a Marine Technology Directorate, to which eight companies will contribute about £100 million over five years.[47]

The second observation to be made about the SRC's policy of selectivity and concentration is that close analysis of the pattern of grant distribution adopted by the council shows little sign of change since the policy was adopted, at least up to 1974. In a highly original demonstration of the power of quantitative methods as a tool of policy analysis, Farina and Gibbons have examined the peer-adjudicated research grants awarded by the SRC between 1964 and 1974 (but not, it should be noted, the later period of severe financial stringency: their choice of dates was a function of the data available at the time the study started).[48] Using a statistical measure of the concentration of resources by grant-awarding committee, they found that over the decade in question only seven of the sixteen committees exhibited significant variations over time in the level of concentration of their resources, and that for all these cases the general trend was for concentrations to decrease. Yet according to the policy of selectivity and concentration (using that term now in the sense intended by the SRC) one would have expected also to find some committees for which the level of concentration increased. A second difference between policy and practice was found to be that the concentration of funds spent by each committee at the level of individual scientists remained broadly constant over the decade. For those committees where the level of concentration in terms of value of grants per scientist did vary, it was in the direction of decreased concentration. Similar stability over the decade was found if one analysed by committee for the concentration of resources in terms of the value of grants received by university and polytechnic departments and by entire universities and polytechnics.

As the authors of this study themselves concluded:

> Statements of policy indicated that the concentration of resources was to increase over time. Concentration was to increase over the full ten years under study, but increases were to be most pronounced in the period after the publication of the pamphlet *Selectivity and Concentration* in 1969/70. Despite this claim, the analysis of awarded grants indicates that the concentration of resources did not increase over time. This was found to be the case when the analysis was performed on grants, scientists, departments and universities/polytechnics . . . Of particular interest is the finding that concentration did not increase over time at the level of departments. Intentions indicated that in the post 1969–70 period selected departments were to act as focal points for the funding of research . . . Apparently, this has not happened.

Yet interestingly, and most importantly, Farina and Gibbons also found that not only did the level of concentration of resources for research grants not change significantly over the decade at whatever level of aggregation one chose to examine, but also that throughout the decade there was already a very high degree of concentration of resources upon a limited number of scientists, departments and universities. For most committees, 10 per cent of the funded scientists, departments or universities received over 50 per cent of available resources. Indeed, in another study the same authors showed that in 1973–74 thirty-six researchers received 23 per cent of SRC expenditure on research grants.[49]

What these findings mean, however, is hard to say. It could be that it takes longer to bring about a change in the distribution of funds than SRC had hoped. Or perhaps the cut-off point of 1974 has failed to show changes deriving from the 1970 commitment to a policy of selectivity and concentration. Or maybe it has taken the harsh regime of 1974 onwards to force change on to the SRC: certainly since 1975–76 there has been a significant increase in the share of the Science Budget spent through the Engineering Board of the SRC, though it should also be noted that the level in 1975–76 was very low, and that by 1977–78 it had only regained ground lost since 1974–75. Or perhaps the existing high degree of concentration means that all the best scientists and all the centres of excellence were already being preferentially supported before the policy of selectivity and concentration was introduced, though in that case it is hard to imagine that they could not have made good use of an even higher degree of concentration, especially during the years since the cut-off point of Farina's and Gibbons's study. The need for the application of this mode of analysis to more recent years, and to the other research councils, is very clear.

Scientific manpower

As well as the support of research, another of the duties of the research councils is the support of postgraduate training, which is part of the wider problem of the overall supply of scientists, engineers and other technical professionals. In both its wider and its more specifically postgraduate aspects, the question of the availability and deployment of the national stock of scientists and engineers became from the outset a major theme of the work of the ACSP. The council, through its Committee on Scientific Manpower, pioneered the collection of statistics on the supply and deployment of, and the demand for, scientists and engineers in Britain. It introduced for this purpose a system of triennial surveys of employers (public and private),[50] the responsibility for which after 1964 first passed jointly to the DES and the Ministry of Technology, and later solely to the Department of Trade and Industry. The surveys have since been abandoned, on the grounds, according to the then Secretary of State for Industry, that 'it would probably be a good thing to withdraw some of the form-filling that companies had to engage in', a reason which the Select Committee on Science and Technology, surely correctly, found 'ludicrous'.[51] Despite criticisms which have since been made of the survey methods used by the Committee on Scientific Manpower and its post-1964 successor,[52] the committee and the ACSP as a whole did succeed in drawing parliamentary and governmental attention to the matter.[53] They also succeeded in obtaining considerable increases in the number of places in science and technology in the universities.[54]

Among the specific issues discussed by the council were the provision (in 1952) of school science teachers, regarded then (as now) as being too low,[55] and the question of broader education for scientists. There may seem little novelty nowadays in the claims that 'the aims of education are [not] necessarily best served by turning out narrow science specialists', or that 'much would be gained if the age of specialisation at school could be deferred', but these remarks, it should be noted, were made in 1954.[56]

On the related theme of higher technological education, which rose to prominence in the late 1940s,[57] the Advisory Council argued that, in the short term, the way forward was to provide more university-educated pure scientists who, with additional postgraduate education in applied sciences, could infuse modern approaches and scientific principles into engineering practice. In the long term 'colleges of applied science similar to the Imperial College ... should be set up ... closely welded into Universities, and providing education up to honours degree standard in both fundamental and applied science'. Such famous technological institutes as those in Massachusetts, California, Zurich and Delft provided models of what was needed in the minds of at least some members of the council.[58] It was not, however, until after the Robbins report, and the transformation of what Robbins had called 'SISTERS' into the new technological universities, that the ACSP in a sense got its colleges of applied science.[59]

It should, incidentally, be noted that the interest shown by the Advisory Council in higher technological education was not mirrored by interest in improving or upgrading the technical colleges. The reasons for this have been discussed by Cotgrove and Price.[60]

The basis for the Advisory Council's emphasis on the provision of high-quality science-based technologists was its belief that the economy would benefit from the availability of such people. Thus in 1953 the council argued that the number of British firms which ranked as technologically advanced by world standards was too small, and that this was partly due to there being insufficient technically qualified people in industry. The blame for this was laid not on inadequate provision of scientists and engineers, but on those large sections of industry which being 'conservative and complacent, have neither missed them nor asked for them. Had the demand been there, it would surely have been matched by a supply of adequately trained men.'[61]

The scientific manpower torch was passed on by the ACSP in 1965 to the CSP. Apart from its inquiries into such specific manpower questions as the provision in the universities for the study of biology in general, and molecular biology in particular, the main focuses of CSP interest in scientific manpower lay with the Dainton and Swann reports.[62] The former was concerned with the flow of science students into higher education, and the latter with the flow into employment of graduate scientists and engineers, and in particular with the question of whether an undue proportion of the best graduates remained in the universities.

The main focus of ABRC interest in manpower questions has been in the support of postgraduate training in the universities. Following up a proposal which had been accepted by the CSP towards the end of its life, the ABRC quickly established a standing committee on postgraduate education. The committee proved useful in June 1974 in advising the DES, through the Board, on its response to the Expenditure Committee's Report on Postgraduate Education of January 1974. The ABRC's rejection (as infeasible) of the Expenditure Committee's call for a close match between the demand from the job market and the supply of places for postgraduate education was reflected in the eventual (1976) response by the DES to the Expenditure Committee.[63]

The actual distribution of postgraduate awards takes place through the appropriate boards or committees of the research councils, with SRC and SSRC, it will be recalled, being the councils which spend the greatest proportions of their budgets under this heading. With £8·8 million of SSRC's budget of £15·6 million in 1978–79 going to postgraduate training, it is easy to see why, when faced with the disproportionately high cut of £1·5 million as its share of the £5 million cut imposed on the research councils in the post-election Conservative budget of June 1979, the council felt it had little choice but to cancel one in four (i.e. 450) of the grants already promised to students for October 1979.[64] It may well have been not too surprised at suffering such a savage cut, since in her days as Secretary of State for Education and Science the new Prime

Minister had been no great supporter of the social sciences.

Ministerial involvement with the research council system

Perhaps because of the greater apparent intelligibility of its work
to lay people, and perhaps also because of the apparently more
immediate political implications of some of the research which it
supports, the SSRC has always been more sensitive than the other
councils to the likely political response to its activities. Andrew
Shonfield, chairman from 1969 to 1971, has recorded how
he felt it prudent to discuss such proposed SSRC ventures as the
establishment of the Industrial Relations Unit with the
Conservative Shadow Employment Minister, and how Mrs
Thatcher at the DES 'had very definite views about the kind of
economists that she liked – and didn't like ... One had to watch
one's step.'[65] Shonfield's successor, professor Robin Matthews,
noted, however, that political pressures on SSRC between 1972 and
1975 were less felt than they had been earlier:

> Mrs. Thatcher ... was not exactly a devotee of the social sciences; but,
> to a greater extent than most politicians, she held in high esteem the
> advancement of basic scientific knowledge, and she was willing to
> stretch a point about including the social sciences under that rubric.[66]

Since 1965 the Secretary of State for Education and Science has
been empowered to direct the work of the research councils. In the
extreme case, this power entitles the Secretary of State to insist
upon or forbid particular lines of research or research projects, and
thus represents a marked change in attitude from that expressed in
the Haldane report in 1918 in relation to governmentally supported
research of general utility.

The implications of Haldane's argument were brought sharply
into focus in 1919 during parliamentary discussions about the
establishment of a Ministry of Health. The minister-designate, Dr
Christopher Addison (an ex-professor of anatomy and dean of
medicine) proposed that the Medical Research Committee should
not be drawn into the new ministry but, in accordance with
Haldane's proposals, should be reconstituted as a research council.
Addison defended his position with a number of arguments, of
which the following was perhaps the chief:

A progressive Ministry of Health must necessarily become committed from time to time to particular systems of health administration.... One does not wish to attach too much importance to the possibility that a particular Minister may hold strong personal views on particular questions of medical science or its application in practice; but even apart from special difficulties of this kind, which cannot be left out of account, a keen and energetic Minister will quite properly do his best to maintain the administrative policy which he finds existing in his Department, or imposes on his Department during his term of office. He would, therefore, be constantly tempted to endeavour in various ways to secure that the conclusions reached by organized research under any scientific body, such as the Medical Research Committee, which was substantially under his control, should not suggest that his administrative policy might require alteration.... It is essential that such a situation should not be allowed to arise, for it is the first object of scientific research of all kinds to make new discoveries, and these discoveries are bound to correct the conclusions based upon the knowledge that was previously available and, therefore, in the long run to make it right to alter administrative policy. ... This can only be secured by making the connexion between the administrative Departments concerned, for example, with medicine and public health, and the research bodies whose work touches on the same subjects, as elastic as possible, and by refraining from putting scientific bodies in any way under the control of Ministers responsible for the administration of health matters.[67]

As Sir Harold Himsworth, secretary of the MRC from 1949 to 1968, later concluded, in winning this battle Addison secured for the nation two valuable benefits:

For Parliament and public alike he secured a continuing source of expert opinion which, because of its independence of commitment to administrative policies and sectional interests, was demonstrably impartial. For research workers he provided a type of organisation which, being scientific, received their professional confidence and thereby enabled the creative ability of the country to be mobilized.[68]

Those who favoured autonomy for the research councils held their own for four decades, the most serious challenge perhaps arising, as will be seen in the concluding chapter, within the Barlow Committee on Future Scientific Policy in 1946. Only with the rise of big science in the late 1950s, coupled with the more *dirigiste* policies of the Labour Party in opposition in the early 1960s, did the principle begin modestly to be challenged, and even with the assumption by the DES of responsibility for the University Grants

Committee and the research councils the idea of autonomy continued to be spoken of highly. Thus it has never yet been admitted that the Secretary of State for Education and Science has used that office's power of direction, and Margaret Thatcher, as Secretary of State from 1970 to 1974, explicitly claimed in 1971 never to have used those powers.[69] Her permanent under-secretary at that time, Sir William Pile, likewise argued:

> I do not think her influence has amounted to saying that this or that should or should not be done; it has amounted to showing an interest in certain activities and hoping and expressing the hope that some would be increased, and that others might be slightly run down.[70]

The practice in Whitehall of discreet consultations at various levels while plans are being prepared makes it easy to grasp the sense in which Mrs Thatcher herself observed in 1971 that the power of direction was one which

> a politician would use sparingly, though of course many discussions take place and usually I would not think that any problem would get beyond the stage of discussion. I doubt very much the power of direction would need to be used.[71]

The case of the CERN 300 GeV accelerator again provides useful illustrative material, this time of the fine line between a ministerial directive and a discussion. To his remarks quoted just above Sir William Pile added that it was Mrs Thatcher's 'interest in the project that enabled the [CSP] to come forward with the proposals which she was able to accept and submit to her colleagues, and which led to joining CERN'. This clearly indicates that there have been occasions when the Secretary of State has displayed an important interest in individual decisions within the realm of policy for science. Support for this claim likewise comes from Mrs Williams's observation in 1968, as Minister of State for Higher Education and Science, that it had been necessary for the government to 'step in' on the CERN proposals.[72]

One can begin to explore the manner of that 'stepping in' from some evidence presented by Sir Frederick Dainton and Dr (later Sir Alec) Merrison, representing the CSP, to the Select Committee on Science and Technology in February 1972.[73] Sir Frederick was then chairman of the CSP, and in 1967–68 had been a member of both the CSP and the Swann working group on the CERN proposals. When asked whether a minister had intervened to prevent money being allocated to the project he replied:

> No, the Secretary of State . . . did not, but I suspect it was just the general paucity of resources at that particular time.

Yet the issue was immediately confused by his reply to the next question:

> You presumably had resources at your disposal and you were prepared to allocate them in this way. Why was there then paucity of resources? Would it not go into your total budget?
> – (Sir Frederick Dainton) It would have done, yes.

Sir Frederick then explained that political elements had, 'quite justifiably', entered into the decision but that as far as he knew no directive had been issued. Of Mr Short's explanation to the CSP in July 1968 of the reasons for the government's decision (see below), he added:

> I think it would have been impossible, in view of what he said, to enter the 300 GeV activity at that time.

Finally, Dr Merrison commented:

> There was not an actual direction from the Secretary of State, but there had been a fairly moving discussion beforehand which led to a particular decision.

The CERN example is complicated by the fact that, in March 1968, after learning privately that the proposal was not acceptable to the government, the chairman of the SRC, Sir Brian Flowers, submitted a private tentative revised plan to the Secretary of State.[74] This plan assumed that a British site be chosen for the accelerator, that there be a substantial reduction in the size of the British nuclear physics community, that the two national high-energy accelerators be closed by about 1980, and that if necessary Britain should withdraw from the existing 30 GeV programme at CERN. On those terms it would be possible to maintain a viable British stake in high-energy physics and to afford the cost of participation within the SRC's forward look for the next five years.

The government's decision against participation came in June 1968, and the new Secretary of State, Edward Short (the third holder of that office since July 1967), gave as the principal reasons that

> in view of its other financial commitments . . . the country could not afford this new commitment. Moreover, once the necessary

international treaty had been signed, there could . . . be no withdrawal
. . . [Also] the Government had to take into consideration the possibility
that costs would escalate.

Further reasons were that the project required a commitment of
resources over a much longer time period than that for which
resources had been allocated to the research councils, and that
there was no short- or medium-term prospect of economic benefit
from the project. Referring to the revised plan put forward by Sir
Brian Flowers, Mr Short doubted whether, in view of the low rating
given by CERN to the possible British site in Norfolk, the
accelerator could be sited in Britain, and added that even this
revised proposal assumed a continued substantial growth of total
resources available to the SRC over ten or more years. Finally, Mr
Short explained that

> The decision in no way altered the understanding that the Government
> did not interfere in the exercise of the Research Councils' own
> judgment on the allocation of resources allocated to them. This was
> their responsibility, and he had no intention of questioning their
> scientific judgment.[75]

That was not, however, the interpretation which many scientists
placed upon the decision, and in Clarke's view the resulting uproar
was

> not so much the result of the decision but of the rejection of the Flowers
> memorandum. Flowers had suggested a means of participating within
> the SRC budget that could reasonably be expected for the next few
> years. The SRC was charged with the job of allocating its own resources.
> Hence several members of the Council saw the Cabinet decision as a
> move which denied the SRC the one function it rightfully possessed. It
> was even proposed that the entire Council resign as a gesture of
> protest.[76]

The decision, on this interpretation, had 'eroded the position of the
SRC'. It should also be noted that the scientists' anger was to a
certain extent increased by the fact that even the two dissenting
chemists on the SRC had been satisfied by the Flowers
memorandum, though on the available evidence that
acquiescence was only formally expressed at the meeting of the
SRC on 19 June 1968 at which Flowers announced the decision and
disclosed the events of the previous months.[77]

The chairman of the SRC's Astronomy, Space and Radio Board
viewed the decision

with the utmost dismay, for two reasons. First, an entire branch of research in physics ... will now inevitably decay relative to world standards. Secondly ... on a vital scientific issue, the Government has taken a decision against the advice of the SRC .. [The decision] raises for the first time a most vital issue of principle as between the political body and its scientific advisers which must cause many of us to give deep thought to our future action.[78]

In similar tone another commentator argued that the decision raised doubts in the minds of those who had 'contributed liberally of their intellectual energies' to the study of the project, and

of the utility of such an immense effort when their unanimous advice is ignored ... It could well be that future historians will single out such decisions as the markers of a new era of mental stagnation, the Dark Ages of the twentieth and twenty-first centuries.[79]

Nature described the abruptness of the decision as 'a departure from reason, not simply a manifestation of incompetence'. It noted that the decision had come 'like the proverbial thunderbolt out of the blue', and that

the confidence of professional scientists in the machinery for the administration of the [science] budget has now been deeply shaken. One result will amost certainly be that the Committees on which the British Government has traditionally relied for advice will become more jealous of their rights.[80]

How fair are these criticisms? Was a new issue of principle raised here? Was the autonomy of the SRC being eroded? It is hard to see how. The proposal plainly exceeded the SRC's delegated authority for capital and foreign currency expenditure; it also involved contributions to, and policy towards, an international organisation. On all these points the SRC was bound to seek the specific permission of the DES before proceeding. Furthermore, it is quite clear that the proposal exceeded the authority delegated to the DES, let alone the SRC. It had to go to the Cabinet, and in strictly formal terms the outcome was entirely proper. The government is not obliged to accept advice, no matter how unanimous or painstakingly gathered it may be.

Nevertheless, it might be argued that a new principle was involved in rejecting such weighty and almost unanimous advice. It is, however, fair comment on that proposition that the safeguards in respect of the rest of science increased as the advice moved up through the research council system, resulting in what Sir Brian Flowers, with hindsight, called the 'impossible "9%" condition',[81] impossible, that is, in the light of the sharp decline in the rate of growth of the science budget from 1968–69. The position reached by the CSP on that point can not have seemed attractive to the government, and although the CSP supported the SRC's Nuclear Physics Board in recommending British participation in the project, it can hardly be claimed that the enthusiasm of the CSP was as straightforward as that of the nuclear physicists. Furthermore, when the SRC and CSP spoke of the project being feasible in terms of the budget which the SRC could reasonably expect, they were, of course, referring to money which the SRC had not yet got. While plans (which were only reasonably firm for the next year or two) existed for expenditure over the years 1968–73, no agreements of even the most tentative kind had been reached on the level of resources for the research councils for 1973–78. For the SRC or the CSP to claim that the project was feasible in terms of certain anticipated growth rates in resources up to 1978 was, therefore, to move well into the unforeseeable future. It follows that technically — and this is the official orthodoxy on this point[82] — there could not have been a governmental directive, since all the government did was decide not to accept certain advice about future funding for the SRC and other research councils. More realistically, however, and in the light of our earlier examination of the distinction between a directive and a discussion, it may be seen that the official orthodoxy conveys but a pale reflection of what actually went on in 1967–68. A clearer assessment of the position is that of Sir Brian Flowers, who has since said:

> When talking of projects involving many millions of pounds and hundreds of jobs, major commitments to public expenditure for future years, and also substantial effects upon our balance of payments and relations with other European countries, plainly no Government can allow an independent agency to spend public money abroad at will.[83]

The role which the ABRC has adopted in relation to big science projects suggests that the research councils and the scientific community have learnt to live with financial constraints upon their activities, and in effect to take the key decisions themselves in the light of the resources likely to be available to them. A case similar to that of the CERN 300 GeV accelerator, were it to arise now, would probably be argued out much more rigorously, not to say ruthlessly, within the ABRC and the 'advice' eventually given to the Secretary of State would almost certainly not include any 'impossible' conditions. The ABRC itself is, however, the product of the greatest ever incursion into the autonomy of the research councils, namely, the post-Rothschild reforms of the early 1970s.

The Rothschild debate

The debate over the CERN 300 GeV project highlighted what ought already to have been clear to the scientific community: free though the research councils were, their autonomy never was and never could be absolute. But that realisation paled into insignificance with what, in 1971, was seen as an unprecedented attack upon the autonomy of the research council system. The uproar that followed the publication of the Rothschild report was in turn unprecedented in volume and range, though by no means all scientists opposed the proposals.

The context in which the report was written included firstly the circulation within Whitehall in 1970 of a confidential report by a committee chaired by Mr Osmond of the Civil Service Department, which recommended the transfer of the Agricultural Research Council to the Ministry of Agriculture, Fisheries and Food. Secondly, the newly returned Conservative government had in 1970 begun a wide-ranging review of governmental activity, with a view to ensuring that as far as possible government business was organised efficiently and on functional lines. Thirdly, and in response to both these stimuli, the Council for Scientific Policy began work in October 1970 on a report on the future of the research council system, which was submitted to Margaret Thatcher in May 1971. Fourthly, it should be remembered that very little time had elapsed since in 1968 the Fulton report had urged that better use be made of scientists in government, and that the lines of accountability within the civil service be clarified. Finally, the early 1970s was a time of considerable disenchantment with science: the research councils were beginning to experience the effects of a sharp decline in the rate of growth of their budgets, and more generally the counter-culture and environmental movements were in full cry, with science as their principal prey. As Shirley Williams put it in February 1971, 'For the scientists the party is over.'[84] Internationally, the mood was much the same, with the OECD report *Science, Growth and Society – a New Perspective*, published in 1971, observing that 'The present situation produces an overwhelming need to reassess the place of science and of particular areas of science, both in cultural terms and as the roots of the technology through which further change, improvement or deterioration will flow'.[85]

Lord Rothschild, formerly a Cambridge scientist and head of Shell Research, became the first head of the Central Policy Review Staff in February 1971. In March 1971 he was commissioned to write by October a report on the organisation and management of government R&D. (There is doubt over whether the report should be regarded as a product of the CPRS or simply of Lord Rothschild.)[86] The report, and the CSP report of May 1971 on the future of the research council system, were published in November 1971 as appendices to a government Green Paper entitled *A Framework for Government Research and Development*.[87] The main points of the Rothschild report were summarised in chapter two, but those relating to the research council system bear repetition and expansion.

Rothschild argued that 'applied R&D, that is, R&D with a practical application as its objective, must be done on a customer–contractor basis. The customer says what he wants; the contractor does it (if he can); and the customer pays.' Applied R&D, therefore, should only be done at the behest of a departmental customer, namely a minister or an official acting on behalf of a minister. According to the DES, Rothschild went on, an 'appreciable' part of the work of the MRC, and a 'major' part of the work of the ARC and NERC was applied. In a well known passage he then concluded:

> But this work had and has no customer to commission and approve it. This is wrong. However distinguished, intelligent and practical scientists may be, they cannot be so well qualified to decide what the needs of the nation are, and their priorities, as those responsible for ensuring that those needs are met.

Accordingly he recommended that funds equivalent to those spent by ARC, MRC and NERC on applied research be transferred, over four years, to appropriate departments which would then spend this money on research commissioned with the research councils but of the departments' choosing. He added two conditions to this recommendation: first, before implementing the proposal, those departments which lacked adequate chief scientist organisations (and would therefore have difficulty in commissioning research) should remedy this defect; and second, the amount paid by the departments to the research councils in the first year of the transitional period should not be less than if no change had occurred, but after that the departments should be free to reduce their payments to the councils, although by no more than 10 per cent per year.

The overall effect of these recommendations would have been that 25 per cent of the funds to be paid by the DES to the research councils in 1971–72 (that proportion to be maintained in the future) would, over four years, be transferred to customer departments as shown in table 6.4.

Table 6.4
Rothschild proposals for transfer of research council funds to customer departments, and actual transfers decided upon by the government, in terms of 1971–72 expenditure (£ million)

Research council	To be paid by DES if old system continued	To be paid by DES under recommended system	To be paid by customer departments under recommended system	Actual sums transferred to customer departments
Science	50·9	50·9	0	0
Social Science	2·2	2·2	0	0
Agricultural	18·7	4·2	14·5 (MAFF)	10·0
Medical	22·4	16·8	5·6 (DHSS)[a]	5·5
Natural Environment	15·3	7·7	7·6 (DOE,[b] DTI, MAFF)	4·5

a Including Scottish Home and Health Department
b Including Scottish Development Department
Sources. Cmnd 4814, table 4, p. 12; Cmnd 5046, para. 50.

Rothschild's proposals as a whole were intended, in line with one of the leitmotifs of the new government, to increase accountability and efficiency in government research and development, and also to improve the quality of scientific advice available in departments and to orient government-supported research more closely towards the national interest. Although the research councils accounted for only one-sixth of government expenditure on research and development, it was Rothschild's proposals for them which drew the fire of much of the scientific community. Quite full accounts of the 'Rothschild debate' having already been written by Williams,[88] only a brief summary will be given here before turning to consider what the effect of the eventual reforms has been.

The debate took place in various forums. *Nature* and *New Scientist* offered much comment.[89] Some forty-five letters on the subject were published in *The Times*, together with four editorials.[90] The Select Committee on Science and Technology held a very thorough inquiry on the subject, taking evidence from, among others, Lord Rothschild, the CSP, the research councils, all the interested government departments, the Royal Society, the Institution of Professional Civil Servants and the Association of Scientific, Technical and Managerial Staffs. The result was a remarkably rich quarry of detailed information about science-government relations in Britain.[91] The House of Lords held a major debate of high quality in which many distinguished scientists took part.[92] Within Whitehall there were meetings between members of the research councils and departments. The government also invited comment on the Green Paper from the councils, the Royal Societies and other interested bodies and individuals, and received submissions from more than four hundred individuals and organisations. Recurrent themes among those opposing Rothschild were the desirability of autonomy for science and the dangers of State control, the high international reputation of the research councils, the degree to which their programmes were already highly responsive to public needs, the limited capacity of government departments to match the scientific expertise available in the councils and, therefore, to make sensible demands of them, and the most unusual (probably unique) style of Lord Rothschild's report, which many found irritating. Much attention was also focused on the validity of the distinction drawn by Lord Rothschild between pure and applied research (and certainly one shortcoming of the select committee's inquiry was its failure to obtain any details of how Rothschild had derived his figures for the cost of applied research supposedly being done by the research councils).

In disputing the validity of that distinction, considerable use was made of an alternative set of categories introduced by the Dainton working group of the CSP in its report on the future of the research council system. (The contrast, incidentally, which was afforded by the publication in the same Green Paper of the Rothschild and Dainton reports – the latter preceded by a quotation from the Book of Common Prayer – provoked much comment: *The Times* found Rothschild 'brisque, brusque, iconoclastic'. whereas Dainton was 'bland, conciliatory, evolutionary',[93] and another journalist commented that the joint publication presented 'a riotous contrast – as though the Pope and the Rev. Ian Paisley's views on the right way to organise a Christian church were placed side by side in a single volume'.)[94] The categories employed in the Dainton report were:

(a) tactical science – the science and its application and development needed by departments of state and by industry to further their immeidate executive or commercial functions . . .

(b) strategic science – the broad spread of more general scientific effort which is needed as a foundation for this tactical science. It is no less relevant in terms of practical objectives of the sort we have mentioned, but more wide ranging . . .

(c) basic science – research and training which have no specific application in view but which are necessary to ensure the advance of scientific knowledge and the maintenance of a corps of able scientists.

The connections between basic and strategic science were regarded as particularly close, complex and subtle, and it was those types of science which, the working group considered, formed the bulk of the scientific activity of the universities and research councils. It was also argued that the strength and flexibility of existing interactions between scientists working in related fields, within these two types of scientific activity, would be damaged if the scientists were dispersed to executive departments; furthermore, because of the multiplicity of users of the work of the research councils, to allocate particular aspects of their work to particular government departments would create difficulties for other interested departments and would fragment existing teams of scientists.

The CSP working group did consider nevertheless that certain changes in the research council system were desirable. It noted that there were a number of policy problems with which the councils individually could not deal. These included the question of whether the boundaries between the research councils were correctly drawn, the problem of the balance of effort within disciplines which spanned more than one council, the need for collaboration between councils on certain subjects (such as pollution), and questions of scientific manpower. The CSP's ability to deal with such matters was constrained by its purely advisory role.

The working group recommended that the activities of the research councils be co-ordinated and administered by a Board of the Research Councils. This would be a statutory body with a charter which would protect the independence of government-supported basic and strategic science and which would empower it to delegate authority to the research councils (and, conversely, to control them much more directly than had hitherto been possible). Subject to the Secretary of State's power of direction, the board would determine broad problems of science policy,

> including any necessary reorientation of that policy and any readjustment of the internal boundaries between Research Councils, and would allocate resources to the individual Research Councils. It would also be able to add to and subtract from the number of Research Councils.

Working under a full-time, independent chairman, the members of the board would include the heads of the research councils, some independent members, the president of the Royal Society, a vice-chancellor, and the chairman of the UGC. In addition, and in order that the board 'may be fully and continually aware of public policy and of those needs of executive departments of government which can be served by the scientific activities of Research Councils and in order that wasteful overlap or duplication may be avoided', there should be representatives from the DES and three other ministries, together with the chief scientific adviser in the Cabinet Office.

Although written before Rothschild's report, the Dainton report was, as has been said, widely used as a source of information and ideas by those opposed to Rothschild. But by no means all scientists were opposed to Rothschild, as again the letters page of *The Times* and the columns of *Nature* and *New Scientist* showed.[95] In the House of Lords debate Lord Zuckerman, who had until a little over a year previously been the chief scientific adviser to the Cabinet, and who was still active within the Cabinet Office, was highly critical of much of what Rothschild had proposed, yet believed that the proposals were a step in the right direction. Furthermore, he argued, 'Practically nothing that Lord Rothschild proposed is not to be found in other Government Reports. He has not made preposterous revolutionary proposals. Indeed, he has not gone far enough, in my view.' As if in illustration of what he meant, Lord Zuckerman had earlier observed that although the last thing he would do would be to destroy the effectiveness of any research council, nevertheless, 'if it is the case that the A.R.C. is the most competent body there is in the field of agricultural research, I cannot help asking why it is not sponsored directly by the Agriculture Departments'.[96] Support for Rothschild also came from Lord Todd, who did, however, suggest that the figure of 25 per cent of research council funds to be transferred to customer departments seemed high.[97]

In the event, with the publication in July 1972 of a White Paper, *Framework for Government Research and Development*,[98] the broad outlines of Rothschild's proposals were accepted, though many of his detailed recommendations were not. The customer–contractor principle was to be extended to all government-supported applied research and development. The scientific capability of departments was to be strengthened, although, as was seen in chapter five, Rothschild's division of responsibilities between policy advice and policy execution was glossed over. £20 million were to be transferred from the research councils to customer departments, not the £27·7 millions recommended. The transitional period, however, was to be three years, not four. Contrary to one of Rothschild's more provocative recommendations, research councils would be free to decline work if they had 'good grounds'. The CSP was to be replaced by the ABRC with a composition close to that recommended by the CSP, but without the executive powers and the full-time chairman, and (contrary to Dainton but in line with Rothschild) without also the president of the Royal Society among its members. Departmental representatives were to become full members of the research councils. As Williams has noted, although the research community may have thought it had won a 'small victory', on the other hand, and focusing on the key issue – the transfer of funds – it would really have been very remarkable (because contrary to all precedents) if the government had insisted on the full transfers proposed by Lord

Rothschild.[99]

Developments since Rothschild

The question of why, after mounting such vigorous and vocal opposition, the scientific community was so unsuccessful in resisting the Rothschild proposals will be deferred until the concluding chapter, and the remainder of this chapter will consider the effects of the 1972 changes and other developments since then.

The judgment in July 1977 of Sir Alec Merrison, who in 1979 became chairman of the ABRC, was that it was difficult to see that the changes had had any substantial effect and that

> such effect that they have had seems to have been for the worse. They have certainly not done the scientists any good, but neither have they done them very much harm (with the possible exception of a good deal of nervousness on the part of scientists working in more fundamental areas).

What had 'unquestionably happened', however, was that an 'unnecessarily elaborate machinery' had been set up to supervise the spending of the money transferred from the research councils. Equally unquestionably, what had not happened was a redirection of research to any conspicuous degree:

> One can ascribe this to the incorrigible waywardness of scientists or to the fact that they were not after all quite so insensitive to the needs of society as some people believed. My own view would be that it is largely the latter. At any rate, society is on balance the loser because of the 1972 reforms.[100]

The reflections of the research councils themselves, and of the ABRC did not, however, accord precisely with Sir Alec's observations. Nor did those of a review of the post-Rothschild arrangements published by the government in March 1979. Sir Alec's point about the greater administrative burden is universally accepted: the MRC reported in 1977 that while 'in general' it could be said that the new machinery linking it to the Health Departments was being 'made to work', nevertheless that machinery had 'imposed heavy additional burdens' not only in terms of administrative time but also, and more seriously, in terms of 'a very great increase in calls on the time of expert advisers, who are limited in number and whose involvement in advisory activities – however desirable – takes them away from the pursuit of research'.[101] The ABRC made similar comments in 1976 and 1978, noting that NERC had experienced particular difficulty because of its considerable number of customers and wide spread of interests, and that ARC and MRC felt that the establishment of chief scientists' organisations in MAFF and DHSS had duplicated many of their own administrative functions.[102] The government itself, in its review of the post-Rothschild arrangements, accepted that there had been administrative costs and that these had been particularly heavy in the case of NERC.[103]

On the question of how the new administrative arrangements were working, the experience of each council varied, and was in any case influenced by the various degrees of financial control exercised by customer departments. The ARC noted in 1975 that although cuts in its budget following the economic crisis in the winter of 1973–74 had made 1974–75 financially the 'least favourable' year in recent times, nevertheless the new administrative arrangements with the Agriculture Departments had 'settled down to steady work and early fears of the disruptive effects of commissioning were shown to be unfounded'.[104] By 1978, however, concern was being expressed by the ABRC that no fewer than 80 per cent of ARC staff were partly or wholly engaged on commissioned work[105] with the effect, as the government's post-Rothschild review put it, that there had been 'some loss of managerial flexibility' for the council and that it had become 'harder to redeploy staff for new or adjusted programmes of non-commissioned work'.[106]

MRC had experienced more difficulty. First, the chief scientist at DHSS, unlike his counterpart at MAFF, had not been given full executive responsibility for research into biomedical and health problems, and second, the Health Departments, lacking appropriate scientific staff, were unable to propose ideas for commissioned research at the rate at which funds were transferred from MRC to those departments. The first problem had led to administrative difficulties and the second, on the government's own account, had resulted in a situation in which the departments 'found themselves largely reacting to proposals from the MRC'. Both problems had been remedied from 1978, the second by accepting a division of responsibility and establishing a procedure whereby each year the departments set out a range of policy and service problems to which biomedical research might be applied, the council then suggesting how their research programmes might relate or be developed in response.[107] MRC remained concerned, however, about the vulnerability of its programmes to sudden cuts in its departmental support. It had experienced at only a few months' notice a cut of £900,000 (or 10 per cent) in the funds expected from DHSS in 1977–78, this having resulted from cuts which the department had had to make in the light of a general reduction in government expenditure, and the secretary of the council argued before the Public Accounts Committee in 1979 that 'the MRC feels a little uneasy ... about this large chunk of their funds which could with political change ... be either decreased or might conceivably ... disappear'.[108]

NERC, however, probably had the greatest difficulty in coming to terms with the new conditions of support for research. Funds had been transferred from the council to four government departments (the departments of Industry, Energy, and the Environment, and MAFF) and to the Nature Conservancy Council (which had been hived off from NERC and transferred to the Department of the Environment in another of the post-Rothschild changes), and it took some time to devise machinery which would allow expression and co-ordination of the differing customer demands. As NERC itself observed in its report for 1975–76:

> It would have been gratifying to be able to record, at the close of the three-year transition phase for transfer of funds, that we had negotiated firm contracts for at least another three-year period to the full extent of the transferred funds. Unfortunately this is not the case, and the resulting uncertainty is making it difficult to carry through efficiently certain of our programmes which requires [sic] advance planning. Charter of specialised vessels for research and survey is an example. Some of the hesitation stems from the uncertainty of the customer Departments about their own financial position. There is also the doubt of the customer Departments as to whether they should continue to support some of the long-range strategic programmes they took over from NERC during the transition period.[109]

But by 1978 the ABRC was able to claim that NERC now had 'satisfactory and productive relationships' with its customer departments,[110] and the government's own review saw 'no risk of management problems which might jeopardise the effectiveness' of the council.[111]

After some teething troubles of more or less severity, coupled with the uncertainty which followed from the unexpected cut in DHSS's funds to MRC for 1977–78, the new arrangements seem, therefore, to have settled down. It is hard to be sure, but it is not apparent that, in general, the morale of research workers employed by the councils, or in receipt of council grants in the universities, has undergone any permanent change. Furthermore, the departments are reported by the ABRC to be satisfied that the commissioned programmes are relevant to their needs.[112] As to whether the commissioned work differs from what the councils would in any case have supported, the judgment of the ABRC is of interest. It considered that the work which the ARC now does on contract is on very much the same lines as that which it was doing before the transfer of funds, 'although the Council considers that there have been beneficial changes of emphasis and attitude towards application of the research undertaken'. The nature of MRC contract work has also changed little, as would be expected from what has already been said about the way in which the initiative over research ideas has lain so heavily with that council. The ABRC considered that there have been greater changes in NERC's programmes, 'a number of which have been adapted to meet the needs of its different customers'.[113]

If it is difficult to detect either any great changes in the programmes of the research councils, or any lasting impact upon the morale of research workers, then at least the one clearly negative outcome of the changes (the administrative costs to the research councils) can, finally, be weighed against the positive benefits of the changes from the viewpoint of the government departments. As early as 1976 the ABRC spoke of the benefits, of growing value for the future, in 'the greater contact now existing between scientists inside and outside government departments', and in 1978 it added that the councils and the Board itself had also benefited from the membership of chief scientists.[114] Universities and polytechnics were also participating in this interchange as commissions placed directly with them by departments grew within the spirit of the post-Rothschild reforms, and as more of their scientists were drawn into the advisory committees set up since 1972.[115]

Of course, the SRC and SSRC have also experienced the effects of more contact with government scientists (through membership of the latter on the councils and on the ABRC), but did not lose control of any of their funds. It is, therefore, ironic that, as regards the contents of the programmes of the research councils, it is the SRC which, according to the government, has since 1972 experienced the greatest shift in the direction of its work. As the 1979 post-Rothschild review put it:

> 'Big' science ... has been cut back and expenditure on engineering research has been greatly increased. In thus adjusting the thrust of its work, the SRC has successfully collaborated with the DOI and other Departments in such areas as research on polymer engineering and marine technology and the training of postgraduates in industry.[116]

How much these changes have owed to financial stringency, how much to the tougher line adopted on priorities by the ABRC, which, unlike the CSP, took up the challenge that the ACSP laid down in its valedictory report (and how much the difference between ABRC and CSP itself owed to the presence of the chief scientists on the former), and how much they owed to concern within the SRC that unless the council appeared fully responsive to national needs it too might go the way of ARC, MRC and NERC, it is impossible to say. Since there now appears to be a consensus that no major changes should be made in the organisation of the research council system for some years, SRC (and SSRC) can probably be less concerned for the moment about the last of those points. As for the other three research councils, they are losing no opportunity to wrest back from their customer departments as much control as possible over their funds. By succeeding in mid-1979 in securing the agreement of MAFF to pay the full economic cost of the use of ARC facilities, ARC has in effect regained control over £2$\frac{1}{2}$ million of its budget.[117] For all, therefore, that the post-Rothschild reforms may have benefited government by improving contact between departments and research councils, and may have made the research councils, through the presence of chief scientists on the councils and the ABRC more aware of national needs, there can be little doubt that the councils would still prefer to revert to the financial arrangements of 1965–72.

Notes

1 *Framework for Government Research and Development* (London: HMSO, Cmnd 5046, 1972), para. 42.

2 *Third Report of the Advisory Board for the Research Councils 1976–1978* (London: HMSO, Cmnd 7467, 1979), para. 10.

3 Cited in A. Landsborough Thomson, *Half a Century of Medical Research* (London: HMSO, 1973), vol. 1, pp. 142–3.

4 Cmnd 7467, *op. cit.*, p. 22.

5 G. Kenner, 'The SRC Chemistry Committee', *Chemistry in Britain*, 6 (1970), p. 466. See also N. Sheppard, 'SRC – policies and procedures', *Chemistry in Britain*, 6 (1970), pp. 374–81.

6 See Select Committee on Science and Technology, Session 1974–75, *Memoranda (Appendices to the Evidence given to the Science Sub-Committee) Part I* (London: HMSO, HC 261–i, 1975) pp. 30, 53, 111.

7 Hugh Heclo and Aaron Wildavsky, *The Private Government of Public Money* (London: Macmillan, 1974), p. 200 and *passim*. For developments since then, and criticism of the public expenditure review process, see Christopher Pollitt, 'The Public Expenditure Survey, 1961–72', and Maurice Wright, 'Public Expenditure in Britain: The Crisis of Control', both published in *Public Administration*, 55 (1977), pp. 127–42 and 143–69.

8 Heclo and Wildavsky, *op. cit.*, p. 24.

9 The description of the budgetary process for the Science Budget is based on *Second Report of the Advisory Board for the Research Councils 1974–75* (London: HMSO, Cmnd 6430, 1976), appendices I–IV, together with information from an interview with Sir Frederick Stewart, 15 December 1976, and a lecture given in Manchester by Professor Geoffrey Allen on 17 May 1979.

10 D. Nelson, 'The Support of University Research by the Science Research Council', *British Journal of Political Science*, 3 (1973), pp. 113–28.

11 *Nature*, 264 (11 November 1976), p. 99.

12 *Nature*, 276 (14 December 1978), p. 657.

13 Cmnd 6430, *op. cit.*, appendix VI, table 2.

14 *Annual Report of the Advisory Council on Scientific Policy 1960–61* (London: HMSO, Cmnd 1592, 1962), paras. 32–8.

15 *Committee of Enquiry into the Organisation of Civil Science* (London: HMSO, Cmnd 2171, 1963), paras. 51, 105 and 112.

16 Norman J. Vig, *Science and Technology in British Politics* (Oxford: Pergamon, 1968), p. 73.

17 House of Lords, *Debates*, 256, cols. 436–446.

18 *Annual Report of the Advisory Council on Scientific Policy 1963–64*, (London: HMSO, Cmnd 2538, 1964), paras. 11–15.

19 R. W. Clark, *A Biography of the Nuffield Foundation* (London: Longmans, 1972), pp. 58–63. Tizard was a trustee of the Foundation until 1950, when he was replaced by Professor (later Lord) Todd. His support for

research in physics was not confined to high-energy work but extended also to radio-astronomy. Clark has concluded that there is 'little doubt' that the Foundation was steered into support of the Jodrell Bank radio telescope in 1952 'largely by Tizard's advocacy'. See Clark, op. cit., pp. 101–6; and Nuffield Foundation, Minutes and Annexed Papers, 1951–52, F.40/3, and Minutes, Nos. II, 664; II, 717; and II, 819.

[20] John Hartland and Michael Gibbons, Britain Joins CERN: An Analysis of the Decision Process 1951–1953, unpublished report for the Steering Group on the Manchester University CERN 28 GeV Study, of the CSP's Standing Committee on International Scientific Relations, November 1972.

[21] Ninth Annual Report of the Advisory Council on Scientific Policy (1955–1956), (London: HMSO, Cmnd 11, 1956), paras. 11–12.

[22] Annual Report of the Advisory Council on Scientific Policy 1961–62, (London: HMSO, Cmnd 1920, 1963), paras. 12–18.

[23] Annual Report of the Advisory Council on Scientific Policy 1962–63, (London: HMSO, Cmnd 2163, 1963), para. 15. On the Brain Drain, see Vig, op. cit., pp. 72, 88, 99 and 129–30; selected correspondence in Minerva, 1 (1963); House of Commons, Debates, 681, cols. 35–168 (July 1963); Emigration of Scientists from the United Kingdom (London: Royal Society, 1963); and The Brian Drain (London: HMSO, Cmnd 3417, 1967).

[24] Annual Report of the Advisory Council on Scientific Policy 1962–1963, loc. cit., paras. 16–17. For Lord Todd's speech, see House of Lords, Debates, 247, cols. 125–33 (February 1963). For the council's final thoughts on the matter, see Cmnd 2538, op. cit., paras. 16–25.

[25] The details given below of the reports of these bodies are taken from The Proposed 300 GeV Accelerator (London: HMSO, Cmnd 3503, 1968). See also Michael Gibbons, 'The CERN 300 GeV Accelerator: A Case Study in the Application of the Weinberg Criteria', Minerva, 8 (No. 2, 1970), pp. 180–91.

[26] Robin Clarke, 'How the 300 GeV decision was made', Science Journal (March 1969), pp. 4–7; and Select Committee on Science and Technology, Session 1968–69, 300 GeV Accelerator (London: HMSO, 1969).

[27] Sir Brian Flowers, 'The Idea of a Research Council', lecture given at Newcastle University (London: SRC, March 1973).

[28] Annual Report of the Advisory Council on Scientific Policy 1958–1959 (London: HMSO, Cmnd 893, 1959), paras. 14–20.

[29] Nature, 184 (1959), p. 1899. See also The Times and The Guardian, 9 December 1959.

[30] Chapman Pincher, Daily Express, 9 December 1959.

[31] In 1959 a Steering Group on Space Research was formed to advise the Lord President. Its exact relationship with the ACSP is not clear, but it seems to have lifted the prime responsibility for this subject from the ACSP. (Cmnd 893, para. 15; and private communication from Lord Todd, 16 July 1973.) The role played by the ACSP in the establishment of ESRO and ELDO also remains unclear. No information is provided in the council's annual

reports, but in 1966 the DES stated that the 'present and planned' scale of British space activity 'stems from the advice' of the ACSP in 1962, 'which endorsed proposals for a build-up of expenditure over about six years on civil scientific space research activities including UK participation in ESRO'. (Thirteenth Report of the Estimates Committee, 1966–67, *Space Research and Development*, London: HMSO, 1967, p. 33 and question 187.)

[32] Council for Scientific Policy, *Report on Science Policy* (London: HMSO, Cmnd 3007, 1967), para. 8.

[33] *Ibid.*, paras. 9–10.

[34] *Ibid.*, paras. 19–20.

[35] 'Report of the Working Group on the Determination of Scientific Priorities', published as Appendix C to *Third Report of the Council for Scientific Policy* (London: HMSO, Cmnd 5117, 1972).

[36] Cmnd 5117, *op. cit.*, para. 10.

[37] *Second Report of the Advisory Board for the Research Councils 1974–75* (London: HMSO, Cmnd 6430, 1976), chairman's covering letter to Secretary of State.

[38] *Nature*, **260** (25 March 1976), p. 273.

[39] This and the succeeding two paragraphs draw heavily on the third report of the ABRC, Cmnd 7467, *loc. cit.*, especially pp. 14–16 and 22–4.

[40] Second Report from the Select Committee on Science and Technology, *Scientific Research in British Universities*, Session 1974–75 (London: HMSO, HC 504, 1975), para. 71.

[41] *Nature*, **279** (21 June 1979), p. 661.

[42] See *SSRC Newsletter*, No. 33 (March 1977), Supplement on Research Initiatives.

[43] David Dickson, *Times Higher Education Supplement*, 7 October 1977.

[44] *Selectivity and Concentration in Support of Research* (London: SRC, 1970).

[45] *Report of the Science Research Council for the Year 1974–75* (London: HMSO, 1975), p. 9.

[46] *Ibid.*, p. 10.

[47] See *Report of the Science Research Council for the Year 1976–1977* (London: HMSO, 1977), pp. 17–18; and *Report of the Science Research Council for the Year 1977–1978* (London: HMSO, 1978), pp. 15–16.

[48] C. Farina and M. Gibbons, 'A Quantitative Analysis of the Science Research Council's Policy of Selectivity and Concentration', *Research Policy*, **8** (1979), pp. 306–38.

[49] See Select Committee on Science and Technology, Session 1975–76, *Second Report on Scientific Research in British Universities* (London: HMSO, 1976), Annex II, 'Selectivity and Concentration in the Science Research Council', p. xviii.

[50] See *Fifth Annual Report of the Advisory Council on Scientific Policy (1951–1952)*, (London: HMSO, Cmd 8561, 1952); Committee on Scientific

Manpower, *Report on the Recruitment of Scientists and Engineers by the Engineering Industry* (London: HMSO, 1955); Ministry of Labour/Advisory Council on Scientific Policy, *Scientific and Engineering Manpower in Great Britain* (London: HMSO, 1956); and the Committee on Scientific Manpower's reports of 1959, 1961 and 1963, Cmnd 902, 1490 and 2146 respectively.

⁵¹ See Select Committee on Science and Technology, Session 1975–76, *University–Industry Relations* (London: HMSO, 1976), para. 4.10.

⁵² See K. G. Gannicott and M. Blaug, 'Manpower forecasting since Robbins: a science lobby in action', *Higher Education Review*, **2**, pp. 56–74; C. A. Moser and P. R. G. Layard, 'Higher Education in Britain', *Journal of the Royal Statistical Society, Series A*, **127**, pp. 499–501; and V. A. Richardson, 'A Measure of Demand for Professional Engineers', *British Journal of Industrial Relations*, **7**, pp. 52–70.

⁵³ See, for instance, the House of Lords Debates on the subject on 15 November 1961 and 11 March 1964.

⁵⁴ A fuller treatment of this subject is given in P. J. Gummett, 'British Science Policy and the Advisory Council on Scientific Policy' (unpublished PhD thesis, University of Manchester, 1973), chapter 5; but see also: G. L. Payne, *Britain's Scientific and Technological Manpower*, (London: Oxford University Press, 1960); House of Commons, *Debates*, **560** (1956), cols. 1750–3; and Sir Solly Zuckerman, 'Scientists in the arena', in Anthony de Reuck *et al.* (eds.), *Decision Making in National Science Policy* (London: J. and A. Churchill, for CIBA Foundation, 1968), pp. 8–13.

⁵⁵ Cmd 8561, *op. cit.*, para. 32.

⁵⁶ *Seventh Annual Report of the Advisory Council on Scientific Policy (1953.1954)* (London: HMSO, Cmd 9260, 1954), paras. 16.17.

⁵⁷ See, for instance, the report of the conference on the subject held by the Royal Society in March 1950 in *Nature*, **165**, pp. 627–9; and G. L. Price, 'The Origins of British Government Policy for Higher Education in Science and Technology: 1943–1964' (unpublished MSc thesis, University of Manchester, 1974).

⁵⁸ *Second Annual Report of the Advisory Council on Scientific Policy (1948–1949)* (London: HMSO, Cmd 7755, 1949), pp. 5–7.

⁵⁹ *Higher Education* (Robbins report) (London: HMSO, Cmnd 2154, 1963), paras. 337 and 383, and Cmnd 2538, *op. cit.*, paras. 4–7 and appendix A.

⁶⁰ S. F. Cotgrove, *Technical Education and Social Change* (London: George Allen and Unwin, 1958), pp. 173–5; and G. L. Price, 'Professional tensions in science and technology: the case of the Colleges of Advanced Technology', *R&D Management*, **9** (1979), pp. 77–83.

⁶¹ *Sixth Annual Report of the Advisory Council on Scientific Policy (1952–1953)* (London: HMSO, Cmd 8874, 1953), paras. 1–5.

⁶² *Enquiry into the Flow of Candidates in Science and Technology into Higher Education* (Dainton report) (London: HMSO, Cmnd 3541, 1968);

and *The Flow into Employment of Scientists, Engineers, and Technologists* (Swann report) (London: HMSO, Cmnd 3760, 1968).

[63] *Second Report of the Advisory Board for the Research Councils 1974–75, loc. cit.*, paras. 40–3; and *Expenditure Committee: Postgraduate Education* (London: HMSO, Cmnd 6611, 1976).

[64] *The Guardian*, 20 June 1979.

[65] *SSRC Newsletter*, No. 29 (November 1975), p. 7.

[66] *Ibid.*, pp. 8–9.

[67] *Memorandum on the Ministry of Health Bill, 1919, as to the Work of the Medical Research Committee* (London: HMSO, Cmd 69, 1919) paras. 10–11; cited in Harold Himsworth, *The Development and Organization of Scientific Knowledge* (London: Heinemann, 1970), pp. 102–3.

[68] Himsworth, *op. cit.*, p. 103.

[69] Select Committee on Science and Technology, Session 1970–71, *Research Councils* (London: HMSO, HC 522, 1971), question 18.

[70] Select Committee on Science and Technology, Session 1971–72, *Research and Development Minutes of Evidence and Appendices* (London: HMSO, HC 375, 1972), question 1258.

[71] HC 522 (1971), *op. cit.*, question 18.

[72] House of Commons, *Debates*, **769** (1968), col. 830.

[73] HC 375 (1972), *op. cit.*, questions 263–70.

[74] Sir Brian Flowers, *op. cit.*, p. 5.

[75] DES Press Statement, cited in Open University, *Science and Society* (Science Foundation Course Units 33 and 34) (Milton Keynes: Open University Press, 1971), p. 43.

[76] Robin Clarke, *op. cit.*, p. 5.

[77] *Ibid.*

[78] Sir Bernard Lovell, *Nature*, **219** (1968), p. 15.

[79] Professor A. R. Bishop, *ibid.*, pp. 15–16.

[80] *Nature*, **219** (1968), p. 2.

[81] Sir Brian Flowers, *op. cit.*, p. 5.

[82] HC 375 (1972), *op. cit.*, appendix 2a.

[83] Sir Brian Flowers, *op. cit.*, p. 6.

[84] Shirley Williams, MP, 'The responsibility of science', *The Times Saturday Review*, 27 February 1971.

[85] OECD, *Science, Growth and Society – a new perspective*, The Secretary-General's Ad Hoc Group on New Concepts in Science Policy (Paris: OECD, 1971), p. 91.

[86] See Roger Williams, 'Some Political Aspects of the Rothschild Affair', *Science Studies*, **3** (1973), pp. 31–46, at pp. 32–3.

[87] *A Framework for Government Research and Development* (London: HMSO, Cmnd 4814, 1971).

[88] Roger Williams, *op. cit.*; and Roger Williams, 'Independence and accountability after Rothschild', *R&D Mangement*, **2** (1972), pp. 131–5. See also L. A. Gunn, 'Government Research and Development', *The Political*

Quarterly, **43** (1972), pp. 225–9.

89 See, for instance, the editorials in *Nature*, **234** (1971), pp. 163–4 and 239–40; **235** (1972) pp. 1–2 and 238–9. See also the thirteen articles on the Rothschild proposals by a wide range of authors published by *Nature* between 17 December 1971 and 18 February 1972.

90 For the editorials, see *The Times*, 6 October 1971; 26 November 1971, 28 February 1972 and 20 July 1972.

91 HC 375 (1972), *op. cit.* See also Select Committee on Science and Technology, Session 1971–72, *Research and Development* (London: HMSO, HC 237, 1972) and *Research and Development Policy* (London: HMSO, HC 308, 1972).

92 House of Lords, *Debates*, **328** (28 and 29 February 1972), cols. 784–925, and 939–1082.

93 *The Times*, 26 November 1971.

94 Nicholas Faith, *Sunday Times Business News*, 28 November 1971.

95 See, for instance, the letters to *The Times* from Professor J. C. Waterlow and Dr E. W. Gill (4 January 1972), and M. Swann, 'Preparation for a Rumpus', *Nature*, **234** (1971), p. 379.

96 House of Lords, *Debates*, **328** (29 February 1972), especially cols. 974–6. See also Lord Zuckerman's second *Times Literary Supplement* Lecture, 'Government needs and expectations', *TLS* (5 November 1971), especially pp. 1386–7. For a further indication of support within Whitehall for the transfer of ARC to MAFF, and also of NERC to DOE, see Sir Richard Clarke, *New Trends in Government* (London: HMSO, 1971), p. 92.

97 *Ibid.* (28 February 1972), especially col. 815.

98 Cmnd 5046, *loc. cit.*

99 Roger Willaims, 'Some Political Aspects of the Rothschild Affair', *loc. cit.*, p. 45.

100 Sir Alec Merrison, 'The concept of usefulness', *Nature*, **268** (1977), pp. 2–3.

101 Medical Research Council, *Annual Report 1976–77* (London: HMSO, 1977), p. 3.

102 Cmnd 6430, *op. cit.*, especially pp. 9–11; and Cmnd 7467, *op. cit.*, section 4.

103 *Review of the Framework for Government Research and Development (Cmnd 5046)* (London: HMSO, Cmnd 7499), para. 35.

104 Agricultural Research Council, *Annual Report 1974–75* (London: HMSO, 1975), pp. 3 and 5.

105 Cmnd 7467, *op. cit.*, para. 39.

106 Cmnd 7499, *op. cit.*, para. 36.

107 *Ibid.*, paras. 37 and 55, and appendix 1D, paras. 6 and 11.

108 Committee of Public Accounts, Session 1978–79, *Minutes of Evidence* (14 March 1979) (London: HMSO, HC 104–viii, 1979), question 1363.

109 NERC, *Annual Report 1975–76* (London: HMSO, 1976), p. 6.

110 Cmnd 7467, *op. cit.*, para. 32.

[111] Cmnd 7499, *op. cit.*, para. 38.
[112] Cmnd 7467, *op. cit.*, para. 35.
[113] *Ibid.*, para. 36.
[114] *Ibid.*, para. 29, and Cmnd 6430, *op. cit.,* para. 11.
[115] Cmnd 7499, *op. cit.*, paras. 46–7.
[116] *Ibid.*, para. 39.
[117] See Committee of Public Accounts, Session 1978–79, *Minutes of Evidence* (19 March 1979) (London: HMSO, HC 104–ix, 1979); and *Nature*, **279** (1979), p. 666.

UNDERLYING THEMES IN SCIENCE – GOVERNMENT RELATIONS

Relations between science and government in Britain have developed in evolutionary fashion. Although from time to time major reports have been written which have sought to take stock of large parts of the machinery for formulating both policy for science and ways of using science and scientists in policy in general, these have either not proposed radical change or, if they have done so, have failed to be fully implemented. A key element in all discussions about the Whitehall machinery of science–government relations has been the idea of the responsibility of a minister for the work of his or her department. This idea, it will be shown, has considerably influenced the possibilities for co-ordination within the field of science policy, broadly defined, and the acceptability within government of the idea of 'science policy' itself.

Discussions about machinery have taken place within a policy environment with several significant features. One of these has been the changing level and nature of public and political interest in science and technology. Another has been the limited degree to which scientists have been encouraged, through education and opportunity, to involve themselves in government. A third has been the capacity of scientists to organise for political influence.

The philosophy of administration which has underlain the machinery for science–government relations, and the policy environment which has influenced developments in that arena, form the two themes of this final chapter.

Ministerial responsibility and science policy

The administrative philosophy behind the machinery of science policy in Britain can best be seen in the light of a discussion of the process of co-ordination within this field. Brickman has suggested that the concept of co-ordination in science policy can be understood in the two senses of co-ordination as process and co-ordination as a state or condition.[1]

Co-ordination as process refers to that which is actually being done to bring about 'co-ordination'. When the term is used in this sense, the focus of interest is the day-to-day mechanics of co-ordination. The variables of co-ordination thus understood include the time frame of the activity (is it concerned with only the next year or the next, say, five years?), the nature of the information which the co-ordinating parties exchange (is it financial, substantive or evaluative?), the comprehensiveness of the activity (does it encompass all the programmes of an agency, or only particular types, such as the large or the small ones?), its scope (meaning the fraction of national R&D activity which is co-ordinated), and the degree of constraint upon agency behaviour (has the co-ordinating process got teeth?).

The co-ordination of French science policy, which is conducted through the machinery of the National Plan, could thus be described as emphasising annual budgetary review and medium-term (five-year) planning of a financial and substantive nature, with high comprehensiveness but incomplete scope (most industrial R&D and much military and high-technology work falling outside the planning machinery), and with a moderate degree of constraint upon agency behaviour. The overall co-ordination of British 'science policy', by contrast, would be much harder to summarise because practice varies so much throughout Whitehall and because no such clear-cut mechanism as the French National Plan exists. At the level of the Department of Education and Science we could, however, say that the Advisory Board for the Research Councils co-ordinates annually and in the medium term, using financial, substantive, and sometimes evaluative, information, with full comprehensiveness (at least in principle; in practice the ABRC would not probe all aspects of a research council's programme), very limited scope (the Science Budget only), but a fairly high degree of constraint over the research councils.

The reason that such a clear-cut summary cannot be given of the overall process of co-ordination of science policy in Britain turns on the question of the style, intentions, even rationality of governmental co-ordination in Britain; in short, on the conception of co-ordination as a state. In this sense of the term, the focus of attention is that which the co-ordinating process seeks to achieve or, in other words, it is concerned with the purpose or intentions of co-ordination. Thus we speak in this sense of the degree to which science policy is 'ordered', is 'coherent and articulated', falls within a 'consistent framework'.

Brickman distinguishes three kinds of 'co-ordination as state': atomistic (which I prefer to call minimal), low and high. Minimal co-ordination is characterised by the absence of any explicit framework against which to judge the suitability of the actions of agencies or departments. Each element within the government navigates as a free agent, aiming only to keep out of the way of others and to keep others out of its way. Any co-ordination which results is of the Lindblomian incremental type, achieved through 'partisan mutual adjustment', where the object is simply to avoid the adverse consequences of others' decisions, or the adverse consequences of one's own decisions on others. It is in this sense that Lord Salisbury once described British foreign policy as being 'to drift lazily downstream, occasionally putting out a boathook to avoid a collision'.

Low co-ordination is characterised by the attempt to apply 'rational-technical' criteria to science policy decisions. That is, the acceptability of proposals is judged against a set of performance criteria which includes avoidance of duplication, rational division of responsibilities, resolution of mutually defeating policies, integration of mutually supportive efforts, and efficient use of human and cash resources. Co-ordinated policy is arrived at by induction from the initiatives of individual agencies: these agencies set their plans in motion, and only then discuss with each other the rationality of their all pursuing all their plans independently of each other.

High co-ordination, finally, is characterised by the attempt to ensure not merely that resources are used according to rational-technical criteria, but that they are being used to optimum effect in terms of overall national goals. This approach involves setting system-wide goals for science and technology by deduction from these national goals. Lower-level science policy goals are in turn deduced from these goals for science and technology. To put the point differently, whereas low co-ordination is a 'bottom up' process, high coordination is 'top down'.

Before beginning to apply these concepts to the British case it will be useful to review briefly what has already been said about moves to introduce co-ordinating machinery into science policy, and to expand upon some of what has already been said. We may begin by recalling that in the 1870s the Devonshire Commission recommended the establishment of a Department of Science, to be responsible for a large part of governmental scientific activity and for acting as a clearing house for information upon work done by other departments. No action was taken, however, until the first world war, when the Department of Scientific and Industrial Research became, in effect, Devonshire's proposed Department of Science. Soon afterwards, in 1918, the Haldane committee took DSIR as the model for what later came to be called research councils, and wrote of the possibility that, if the number of research councils grew, responsibility for them (but not for all governmental scientific activity) might be transferred from the Lord President to a separate Department of Intelligence and Research, although the Committee of Civil Research, which operated for a few years in the 1920s, was not what the committee had in mind.

The emergence in the 1930s and 1940s of various groups of scientists concerned, in one way or another, with the establishment of closer relations between science and government, coupled with the experience in the second world war of what science actually could contribute to such a relationship, led at the end of the war to pressure from inside and outside government for some sort of reform of the co-ordinating machinery.[2] This point was particularly firmly pressed from 1943 by the president of the Royal Society and chairman of the Scientific Advisory Committee to the Cabinet, Sir Henry Dale, and from soon after the 1945 election (with the return of a Labour government) by Professor Zuckerman and Sir Henry Tizard. Despite reluctance on the part of the other members of the Scientific Advisory Committee (chiefly the heads of the three research councils), Dale succeeded in the final days of his presidency in persuading certain key officials and, through them, Herbert Morrison, the new Lord President, that the time was ripe for a review of the central machinery for science policy. The nub of Dale's argument was that the composition of the Scientific Advisory Committee (viz. the secretaries of the three research councils and three officers of the Royal Society) was too narrow. Accordingly, to the terms of reference of a committee which was already being planned, under Sir Alan Barlow of the Treasury, to review the question of scientific manpower, there was added at the last minute a requirement to review the central arrangements for formulating science policy.

The debate which was conducted in 1946 within the Barlow Committee on Future Scientific Policy is worth discussing in a little detail here because it epitomised the debates over the co-ordination of science which were to occur for the next three decades. For the sake of brevity, the discussion will be considerably simplified; G. L. Price and I have published a fuller account elsewhere.[3]

Within the Barlow committee's discussions, three main lines of argument may be identified. A radical position, associated with Professors Blackett and Zuckerman (both members of the committee), and to some extent with Dale and Tizard, argued for strong central co-ordination of all government-supported scientific activity. In a memorandum to Morrison, entitled 'Machinery for Central Direction of Scientific Effort',[4] Zuckerman proposed an active scientific staff of perhaps ten members at the centre of government, with extensive powers for both inquiry and the execution of plans. As well as scientific manpower, it would oversee the planning of public and private research in the civil, military and industrial fields; it would cross departmental boundaries to co-ordinate departmental views on scientific aspects of public policy; it would handle international scientific relations and policy regarding scientific information, matters normally regarded as the province of the Royal Society; and it would seek to rationalise the ad hoc activities of the many official and semi-official scientific committees and organisations. The head, and perhaps three others, of this staff would be senior scientists of repute, and the head might be chairman of all the major governmental scientific advisory committees, defence and civil, and might also serve on ministerial committees and on the Chiefs of Staff Committee.

A more moderate position was outlined in evidence to the committee by Sir John Anderson, the distinguished former official and wartime minister, with whom Barlow had worked closely while Anderson was Chancellor of the Exchequer, and with whose views on this subject Barlow was broadly in sympathy. Anderson argued that the Lord President should retain his current responsibilities for science but that this arrangement should not detract from the responsibilities of departmental ministers for maintaining their own scientific organisations. The Lord President should have a staff which, as distinct from the characteristics desired for it by the radicals, should be small, non-specialist, and headed by a senior official from the Cabinet Office who should not be a recognised scientist but should have an understanding of science. There should also be a standing advisory committee of some seven members, with a wider representation than the Scientific Advisory Committee. No governmental scientists or secretaries of research councils should be members, nor should the secretaries of the Royal Society automatically be members. Such a committee, argued Anderson, would go a long way towards demonstrating the determination of the government 'to put science in its rightful place in the planning of our educational, social and economic system'. Anderson also argued, in contrast with the proponents of the centralisation of science policy, that while the Lord President's staff should be 'cognisant of scientific matters', they should not be in a position to set up as rivals to departmental scientific staffs.

In addition to the radical position, which was characterised by its desire for a strong central scientific staff with wide powers, and the moderate position, which attempted to balance the need for a central staff with respect for the tradition of ministerial responsibility, there was a third position which feared that even the moderates went too far in reducing the importance of the Royal Society and the secretaries of the research councils in the formulation of scientific policy. This position was most explicitly defended on the Barlow committee by Sir Alfred Egerton, one of the secretaries of the Royal Society. As a member himself of the Scientific Advisory Committee, Egerton rejected Dale's argument that the composition of that body should be increased to include four or five independent members. Furthermore, he expressed concern about the tenor of Zuckerman's proposals. Specifically, he was 'most anxious to avoid the too definite planning of research by a Board or Committee or even the direction of it into definite channels'. He was also unhappy with Zuckerman's proposal that the central machinery should guide scientific relations with other countries; science, said Egerton, 'should combat the tendencies which prevent it being international (e.g. Russia, Nazi Germany)'. On behalf of himself and some fellow members of the Royal

Society, Egerton later explicitly opposed the idea of a central science policy committee, arguing that such a committee might become too authoritative and begin to encroach on the responsibility of the Royal Society for promoting all branches of natural knowledge.

It is not necessary for present purposes to pursue in detail the subsequent course of these discussions. It suffices to note first that the interested politicians (including the Prime Minister and Lord President) and officials were broadly in favour of some changes in the central machinery for science policy, roughly along the lines suggested by Anderson. That, together with the composition of the Barlow committee (with a moderate reformer in the chair, and radicals comprising at least half the membership of the committee), meant that the conservative policy of 'no change' was lost from the outset. Second, the option of establishing a Ministry for Science was never open to the committee. Morrison and the Prime Minister had openly rejected this possibility, and it met little favour when it was raised with officials. It is in any case doubtful whether any members of the Barlow committee would have favoured it. The Whitehall tradition of the responsibility of each minister for the work of his own ministry was cited time and again as the reason for this opposition. The options which were seriously open to discussion were, first, the relative merits of a chief scientific adviser versus a central advisory committee; second, the structure and functions of any central scientific secretariat; and third, liaison between defence and civil scientific policy.

The outcome was the establishment of the Advisory Council on Scientific Policy, linked with the Defence Research Policy Committee (set up at about the same time through a separate but not entirely independent sequence of events) through the chairmanship of both by Tizard and by some overlap in secretariats. Despite the success of the radicals in getting into the Barlow committee's report a (somewhat ambiguous) recommendation for a large central scientific secretariat, the secretariats eventually established for each committee were rather small. This was not, as has been suggested,[5] because of Treasury opposition, but because of the insistence of the Ministry of Defence that it needed its own secretariat for the DRPC, coupled with Morrison's desire to build up the scientific side of the Office of the Lord President. It was thought wasteful to establish a third secretariat in the Cabinet

Office to serve the ACSP, and so the Lord President's staff assumed that responsibility.[6] No doubt it all seemed perfectly reasonable at the time, but the result was that the hopes of those who favoured a strong co-ordinating focus for science–government relations in Whitehall, and who had arguably got closer to the fulfilment of this dream than any before or since (the Trend committee apart), were dashed at the last minute on the rocks of departmental independence.

The influence of the ACSP and the DRPC, as was seen in chapter two, is hard to assess but was significant in certain areas, and conspicuous by its absence in the major field of atomic energy and in other technological areas. Its lack of responsibility for advice on finance also denied to the ACSP the supreme weapon of a co-ordinating body. The growth during the 1950s of government expenditure on science, coupled with doubts in both major parties about the cost-effectiveness of this expenditure in relation to economic growth, coincided with concern inside the ACSP and the Treasury about the absence of machinery (the appointment of a Minister for Science notwithstanding) for establishing priorities in science policy. Thus, against a background of debate within the main opposition party about the purposeful use of science and technology, the Trend committee got under way, and found:

first, that the various agencies concerned with the promotion of civil science do not, in the aggregate, constitute a coherent and articulated pattern of organisation; second, that the arrangements for co-ordinating the Government's scientific effort and for apportioning the available resources between the agencies on a rational basis are insufficiently clear and precise.[7]

The Trend committee proposals for a strong Ministry for Science, advised by a revamped ACSP, were, however, put aside by the victors of the 1964 election. Enhanced co-ordination within ministries (especially the DES and the Ministry of Technology) became possible, but co-ordination between the scientific activities of different ministries was not helped by the 1964 reorganisations. The appointment of Sir Solly Zuckerman as chief scientific adviser to the government was also designed not to improve co-ordination but only advice at the centre.

In the 1970s the post-Rothschild reforms reduced somewhat the scope of DES control over the research councils, tightened the bonds between research councils and other ministries, and strengthened the machinery for scientific advice and for the formulation and implementation of research policy within certain departments. The Rothschild proposals also provided an occasion for the Select Committee on Science and Technology to press, unsuccessfully, for the appointment of a co-ordinating minister of R&D with a seat in the Cabinet and with statutory power to examine and approve all government research and development.[8]

In 1976 the status of the Cabinet's science adviser was reduced when that office was moved sideways into the CPRS, and at the same time the Advisory Council for Applied Research and Development, and the Committee of Chief Scientists and Permanent Secretaries (under the chairmanship of the secretary of the Cabinet), were set up. These changes were 'designed to strengthen the machinery for co-ordinating scientific advice to the Government',[9] but not, it seems, directly to co-ordinate decision-making for science.

Having brought this review of the central machinery for science up to the time of writing, let us now relate these events to the idea of co-ordination as a state or condition. To do this, we should first consider the principle that lies behind the organisational pattern of British government.

Chester and Willson have observed that there are four main ways in which governmental powers and activities may be grouped for administrative purposes:[10]

1. By class of persons, or clientele, dealt with – e.g. children, pensioners, local authorities.
2. By major purpose, or function – e.g. education, health, defence.
3. By area served – e.g. Scotland.
4. By kind of work or administrative process – e.g. legal, research, printing.

The distinction between the first two of these dates back to Aristotle, and was given prominence by the Haldane committee in 1918, which favoured the functional approach. It has remained since then, as before, the predominant organisational principle in British government. Accordingly, departments have generally been organised on functional lines, with the minister in charge being theoretically responsible for ensuring that all activities (such as research) that are relevant to the function of his department are performed as appropriate. Co-ordination, of a minimal to low type, has occurred at the financial and policy levels through the Treasury and, at the policy level, through the Cabinet Office since its establishment by Lloyd George. Since the 1940s cabinet committees have also played an important co-ordinating role. Furthermore, on international matters, the Foreign Office has always played an important role and, since 1968, the Civil Service Department has co-ordinated the use of manpower in government departments.

In the context, then, of belief in functional organisation and considerable ministerial autonomy, one does not need to look for any anti-scientific sentiment in British government to account for the low level of interdepartmental attention to science and technology. Just as the *dirigiste* tradition in French government dating from the eighteenth century made it seem natural for science policy to be co-ordinated through the machinery of the National Plan,[11] so in Britain the traditions of government have made it seem natural *not* to seek to co-ordinate science policy (or any other kind of policy) interdepartmentally at other than a minimal or low level. Attempts to go beyond this (as in 1946, or in the pressure in the 1970s from the Select Committee on Science and Technology for a Minister of R&D) have failed because they have gone against the grain of the traditions of functional organisation and relative decentralisation of decision-making. Thus, to the recommendation of the select committee that there should be a Cabinet minister with statutory power to examine and approve all government research and development, since

> unless there is one Minister ... who would make recommendations ... on the range, structure, and balance of the Government's research and development as a whole, there can be no proper scrutiny of national objectives and how they should be defined,[12]

the government replied, in terms that would have been familiar both to Haldane and to the Barlow committee,

> Departments should be organised by reference to the tasks to be done and the objectives to be met. Each department should be a complete and coherent organisation for dealing with its executive tasks and should have all the facilities necessary for this, including the right and means to commission the research and development it needs to fulfil its tasks. But with the right goes also the responsibility. Each Department must be accountable for the effective use of the Vote it receives for the pursuit of its tasks. The Minister ... is thus fully accountable for ensuring

that his policy objectives are properly backed by all necessary facilities, including research and development. But he could not carry this responsibility if the authority for approval of part of these proposals was placed elsewhere, with an independent Minister possessing the power to adjudicate between departmental research and development programmes.[13]

In other words, and as was made plain in 1972 by the Lord Privy Seal and the chief scientific adviser to the Cabinet, British policy is to have no unified national science policy, outside the area of policy for science (i.e. the field overseen by the ABRC), but to have research policies within each functional area of government.[14] In Britain, therefore, the term 'science policy' has come to refer to the unplanned sum of sectoral research policies. Such co-ordination as occurs between these research policies depends, essentially, upon the web of connections between officials in Whitehall, and indeed this is not to be underestimated as a method of ensuring minimal and low co-ordination. In their study of the public expenditure process Heclo and Wildavsky wrote of the 'Whitehall village' in which key officials, knowing each other well, can have such trust in each other's judgment that

> every sum need not be redone, many details can be confidently overlooked, advance warnings can reduce uncertainty, informal chats will distinguish the real fire from smoke-screen issues, and political administrators can more confidently bypass most that goes on.[15]

Such highly developed informal relations can not only help to resolve one of the main questions faced by many theories of decision-making – namely, how decision-makers with limited resources of time, intellect and information cope with the complexity and uncertainty of public decision-making – but can also (if the case of officials dealing with public expenditure is not unique) provide a highly effective means of co-ordination at the minimal and low levels. In a village everyone knows everyone else's business, and according to Alexander King, who was the first secretary of the ACSP, such a state was easily achieved in British science policy circles before 1939:

> up to the Second World War, the size of the British science system was small enough for internal adjustments and policy direction to be in the hands of a few, outstanding personalities belonging to the same coterie. Coherence and mutual understanding were probably achieved rather effectively, if utterly informally, through frequent, easy, but often

unplanned contacts between the leading figures of the Royal Society, the research council secretaries, and senior civil servants, all of whom were habitués of the Athenaeum Club.[16]

Whether, however, such arrangements will be adequate in the 1980s seems an open question to which we shall return below. For the moment let us note that Freeman has argued that, since the setting of priorities is a question of fundamental importance in any democracy, to leave the main priorities in science and technology policy entirely to departments is unacceptable.[17] Given, however, the organisational tendencies of British government throughout this century, it seems unlikely that there will be any major change in the short or medium term. Haldane's characterisation of the British mode of administrative reform – 'Improvisation, with a bias towards the minimum rather than the maximum'[18] – continues to apply today in the field of science–government relations, as in others.

The policy environment

Beyond the details of the machinery of science–government relations, whether at intra- or interdepartmental level, lies the environment within which those relations are fostered. In broad terms the OECD report *Science, Growth and Society* distinguished three phases of the overall political climate in which science has operated throughout the OECD countries since 1945.[19] The first period extended to the early 1960s and was characterised by high public faith in the efficacy of science and high political prestige of scientists, especially in the United States and Britain. The second phase extended from about 1961 to 1967 and was characterised by the emergence of economists and systems analysts as significant influences upon science policy. Government attitudes towards science and technology moved from euphoria towards concern about rational resource allocation and the role of science and technology in economic growth. It was still a period of optimism about the social and economic value of science and technology. The third phase began in the late 1960s in Europe (and earlier in the United States), when a mood of disenchantment with science and technology set in, budgets became tighter, and scientists lost some of their influence and credibility in government and before the public.

It should already be clear that, in general terms, the first and third of those phases have influenced British science policy. That the second has also made its mark ought also to be clear, and can be further shown by briefly considering the language used by the Council for Scientific Policy in the 1960s. In commenting on the Swann report, the CSP observed that the committee's work would make it possible 'for the first time to study the relationship between the flow of highly qualified manpower into employment and the growth of basic research as an interrelated system'.[20] Elsewhere the council's first chairman wrote of the need for a fuller understanding of 'the mechanics of scientific growth', and the council itself wrote that the main objective of the various science policy studies which it had set in train was to 'arrive as soon as possible at a synthesis of views on how scientific expenditure grows and the criteria by which that growth can be measured and justified'.[21] The tendency towards making a science of science policy can most clearly be seen in the closing paragraph of the council's first report, in which it indicated in general terms how its studies of science policy issues might fit together:

> it is possible to envisage that the part of Research Council expenditure devoted to support of general research in the universities (training awards and the majority of Research Grants) should rise by an amount composed of 'university growth' plus the appropriate 'sophistication factor'; and that the rest of research expenditure not directly associated with teaching would have to be justified either on economic, humanitarian, or social grounds ... or on intrinsic scientific grounds ... To this would have to be added the level of contribution to international schemes ... All will have to be set within a pattern which is unlikely to denude other important sectors of the economy of essential highly qualified manpower. It will take time, and the prolonged co-operation of the Research Councils and many other organisations, to develop such a pattern in place of the present pattern of unco-ordinated development; but we believe that achievement of a solution is the prime requirement of scientific policy at the present time.[22]

One wonders which came first: the words or the implicit equations.

With the transition from the second to the third phase, and the associated replacement of the CSP by the ABRC, the search for what could almost be seen as a mathematical model of the growth of science and its relations to its input and output variables came to an end. There has, however, carried over into the third phase an important residue of the systems approach of the second, namely the emphasis placed now upon explicit planning of developments, at least in the area of the Science Budget. Rose and Rose argued in 1969 that 'common sense demands that if science spending is to be limited, it should be done explicitly rather than implicitly',[23] and here certainly the attempt by the ABRC to spell out the terms in which its decisions are taken must be regarded as a step forward. It is also possible, but too soon to be sure, that the stabilisation which is currently being sought in the growth (or more recently decline) curve of the Science Budget marks in Britain the onset of a fourth phase in post-war science policy, in which governments, having taken the measure of science, no longer regard it euphorically but do consider it to be one important contributor to the quality of national life, and no longer regard it as homogeneous but single out certain areas for special attention (micro-electronics and biotechnology being among the current front runners).

Within these broad international changes in the environment of science–government relations, certain specifically British features are also noteworthy. Of particular significance has been the limited degree to which scientists have been encouraged, through opportunity and education, to involve themselves in government, as can be seen with reference to the scientific civil service and scientific advisory groups in general.

As has been seen, the view gained ground within the civil service in the 1920s that the closest official advisers to ministers should have general administrative rather than specialist skills. Attempts to draw specialists into closer contact with ministers, and to give them wider departmental responsibilities, have been made from time to time, most recently in the form of some of the post-Fulton and post-Rothschild reforms (and yet another official inquiry into the scientific civil service was taking place at the time of writing).[24] The failure of some of the post-Fulton schemes to attract scientists into administration has, as we have seen, been officially attributed to several factors, which include the reluctance of scientists to move outside their specialism, apparent deficiencies in one of the schemes (that for Senior Professional Administrative Trainees), and the fact that most administrative posts arise in the London area.

All schemes of this sort can be expected to have some unforeseen deficiencies, or to suffer from certain contingent factors (such as the variable attractiveness of working in London). Underlying these difficulties, however, may well be not only a still over-rigid distinction between the specialist and generalist roles, but also a more fundamental problem which is rooted in the British system of education. I mean by this that to be educated as a scientist or engineer in Britain involves almost total concentration upon those specialisms during the last two years at school and the three to six years at university. Nothing in that education prepares a person for any other career than that of scientist or engineer, and it should not be surprising if, having undergone such an initiation, a person wishes to capitalise to the full on his or her investment of time and energy. Despite, as has been seen, the warning from the ACSP in 1954 about the dangers of 'turning out narrow science specialists', the structure of a British science education has not changed markedly since then, and although within that structure the curricula have changed, at school level at least, some of them may well be more demanding now than in 1954. If nothing in their education has awakened them to the possibility that administrative work may be at least as fulfilling as technical, young scientists and engineers can be forgiven for not seeking administrative experience early enough in their careers to stake their place in the competition later for senior administrative posts. To say this is not to argue that the structure of opportunities in the civil service is unimportant, but only that, even if the structure were improved, the educational system may still impede the better use of scientists in Whitehall.

As has been seen, scientists have been invited into Whitehall not only as permanent civil servants but also as temporary advisers and members of relatively autonomous bodies such as the research councils. Here again, the structure of the educational system has been significant in so far as, on the limited data available, a few universities seem to have predominated as the training ground for these advisers (probably because their reputations as centres of scientific excellence at the time when these future scientific leaders were being educated attracted the best students to them), and also as the places of employment of those of them who have been academics. To say this is not to impugn the quality of those advisers, or of the education in science which they received, but only to wonder whether it would not be in the best interests of British science and British government to broaden the base of experience which is being tapped. Interestingly, this is not a question that has attracted much attention among scientists, even though a decade ago Rose and Rose warned of the dangers of 'the disenfranchisement of the non-establishment scientist, and still more of the non-scientific public',[25] and this suggests that a few observations on the political organisation of scientists in Britain are in order.

Within the environment that surrounds and shapes a nation's science policy, the capacity of the scientific community to make its voice heard on relevant issues is clearly important. But sheer vociferousness is not sufficient for winning political battles, as was made plain in 1972 by the failure of the scientists who opposed Rothschild's proposals to wring many concessions from the government, despite a campaign which was unprecedented in its fierceness. One reason for their failure in this case may have been that the opposition was mobilised rather late in the day. It will not be possible to be sure about this before the year 2001 (barring a change in the rules governing inspection of official records), but it may be that the CSP – which should have been the main guardian in Whitehall of the interests of the research councils and their beneficiaries – did not itself realise what was in the wind until rather late on. It must be emphasised that this is a speculation, but it is based on some indications that the CSP was not quite fully in touch with Whitehall thinking about science, such as the disappointment expressed in 1972 by Lord Helsby, head of the civil service from 1963 to 1968, about the detachment which, he argued, the CSP had maintained from the programmes of the research councils: the implication of his remarks was that senior civil servants had hoped for a more interventionist role from the council.[26]

Other reasons for the failure of the opposition to Rothschild are more clearly rooted in the lack of unanimity within the scientific community (which was discussed in chapter six), and in its lack of political organisation. Scientists are split by discipline, by place of work (within the public sector alone there are government research establishments – in turn divided by ministry – university laboratories, and research council units and establishments), and by professional association or union (IPCS, ASTMS and the AUT being the main three). There is, in short, no one body through which the views of scientists as a whole – even within the public sector — can be channelled into the political arena. Although the government frequently turns to the Royal Society for the 'scientists' view', it is doubtful how far the opinions of that august but self-selected body can be taken as representative of scientists as a whole. In Haberer's terms, the Royal Society is composed of 'paradigmatic leaders', chosen for their eminence in their fields, rather than 'institutional leaders', chosen to deal with the 'organisational and political imperatives' with which science must now contend.[27]

Related to this point, Vig concluded of the 1959–64 debate about the machinery for formulating policy for both science and technology that the decentralised nature of science policy has not been conducive to organised representation of scientific interests – 'The particularity of the scientists' concerns makes them an "interest group" only in the broadest and loosest sense of the term'[28] – while Moodie and Studdert-Kennedy, referring to the same case, considered that 'scientists constitute a public, albeit a public with certain organizational nuclei, rather than an organized and fully-fledged pressure group. As against this somewhat divided interest, the Government is well placed to take the initiative.'[29] Comparing the 1959–64 debate with that of 1971–72, Williams concluded that in the later case scientists were again more of a 'special public' than a pressure group, though demonstrating more of a capacity to act in groups than in the earlier case, and showing less reluctance to press their views in any available forum.[30] More recently, as we have seen, the IPCS demonstrated in 1979 its capacity to adopt traditional trade union tactics in fighting for a pay claim, but it is unlikely both that any other public sector scientists' union could apply similar pressure and that IPCS would use its strength on broader issues not directly relevant to the pay and working conditions of its members.

In the absence, then, of a single voice to speak for scientists in government departments and research establishments, and for the employees and beneficiaries of the research councils, there is also lacking a single focus for generating and guiding debate about the conduct in general of science–government relations. Thus the 'disenfranchisement of the non-establishment scientist' is nowhere seriously discussed. The question of whether working scientists as a whole should have some say over who should serve on governmental and research council committees (possibly, as in certain committees in Japan, Yugoslavia and France, through elections)[31] is not an issue in Britain. Nor is attention paid to the possibility of governmental agencies regularly canvassing the opinions of working scientists on the question of what their research needs are. The possibility, as is the practice with the US National Science Foundation, of making referees' reports (without the name of the referee) available to scientists whose research grant applications are rejected, is not discussed.[32] And so on. The point here is not that these possibilities necessarily represent an improvement on present British practice. Rather it is that, in the absence of any one organisation concerned to protect the interest of all scientists within the public sector, questions about the overall working of science–government relations tend not to be raised in any coherent way. The initiative rests with the governmental agencies and committees, and there are no strong countervailing forces.

In conclusion

The quality of British science has won world-wide admiration in the past and continues to do so today. In so far as one can judge impressionistically from the press and from personal contacts among scientists in the public sector, morale among scientists is fairly good, but shows plenty of scope for improvement. The post-Rothschild reforms are settling down, and appear to have produced some beneficial changes in attitude in government departments and in the research community, although, since among the research councils it is SRC which has made the greatest changes in its programmes (not necessarily entirely because of the reforms), it remains doubtful whether the transfer of resources from ARC, MRC and NERC was really necessary in order to achieve what has been achieved: perhaps all the other changes *without* that one would have done as well. How long, however, the quality of British science can remain high in the straitened circumstances which have attended basic research since 1974 remains to be seen. It is not really much consolation to know that other countries have been similarly affected: to take up just one implication of this situation, the generally low availability of posts for scientists in universities and related research institutes throughout Europe means, in the words of the president of the European Science Foundation, Lord Flowers, that 'we are in danger of starving ourselves of fresh talent ... If we are to avoid sinking into mediocrity we must recognise that real talent has to be carefully fostered and generously nurtured.'[33]

This chapter began by discussing a question of machinery of government, namely the effect of the British administrative philosophy of ministerial responsibility upon the possibility of a co-ordinated science policy. It then considered some features of the environment within which science policies in Britain are formulated and implemented. In a sense, environment is more important than machinery: much can be done if the environment, or climate, is favourable even though on paper the machinery may look inappropriate. A key element in that environment is the availability of adequate resources, but more money in itself will not help government to improve the quality and use made of science and technology unless it is coupled with further efforts to break down those barriers which tend to insulate science from society: indeed, more money *without* those renewed efforts could be damaging if it encouraged the scientific community to turn inwards on itself in relief at the passing of the need to appear socially responsive.

I have in mind here particularly the barrier between the 'two cultures', which stems from the educational system and has implications both for the use made of scientists in government and for the demands placed by the public upon science, and also the barriers between the workplaces of scientists, be they in industry, universities, research council establishments or government departments, which impede the easy interchange of people and hence ideas. More interchange of people could encourage greater openness in the system of government in general (and not simply with reference to science–government relations), and this would be no bad thing from the points of view both of greater public accountability in government and of ensuring that policy makers were as well informed as possible. It would be harder to lay charges of government by an aloof mandarinate if Whitehall were seen actively to canvass a wider range of views on all subjects than it does at present, and if activity within Whitehall were more open to public scrutiny. Much the same points were being made by Rose and Rose a decade ago,[34] and there is every reason to emphasise them with equal force today, but as a final caution one should add that the required transformations will take decades to bring about. Just as in the argument about industrial democracy, so also in the argument that Whitehall should be more open to outside influences, it must be recognised that a lengthy learning process is involved. It is, for instance, easy for hard-pressed officials to say that outsiders are insufficiently versed in administrative processes or problems to be of very much use to them, but that is likely to remain the case until enough outsiders have had sufficient contact with Whitehall to develop the necessary sensitivities.

To return, finally, to the question of machinery for science policy, it must be emphasised that there is in Britain no adequate national institutional focus for thinking about the state and direction of science and technology as a whole. If, as for instance Henry Kissinger has argued,[35] science and technology will be the principal national resources of advanced industrial states in the coming decade, this is an omission which Britons should be really sure they wish to accept.

What form might such an institutional focus take? A Ministry of Research and Development, acting 'horizontally' across the grain of the 'vertical' spending departments in Whitehall would be a possibility, and the recent French analysis,[36] conducted under the auspices of the Minister of Science, Pierre Aigrain, of the strengths, weaknesses and value of each branch of French science, shows what such a ministry could do. However, the strong functional orientation of British government makes it unlikely that such a ministry would be countenanced in Whitehall in the foreseeable future, even though it is not obvious why, if conventions have been established which allow the Treasury and the Civil Service Department to act horizontally without reducing the accountability of spending ministers, another ministry could not in time do likewise.

Within the legislature, the Select Committee on Science and Technology provided another basis for a focus, but one with many limitations, and in any case the committee no longer exists.

Within the executive, there is now the Committee of Chief Scientists and Permanent Secretaries, but I do not regard this as an adequate focus, partly because of the Whitehall reaction against thinking in terms of a national science policy, partly because its members are unlikely all to be able to meet very often and are also unrepresentative of the scientific community as a whole, and partly because it remains an unknown quantity outside Whitehall.

On the periphery of the executive, and mediating between it and the wider scientific community, are the Advisory Council for Applied Research and Development and the Advisory Board for the Research Councils. These are at present too restricted in their terms of reference to provide an ideal focus, and the former also seems to have a predeliction for inquiries into particular and limited, though important, issues of technology policy, such as problems of innovation, micro-electronics and biotechnology, and is completely detached from the financing of all aspects of governmentally supported research and development.

The ABRC perhaps offers more promise. Its membership is relatively wide-ranging, including departmental chief scientists, heads of research councils and independent scientists. Furthermore, it is apparently interested in broadening the scope of its work beyond the transitional difficulties of the post-Rothschild reforms and the budgetary problems of 1974–79.[37] Its standing appears good in Whitehall and in the wider scientific community. It may, therefore, lie within the capacity of the Advisory Board to emulate and improve upon the former Advisory Council on Scientific Policy in producing an authoritative annual report on many aspects of the state of science and technology in Britain and, like the Advisory Council's, these reports could well prove useful both as sources of information and as stimuli to debate in Parliament and in the media. That in itself would be a step in the right direction. If ways could be found to broaden the Advisory Board's terms of reference, perhaps by making it report through the Cabinet Office to a ministerial cabinet committee on science and technology as well as to the Secretary of State for Education and Science, and by giving it access (difficult though it would be to ensure this) to relevant departmental papers, that would be a further improvement. Finally, ways might also be sought of linking more working scientists into its deliberations, so that its pronouncements on policy would not have the air of diktats handed down from on high. Its aim would be, through consultation, forethought and persuasion, to seek to match scientific potential with national need, in the way that the post-Rothschild reforms have tried to do sectorally, but on a higher governmental plane.

One can already imagine the objections that will be raised to such an untidy scheme on the grounds of functional organisation. But as Salomon argued in 1977:

Must one . . . simply accept the fact that science policy ceased to have a *raison d'être* at the end of the last decade because it had to take account of a series of peripheral ventures undertaken by public and private executive bodies in the framework of their respective responsibilities? In this perspective, budgetary arrangements might be enough to ensure the co-ordination and control of certain activities. Yet the problems are still there, and if past science policy has not been able to achieve all that was expected of it, it is rather for lack of long-term means of persuasion, and long term perspectives, than because its function has not been defined.[38]

If there is merit in the principle of functional organisation, other countries seem also to have found merit in the idea of a co-ordinated national science policy. The modest proposals made here recognise the strength of commitment within Whitehall to functional organisation while offering the bones of a measure which, while falling short of the appointment of a Minister of R&D or even of a central scientific secretariat, might offer some of the advantages of a more co-ordinated approach. These proposals seek the best of both worlds, in the belief that science and technology are too important as national, and global, resources to risk their sacrifice to unbending administrative principle.

Notes

[1] Ronald Brickman, 'Interagency Coordination in Science Policy: A Comparative Study of Theory and Practice', paper presented to the American Political Science Association, September 1977. A revised version of this paper is forthcoming in *Policy Sciences* under the title 'Comparative Approaches to R&D Policy Co-ordination'.

[2] For references on this point additional to those given in chapter two, see Philip Gummett and Geoffrey Price, 'An Approach to the Central Planning of British Science: The Formation of the Advisory Council on Scientific Policy', *Minerva*, **XV** (No. 2, 1977), pp. 119–43, at pp. 121–4. The discussion of the origins and work of the Barlow committee draws heavily on this paper.

[3] *Ibid.*

[4] A version of this memorandum has been reprinted as appendix 7 in Lord Zuckerman, *From Apes to Warlords: The autobiography (1904–1946) of Solly Zuckerman* (London: Hamish Hamilton, 1978).

[5] Hilary and Steven Rose, *Science and Society* (Harmondsworth: Penguin Books, 1970; first published by Allen Lane, 1969), p. 74. See also chapter two above.

[6] Gummett and Price, op. cit., pp. 139–42.

[7] Committee of Enquiry into the Organisation of Civil Science (London, HMSO, Cmnd 2171, 1963), para. 43.

[8] First Report from the Select Committee on Science and Technology, 1971–72, Research and Development (London: HMSO, HC 308, 1972), paras. 25–40.

[9] Review of the Framework for Government Research and Development (Cmnd 5046) (London: HMSO, Cmnd 7499, 1979), para. 6.

[10] D. N. Chester and F. M. G. Willson, The Organization of British Central Government 1914–1964 (London: George Allen and Unwin, for Royal Institute of Public Administration, 1968), p. 399.

[11] For details of central co-ordinating machinery in France and Canada, see Robert Gilpin, France in the Age of the Scientific State (Princeton: Princeton University Press, 1968); 'France puts science under the microscope', Nature, 280 (1979), pp. 98–9; P. Aucoin and R. French, 'The Ministry of State for Science and Technology', Canadian Public Administration (fall 1974), pp. 461–81. For an idea of the scope of the West German Bundesministerium für Forschung und Technik, see Department of Trade and Industry, 'The Federal German Science Budget for 1974', Science Abroad, GER 131 (London: Department of Trade and Industry, 1973).

[12] Select Committee on Science and Technology, HC 308 (1972), loc. cit., para. 26.

[13] Select Committee on Science and Technology, Government Observations on First and Fourth Reports, Session 1971–72 (London: HMSO, Cmnd 5177, 1972), para. 7.

[14] Select Committee on Science and Technology, Session 1971–72, Research and Development Minutes of Evidence and Appendices (London: HMSO, HC 375, 1972), pp. 375–81.

[15] Hugh Heclo and Aaron Wildavsky, The Private Government of Public Money (London: Macmillan, 1974), p. 23.

[16] Alexander King, Science and Policy: The International Stimulus (London: Oxford University Press, 1974), p. 11.

[17] Christopher Freeman, The Economics of Industrial Innovation (Harmondsworth: Penguin Books, 1974), p. 306.

[18] Cited in A. G. Jordan, J. J. Richardson and R. H. Kimber, 'The Origins of the Water Act of 1973', Public Administration, 55 (1977), p. 332.

[19] OECD, Science, Growth and Society – A New Perspective, report of the Secretary General's ad hoc group on new concepts in science policy (Paris: OECD, 1971), pp. 39–40.

[20] Council for Scientific Policy, Second Report on Science Policy (London: HMSO, Cmnd 3420, 1967), para. 74.

[21] Council for Scientific policy, Report on Science Policy (London: HMSO, Cmnd 3007, 1966), p. iii and para. 36.

[22] Ibid., para. 37.

[23] Rose and Rose, op. cit., p. 263.

[24] See Cmnd 7499, loc. cit., para. 33; and Civil Service Department press release, 27 April 1979.

[25] Rose and Rose, op. cit., p. 266.

[26] Lord Helsby, House of Lords, Debates, 328 (1972), cols. 1038–9.

[27] Joseph Haberer, 'Politicalization in Science', Science, 178 (1972), pp. 713–24, at p. 714; see also his Politics and the Community of Science (New York: Van Nostrand Reinhold, 1969).

[28] Norman J. Vig, Science and Technology in British Politics (Oxford: Pergamon, 1968), pp. 126–39.

[29] Graeme C. Moodie and Gerald Studdert-Kennedy, Opinions, Publics and Pressure Groups (London: Allen and Unwin, 1970), p. 86.

[30] Roger Williams, 'Some Political Aspects of the Rothschild Affair', Science Studies, 3 (No. 1, 1973), pp. 31–46, at p. 41.

[31] King, op. cit., pp. 55–6; and E. Caty, G. Drilhon, G. Ferné and S. Wald, The Research System: Comparative Survey of the Organisation and Financing of Fundamental Research, Vol. 1, France, Germany, United Kingdom (Paris: OECD, 1972), p. 102.

[32] National Science Foundation, Grants for Scientific Research (Washington, D.C.: National Science Foundation, NSF 78–41, 1978), p. 11.

[33] European Science Foundation, Report 1978 (Strasbourg: European Science Foundation, 1979), p. i.

[34] Rose and Rose, op. cit., pp. 264–9.

[35] Cited in Science and Technology in the Department of State, report prepared for the Subcommittee on International Security and Scientific Affairs of the Committee on International Relations, U.S. House of Representatives (Washington, D.C.: USGPO, 1975), p. 35.

[36] See Nature, 280 (1979), pp. 98–9.

[37] See Cmnd 7499, loc. cit., para. 43.

[38] Jean-Jacques Salomon, 'Science Policy Studies and the Development of Science Policy', in Ina Spiegel-Rösing and Derek de Solla Price (eds.), Science, Technology and Society: A Cross-disciplinary Perspective (Beverly Hills, California: Sage Publications, 1977), pp. 62–3.

Index